A Brotherhood of Arms

A Brotherhood of Arms

Brazil–United States Military Relations,
1945–1977

Sonny B. Davis

UNIVERSITY PRESS OF COLORADO

© 1996 University Press of Colorado
Published by the University Press of Colorado
P.O. Box 849
Niwot, Colorado 80544

The University Press of Colorado is a cooperative publishing enterprise supported, in part, by Adams State College, Colorado State University, Fort Lewis College, Mesa State College, Metropolitan State College of Denver, University of Colorado, University of Northern Colorado, University of Southern Colorado, and Western State College of Colorado.

The paper used in this publication meets the minimum requirements of the American National Standard for Information Sciences — Permanence of Paper for Printed Library Materials.
ANSI Z39.48-1984

Library of Congress Cataloging-in-Publication Data

Davis, Sonny B., 1948–
    A brotherhood of arms: Brazil-United States military relations, 1945–1977 / Sonny B. Davis.
        p.   cm.
    Includes bibliographical references and index.
    ISBN 0-87081-418-4 (cloth: alk. paper)
    1. Brazil — Military Relations — United States. 2. United States — Military relations — Brazil. 3. Military assistance, American — Brazil. 4. Brazil — Politics and government — 20th century. I. Title.
UA619.D38   1996
355'.03281 — dc20   95-42691
                                                                        CIP

10 9 8 7 6 5 4 3 2 1

To Rebecca Davis,
with love

Contents

Preface

Scholars of Brazil–United States relations have provided a good understanding of the ebb and flow of political relations between the two Western Hemisphere giants. Less understood is the special relationship that existed between the military establishments of Brazil and the United States. With the exception of Frank McCann's seminal work *The Brazilian-American Alliance*, few works investigate in any detail the role military diplomacy played in the creation of close ties. Whereas McCann's study examined the World War II period, this book focuses on Brazil-U.S. military relations in the post-war era, particularly emphasizing the roles of the Joint Brazil–United States Defense Commission and the Joint Brazil–United States Military Commission.

Chapter 1 offers a synopsis of the birth of the special military relationship. The following chapters detail military ties in the context of the cold war. In those chapters I analyze Brazilian and American motivations for maintaining a close relationship, the evolution of military relations, and the demise of the formal alliance that held the Brazil and the United States militaries together from 1942 until 1977.

Readers will no doubt point to the deterioration in overall Brazil–United States relations to argue that the specialness of ties ended with the Allied victory in World War II. I confess to suffering from that same idea until I looked at the military relationship more closely. What I found was a natural evolutionary process that reflected a specialness sculpted within the growing complexity of a world affected by the schisms wrought by the cold war. It is in that intellectual framework that this work attempts to bring meaning to Brazil–United States military diplomacy.

This work is broadly conceived and looks at the major issues around which military diplomacy between Brazil and the United States was conducted. Although I use Brazilian sources, most of my effort went into the use of U.S. documents and secondary materials. As a result, my analysis of Brazilian motivation borrows heavily from mentors with longer years of study on and in Brazil. It is my hope, however, that this book will stimulate other scholars to devote efforts toward a greater understanding of the Brazilian-American military alliance.

As can be imagined, a work of this nature requires the assistance of numerous individuals. The staffs of the Harry S. Truman and John F. Kennedy Libraries provided hours of help. I owe a large debt to David Keogh of the U.S. Military History Institute, Salvador Velez and his staff at the Inter-American Defense College, and John Taylor and Edward Barnes of the National Archives. Their aid in sorting through the records was invaluable. At the U.S. Embassy in Brasília Lieutenant Colonel Daniel Mason graciously offered me insight into the later workings of the Joint Brazil–United States Military Commission and overall military relations. The staff at the Western State College of Colorado Library cheerfully provided assistance whenever it was needed. Dr. Claude Fouillade kindly consented to offer an outsiders view of the manuscript. Many thanks go to Jess Lionheart and Jody Berman of the University Press of Colorado. This work has been enriched because of their efforts.

The intellectual underpinnings of this work have benefited from individuals of which there are too many to mention. Recognition must, however, be offered to a special few. Many thanks to Dr. Edward Byrd, who first introduced me to the joys and pains of research and writing. Words cannot express my gratitude to Michael Conniff and Frank McCann, mentors, colleagues, and friends. Late afternoon and evening discussions with the latter offered me a four-year seminar on Brazil and Brazil–United States relations. Whatever of value this book contains is a direct result of their guidance. Any mistakes or errors in analysis, however, rest with me.

Special thanks go to Dr. Earl and Mrs. Ann Kilpatrick, to S. B. and Betty Davis, and the late Fredia Davis for their nurturing and encouragement of my intellectual pursuits. Finally, I wish to thank my wife, Rebecca A. Davis, for sharing her technical skills and for always being there when needed. Her sacrifice in producing this work has been far greater than my own.

Sonny B. Davis

Introduction

On the morning of March 12, 1977, Brazilians awoke to newspaper reports that their government would not renew the military agreement that had allied Brazil and the United States since 1952. The decision came three days before the military accord's twenty-fifth anniversary. According to an Itamaraty (Foreign Ministry) spokesman, Brazil would not renew formal ties because of the American government's linkage of human rights with military assistance. Support for the break came from a broad section of the Brazilian elite, including such staunch pro-Americans as diplomat Maurício Nabuco and Generals Nelson de Melo and Idálio Sardenberg.[1] Newspaper articles date the military alliance to the 1952 Military Defense Assistance Agreement. In reality, the decision to break the accord ended thirty-five years of formal military relations.

The worsening situation in Europe in the 1930s stimulated the administration of Franklin D. Roosevelt to secure economic and security cooperation from Latin America through the Good Neighbor policy. To deny potential enemies a foothold in the Western Hemisphere and access to Latin America's vast resources, security relationships with key countries were vital. Brazil became the focus of intense U.S. efforts to obtain a close military relationship because of its strategic geographical location and wealth of raw materials.

The Roosevelt administration's desire to strengthen economic, political, and military ties with the largest South American country meshed well with President Getúlio Vargas's (1932–1945, 1950–1954) aim of developing his country. Until Brazil moved into the U.S. orbit, however, Vargas carefully balanced relations with the Axis powers and the United States, playing each against the other to his country's advantage.[2] Brazil already had formed an unwritten diplomatic alliance with the northern giant earlier as a result of the efforts of the Baron Rio Branco. When Vargas committed Brazil to a military alliance with the United States in 1942, it added a new dimension to the realignment away from Europe. As trade patterns shifted, so too did political and military ties.[3] The move to the U.S. sphere might not have been as psychologically difficult as might be imagined, for Brazilian society was a paternalistic one in which patron-client relationships dominated. In allying with the United States, especially militarily, Brazil shed its old European patron for a new American benefactor.

The evolution of a closer relationship proceeded slowly until Nazi successes in Europe in late 1939 created a sense of urgency. Brazilian and American diplomats and military officials worked to prepare for expected entry into the conflagration engulfing the Old World and the Far East. The pressing need to secure Brazil's friendship made economic and military assistance a top priority in U.S. policy toward Latin America.[4] Expansion of world conflict led both nations to seek alliance because of the common goal of self-preservation, although perceptions on how best to secure the South Atlantic often differed.

Although close economic ties had a long history, it was not until the Japanese bombed Pearl Harbor in 1941 that military relations reached a high point. U.S. military personnel and matériel began to enter Brazil in increasing amounts, while U.S.-built air bases provided the means for ferrying war supplies to Europe and North Africa, patrolling the South Atlantic against submarines, and defending Brazil from invasion. In addition, U.S. officers trained their Brazilian comrades in U.S. military methods and use of U.S. military equipment.[5]

The instruments of the new military relationship were the Joint Brazil–United States Defense and Military Commissions (JBUSDC and JBUSMC). Created in 1942 to oversee mutual defense and security, the commissions were central to bilateral military relations and to the preparation of Brazilian forces for war. When the first elements of the Brazilian Expeditionary Force (FEB) landed in Naples, Italy, on July 16, 1944, to take part in the Allied campaign, the Brazilian-American military alliance reached a closeness unmatched by any other Latin American country.[6]

After the end of world conflict both countries based their postwar political-military relations on perceptions of national self-interests, but close ties remained a hallmark of Brazilian and U.S. foreign policy. Whereas the United States believed the alignment would result in Brazilian support of U.S. economic, political, and military policies, Brazil counted on U.S. help in enhancing its position in South American affairs by assisting in the modernization of its military and economy.[7]

Each side attempted to satisfy the other's expectations, but internal and international pressures prevented either country from doing so to the hoped-for degree.[8] U.S. commitment to anti-communist ideology placed Latin America last in assistance priority, which often clashed with Brazilian desires for U.S. aid.[9] At the same time, the rise of nationalism and the belief that the United States had not provided the help Brazil needed led to opposition to the U.S. connection. As a consequence, the relationship adapted, often with difficulty, to the changing post-war environment.

Strains in relations resulting from adjustment did not persuade a powerful segment of the Brazilian military to loosen institutional attachment to its U.S. colleague. Much like medieval knights linked by the potential for violence inherent in their careers, the relationship between U.S. and Brazilian officers was a brotherhood of arms.[10] The brotherhood, however, did not signify concurrence in all military matters. International and internal politics in both countries affected cooperation. When national and institutional goals coincided, as in the case of post-war defense roles, the establishment of the Escola Superior de Guerra (ESG), the 1964 military coup, and intervention in the Dominican Republic, the two militaries came to a concordance. When objectives diverged or, in Brazil's case, when institutional integrity was threatened over issues such as U.S. requests for Brazilian troops in Korea and Vietnam, the two countries went in different directions.

An underlying theme throughout the formal relationship was the question of military assistance. The quantity and quality of U.S. aid colored negotiations over all bilateral military issues. Nowhere was this clearer than in discussions for a missile-tracking station on Fernando de Noronha Island and for radio and long-range navigation (LORAN) radar sites in the Northeast.

Relations worked through a number of channels, although the JBUSMC became the most prominent symbol of Brazilian–United

States military ties in the years following World War II. The commission, located in Rio de Janeiro, and its Washington counterpart, the JBUSDC, dealt with most aspects of bilateral military relations under the 1952 Mutual Defense Assistance Agreement. Officers from both countries sat on the commissions and shared offices in various departments and ministries, thereby enjoying much personal contact. In the 1960s the U.S. delegation of the JBUSMC also acted as the U.S. Military Group, a centralized command formed to coordinate the efforts of military advisers. U.S. officers also maintained regular liaison with non-military Brazilian government agencies.[11]

Close contact did not eliminate the constant adjustment necessary for the maintenance of the relationship. The ebb and flow of post-war ties often made adaption difficult and created misunderstandings. Nevertheless, the U.S. connection remained a staple of Brazilian military policy until Brazil progressed to the point where formal ties had little meaning. The joint Brazil–United States effort in the Dominican Republic in 1965 represented the last manifestation of the old alliance.[12]

One of the factors affecting military collegiality was Brazil's evolving nationalism. Despite close military ties, starting in the 1950s Brazil and the United States increasingly moved in separate geopolitical circles. Brazil's decision not to send troops to Korea indicated the impetus to move away from the U.S. sphere, and the refusal to participate in the Vietnam War confirmed the trend. Equally important was Brazil's developing industry. With the development of indigenous war matériel industries, Brazil was able to fulfill its needs, which allowed a gradually weaning from U.S. tutelage. The ability to provide for itself coupled with a desire to pursue an independent course in world affairs made possible Brazil's decision not to renew the accord in 1977. The decision was simply the formal recognition of a changed relationship in which there was no incentive to continue a sentimental military agreement.

The military connection continued after the demise of the accord but bore little resemblance to earlier ties. Brazilian economic and political development and the erosion of U.S. dominance of the non-communist world led to an end of the old patron-client military relationship. The destruction of the accord in 1977 ushered in a new era in which the Brazilian military was no longer a supplicant but was rather a junior partner in the brotherhood of arms.

NOTES

1. "Brasil denuncia acordo militar com EUA," *O Jornal do Brasil*, March 12, 1977, 1, 19–22; Nabuco aplaude o ato de Geisel," *O Jornal do Brasil*, March 12, 1977, 19. Nabuco was a former ambassador to the United States. De Melo and Sardenberg were former chiefs of the Joint Brazil–United States Military Commission, the primary vehicle in bilateral military relations. Interestingly, three days before the announcement of the break Tancredo Neves, future short-lived president of Brazil, had warned of problems in the Brazilian-U.S. relationship. Neves noted that human rights, nuclear energy, and economic assistance were points of friction between the two countries. See "Tancredo ve tres pontos de atrito entre Brasil e EUA," *O Jornal do Brasil*, March 9, 1977, 15. Because Latin Americans are sensitive to use of the term *American* to refer solely to matters pertaining to the United States, "U.S." or "United States" will be used in this work except in cases where clarity is served by use of "American."

2. Frank D. McCann, Jr., *The Brazilian-American Alliance, 1937–1945* (Princeton: Princeton University Press, 1973), 7–9; Paulo Pinto Guedes, "E fomos para a guerra," in *Getúlio, uma história oral*, ed. Valentina da Rocha Lima (Rio de Janeiro: Editora Record, 1986), 212; and Gerson Moura, *Autonomia na dependência: A política externa brasileira de 1931 a 1942* (Rio de Janeiro: Editora Nova Fronteira S.A., 1980), 62–66, 142.

3. E. Bradford Burns, *The Unwritten Alliance: Rio Branco and Brazilian-American Relations* (New York: Columbia University Press, 1966), 160–162; José Honório Rodrigues, "The Foundations of Brazil's Foreign Policy," in *Latin America International Politics: Ambitions, Capabilities, and the National Interests of Mexico, Brazil, and Argentina*, ed. Carlos Alberto Astiz (Notre Dame, Ind.: University of Notre Dame Press, 1969), 209–210; and Frank D. McCann, Jr., "Brazilian Foreign Relations in the Twentieth Century," in *Brazil in the International System: The Rise of a Middle Power*, ed. Wayne A. Selcher (Boulder, Colo.: Westview Press, 1981), 1.

4. Stetson Conn and Byron Fairchild, *The Framework of Hemisphere Defense* (Washington, D.C.: Office of the Chief of Military History, Department of the Army, 1960), 173–174; and Edwin Lieuwen, *U.S. Policy in Latin America: A Short History* (New York: Praeger, 1965), 75.

5. McCann, *Brazilian-American Alliance*, offers the most complete work on the period.

6. Ibid., 402–442.

7. Ibid., 304–305; "Current Status of the Military Aspects of Brazilian-U.S. Relations," March 28, 1949, RG–319, Plans and Operations Division (hereafter P&O) Decimal File, 1949–February 1950, 091 Brazil, Box 534, National Archives (hereafter NA); and William Perry, "The Brazilian Armed Forces:

Military Policy and Conventional Capabilities of an Emerging Power," *Military Review* 58:9 (September 1978): 11.

8. The United States only grudgingly helped Brazil economically. Much more effort went into providing the Brazilian military with equipment and training.

9. Albert Fishlow and Abraham F. Lowenthal, *Latin America's Emergence: Toward a U.S. Response* (New York: Foreign Policy Association, 1979), 28.

10. Many Brazilian officers in the cold war era agreed with geopolitician General Golbery do Couto e Silva that a communist threat to the United States was an indirect menace to Brazil. See General Golbery do Couto e Silva, *Aspectos geopolíticos do Brasil* (Rio de Janeiro: Biblioteca do Exército Editora, 1957), 51–60. General Estevão Leitão de Carvalho was the first to use the phrase *a brotherhood of arms* in describing the Brazilian-U.S. military relationship; he did so at a September 1944 luncheon address at West Point. According to Leitão de Carvalho, there was a "brotherhood of arms between our two armies, on whose shoulders rests the main responsibility of the defense of peace on our continent." See "Address of General Carvalho," September 7, 1944, RG-218, JCS Military Commissions U.S.-Brazil, 33-18, DDC 1350, Visits, Box 1, NA.

11. John Child, *Unequal Alliance: The Inter-American Military System, 1938–1978* (Boulder, Colo.: Westview Press, 1980), 64; and Major Colin K. Winkleman and Captain A. Brent Merrill, "United States and Brazilian Military Relations," *Military Review* 63 (June 1983): 63.

12. Some scholars contend that the specialness of the old alliance ended with the inception of the cold war. See Stanley E. Hilton, "The United States, Brazil, and the Cold War, 1945–1960: End of the Special Relationship," *Journal of American History* 68:3 (December 1981): 599–624. Hilton's premise may be true regarding economic ties, but the military relationship remained close.

.. 1 ..

Interwar Years: Prologue to Special Ties

U.S. defense planners achieved an important goal when Brazil and the United States agreed to a secret military alliance in May 1942. The proximity of the northeast bulge to Africa and easy access to the South Atlantic Ocean from its ports made Brazil vital to the U.S. hemispheric defense scheme.[1] With the agreement, defense of the southern approaches became a joint effort from which future relations evolved. The regularization of military ties had not been a simple process, for the rivalry between Germany and the United States for economic, military, and political influence complicated efforts. U.S. attempts to woo Argentina and the question of military assistance added obstacles to closer ties. In the process an opportunistic Brazilian government sought the rewards of the courted to modernize the economy and military.[2] By the late 1930s, however, Brazilian and U.S. interests had coalesced to a point that made close ties possible.

EARLY RELATIONS

Brazilian-U.S. military relations date from 1914, when the United States supplied a naval officer to serve as an instructor at the Brazilian Naval War College in Rio de Janeiro. U.S. presence at the school later expanded, and in 1922 the United States agreed, over the protest of Argentina, to provide a nine-man naval mission to assist in the reorganization of the Brazilian Navy. In 1926 the U.S. Congress passed legislation that allowed U.S. Army personnel to work with Brazilian forces, but it was not until the 1930s that a small mission became operational.[3]

The modest relationship suffered a minor setback in 1930, when Getúlio Vargas assumed the presidency following the revolt that ousted President Washington Luís (1926–1930). During the conflict the United States sold the Luís government military equipment but refused to grant the rebels belligerent status or access to arms and ammunition. In retaliation the Vargas government terminated the naval mission for a two-year period. Although the re-establishment of the mission in 1932 did not signify an expanded relationship, it provided the foundation on which formal military ties were built.[4]

As the world slipped toward war in the 1930s, a formal alliance came closer to reality. New agreements in 1936 called for U.S. Navy and Army officers to advise the Brazilian Navy and Army. Another arrangement in 1937 between Brazil's Ministry of the Navy and the U.S. Navy Department provided for the U.S. Navy Mission in Rio de Janeiro to assist the Brazilians in building three destroyers with American designs and materials.[5]

ROADBLOCKS TO APPROXIMATION

Major barriers prevented a formal military alliance despite the 1936 and 1937 arrangements. A perception among Brazil's military leaders that the United States ignored their concerns, particularly in regard to Argentina, worked against closer approximation. Argentine military expansion from the end of the 1930s to the mid-1940s spurred a similar response from Brazil. A strengthening of the military, however, required foreign assistance. While Germany and Italy supplied Brazil with arms and equipment under favorable terms (in 1938 Army Chief of Staff General Pedro Aurélio de Góes Monteiro arranged with Germany a $100 million arms barter deal), U.S. law prohibited the United States from following suit. To the Brazilian military it appeared that an isolationist United States was insensitive to its fear of a rearmed Argentina.[6]

Fear of a powerful Argentina fueled Brazilian desires for a modern, well-equipped military and for U.S. assistance. The inability of the United States to supply arms and equipment, as well as U.S. demands that Brazil pay its debts, caused resentment among Brazilian military leaders. An agreement with Washington that called for Brazil to cut its national budget to pay debts, which would therefore limit resources available for national defense, also angered the military hierarchy. Worse for the Brazilians was a decision not to provide U.S.-built destroyers to the Brazilian Navy.[7]

In response to a U.S. offer made to all the Latin American republics, Brazil wanted to lease six decommissioned destroyers. Opposition to the idea arose immediately, as the Argentine government protested the Brazil-U.S. arrangement. Arguing that the lease of ships to Brazil would upset the region's naval equilibrium, the Argentine government pressured the United States to cancel the deal. The situation so alarmed the U.S. ambassador in Buenos Aires, Alexander W. Weddell, that he cabled Washington about his fears that Argentina would go to war against its neighbor if Brazil received the ships. Great Britain also opposed the transfer because it threatened British monopoly of the sale of naval vessels to the states in the region. According to London, consummation of the ship lease would violate the capital ship limitations clause of the Washington and London Naval Treaties of 1922 and 1936.[8]

The combined pressure of Argentina, the U.S. ambassador, and Great Britain was formidable. Despite Brazilian assurance that the destroyers were for training purposes only, the United States withdrew the offer, and Brazil did not receive the vessels.[9] The whole episode, as well as later Argentine-U.S. relations, caused bitter feelings among the Brazilian military. The political-diplomatic atmosphere gave little indication in the 1930s that Brazil and the United States would form a military alliance.

Brazil-Argentina competition created further impediments to a Brazilian-American military alliance in the latter half of the 1930s. Shortly after the collapse of the destroyer deal, the United States agreed to send eight military aviation instructors to Argentina and to allow Argentine naval officers to serve aboard U.S. Navy vessels. The Brazilians reacted to the news by charging Washington with abandonment of a friend to help Brazil's enemy. The Department of State claimed that equality of treatment and inter-American solidarity were the motivations for the decision and suggested that the situation was similar to the 1936 mission agreements that had sent U.S. advisers to Brazil.[10]

Lost on the Department of State was the impact of the failed destroyer deal and the importance of the Brazil-Argentina rivalry. U.S. actions seemed contrary to Brazil's understanding of the "unwritten alliance." Brazil's ambassador, Oswaldo Aranha, tried to kill the arrangement by appealing to the United States to honor the "special relationship" between the two countries on the grounds that Argentina would use the skills learned from the Americans to make war on his nation. Aranha's argument fell on deaf ears. The U.S. Navy vetoed the service of Argentine officers aboard its vessels for security reasons unrelated to Brazilian desires, but the aviation instructors went to Argentina.[11]

Aranha believed a special relationship existed between his country and the northern giant, but the United States was pursuing a multilateral approach in its military relations with Latin America. Such an approach placed Brazil on a level equal to the smallest Spanish-speaking country. The multilateral policy indicated that by 1938 Brazilian-U.S. military ties were tenuous, not special. Military agreements were minor and had little impact on overall relations. The lack of will to treat Brazil differently made the Brazilians skeptical and prevented expansion of the relationship. Indeed, in the 1930s the Brazilian General Staff viewed the United States as a potential enemy.[12] Events on the world stage had yet to reach a point where the interests of the two countries coincided. Nevertheless, 1938 was an important year, for the machinery that deepened military and political relations was put in motion.

NEW APPROACHES FOR OLD GOALS

In 1938 fear of German, Italian, and Japanese influence spurred Secretary of State Cordell Hull to argue for greater U.S. military assistance to Latin American nations as a counterweight to non-U.S. inroads. The Department of State proposed a program that included attendance and visits of Latin American officers at U.S. service schools and installations and supplying of armed forces publications, aircraft, and naval vessels to the region's militaries. The War Department supported the proposal and suggested an increase in the number of military attachés and promotion of U.S. arms sales in the hemisphere as well.[13] All would be accomplished through bilateral arrangements with countries in the region considered important, which seemed to run counter to the earlier espoused multilateralism.

These suggestions differed from previous policies in method but were anchored in the goals of the Monroe Doctrine. Maintenance of U.S. influence for economic and security reasons drove the new approach. President Franklin D. Roosevelt agreed with the State and War Departments and created the Standing Liaison Committee to coordinate and supervise implementation of the plan. Adhering to the intent of Good Neighborism, the policy eschewed direct intervention but kept the objectives of obtaining markets for U.S. goods and securing the hemisphere through trade and military agreements. U.S. security plans assigned the Latin American militaries the roles of protecting U.S. access to natural resources and rights of transit or allowing permanently based military personnel if that could be achieved. To realize those aims, the task of the Latin American militaries was to maintain internal order. Brazil's size, abundance of natural resources, and strategic location placed it at the center of the scheme.[14]

Ironically, the previous year the United States declined an invitation from President Getúlio Vargas to forge closer military ties. The proposition fit Brazil's plans to develop its military, but the United States was unprepared to embark on such a course at the time.[15] Refusal to adopt the Vargas plan caused Brazil to turn to Europe for arms and equipment until the outbreak of war in 1939 forced a return to accommodation with the United States. Legal restrictions prevented the United States from providing Brazil with military assistance, but the German invasion of France in June 1940 changed matters. A fearful U.S. Congress quickly passed the Pittman Resolution, which repealed the prohibitions on arms sales and allowed the sale of military equipment on a cash-and-carry basis. The resolution failed to immediately produce the arms desired but helped prevent Brazil from moving into the Axis camp.[16]

DISCUSSIONS ON MILITARY TIES

Although the cash-and-carry policy and world conditions precluded close military cooperation with Brazil in the late 1930s, the seeds from which future relations grew were planted at the 1938 Eighth Inter-American Conference in Lima, Peru. Brazilian-U.S. collaboration was instrumental in obtaining from conference delegates the Declaration of Lima, which pledged all the hemisphere's countries to act collectively in the event of aggression from a non-American state. Soon after the conference President Roosevelt called for high-level talks aimed at drawing Brazil and the United States closer. Most important among the topics proposed for discussion was U.S. assistance to the Brazilian military. President Vargas and Ambassador Aranha responded quickly and favorably, hoping economic and military aid would follow immediately. The goal of the United States was Brazilian agreement regarding the security of the important northeast bulge in Brazil.[17]

Aranha went to Washington in February 1939 to pursue the matter, where he obtained an agreement on economic assistance that had military implications. Brazilian military leaders accepted the economic aspects of the arrangement but condemned the deal in general because it restricted their ability to buy weapons from Germany. Under the terms of the accord Brazil agreed to resume debt payments suspended after the 1937 coup that had consolidated the rule of Getúlio Vargas. Resumption of debt payments meant a restriction of capital available for military purchases and linked the Brazilian currency to the dollar. Most important, the barter arrangement with Germany would be curtailed. The latter particularly galled the military because Aranha had not raised the issue of rearmament assistance with the U.S. negotiators.[18]

Military anger with Aranha over the arrangement failed to recognize that the ambassador's efforts opened the door to a wider relationship. Hoping to counter the negative effects of a 1938 German invitation to Army Chief of Staff General Pedro Aurélio de Góes Monteiro to come to Germany and participate in maneuvers, Aranha proposed an exchange of visits by Góes Monteiro and U.S. Army Chief of Staff General George C. Marshall. Marshall readily accepted, for Brazil's geographic location made it strategically important if Germany conquered Europe and moved to control Africa. The northeastern city of Natal was a short eight-hour flight from West Africa, and U.S. Army planners lacked confidence in the Brazilian military's ability to defend the bulge area. Marshall believed that U.S. soldiers would have to secure the area, which would require Brazilian cooperation. That cooperation hinged to a large degree on Góes Monteiro, who had great military and political influence; he had been Vargas's chief of staff in the 1930 revolution and had suppressed the 1932 São Paulo revolt. His voice carried weight with civilian and military leaders.[19]

Marshall and his staff went to Rio de Janeiro in May 1939 to discuss joint military interests with Góes Monteiro and Minister of War Eurico Gaspar Dutra. The goal of the Americans was to establish lines of communications from Natal to Dakar, French West Africa, via Ascension Island. Marshall's principal aim was to secure transit privileges and permission to station U.S. troops in Brazil should the situation warrant such action.[20]

OBSTACLES TO AGREEMENT

Two formidable obstacles, one philosophical and the other military, had to be overcome before agreement could occur. The first required re-orientation in the views of Dutra and Góes Monteiro, both of whom admired the German military and believed Nazi victory in Europe was a forgone conclusion. Special efforts had to be made to obtain Dutra's acceptance. One of Vargas's most important military supporters and a classmate of Góes Monteiro, Dutra was a Germanophile who liked the disciplined nature of the German dictatorship. Representative government interested Dutra little, but his influence in military and civilian circles was substantial.[21]

Strategic differences made the military obstacle more complicated. While U.S. defense planners focused on the northeastern bulge, the Brazilians felt their greatest danger lay in possibile invasion from traditional enemy Argentina. Potential subversive activities from the large Germanic population in the south also worried military leaders but to a lesser extent. In addition, although Brazil had no fear in offering the use of air and sea bases at Natal and Fernando de Noronha Island, it rejected the idea of U.S. troops on Brazilian soil. Defense of the nation was the responsibility of the Brazilian Army, not foreigners. The integrity of Brazilian sovereignty was non-negotiable.[22]

Although U.S. military negotiators pursued diplomatic means to obtain cooperation, they had little confidence in the Brazilian military's ability to defend against an attack. As a result, U.S. planners made unilateral plans to secure the country. When reports of coup plotting by pro-Nazi officers in Argentina and a possible German offensive toward Brazil reached Washington, U.S. Army strategists quickly developed the "Pot of Gold" plan. Under the plan if invasion seemed imminent, a one-hundred-thousand-man force would be rushed to a variety of locations from Belém to Rio de Janeiro with or without Brazilian permission.[23] The practicality of the scheme was questionable given the level of U.S. military capabilities, but it provides a measure of U.S. fears. Negotiations moved too slowly to soothe worried U.S. officials who ascribed pro-German influence to Brazil's southern defense orientation. Therefore, U.S. intervention seemed necessary even if it angered the Brazilians.

Brazil–United States military discussions resolved little until German advances in the Low Countries and France in mid-1940 stimulated the Brazilians to intensify discussions on military aid. In a May meeting Ambassador Aranha informed his U.S. colleagues that Brazil was prepared to "cooperate 100% with the United States in plans for military and naval defense or to repel aggression, and even to cooperate with the United States in war." To underscore Brazilian concerns, Góes Monteiro requested that Lieutenant Colonel Lehman Miller, the new U.S. Military Mission chief, be dispatched quickly to Rio de Janeiro to continue assistance negotiations.[24] Brazilian-U.S. interests moved ever closer as Nazi successes in Europe multiplied.

Despite the new urgency, major problems continued to hamper close military ties. The United States still saw hemisphere defense as a collective venture despite accepting the concept of arrangements with individual countries, while Brazil sought a special bilateral relationship as the best guarantee of its security from either a German or

an Argentine threat. The Brazilian military agreed to full cooperation, but only on issues between the two countries; schemes of continental defense were of no interest to Brazil. Ambassador Jefferson
Caffery reported that the Brazilians agreed to "go all the way [with
the United States] but did not want to get tied up with any other
country or countries." Lehman Miller was unconvinced. He argued
that, even though field- and company-grade officers leaned toward
the United States, the Brazilian high command had pro-German
sympathies.[25]

THE QUESTION OF ASSISTANCE

Miller's analysis of the high command was faulty; pro-German
sympathy was less important than were arms and equipment for
national security. Brazil's military leaders were ready to cooperate
but were skeptical about U.S. assistance because of the high arms
prices and the cash-and-carry policy. Besides, the U.S. Congress had
yet to pass legislation allowing assistance, and the United States
lacked industrial plants to produce arms. The value of an alliance
with the United States was doubtful. Minister of War Dutra was
especially wary. He confirmed the military's cooperative disposition
but emphasized the need for arms, airplanes, coastal defense artillery, and motorized equipment.[26] Aranha was more direct. He
bluntly told the U.S. ambassador that "you [Americans] hold conversations with us and the Germans give us arms." Either the United
States provided military aid, or Brazil would be forced to rely on
Germans arms, with the attendant instructors and influence.[27]

The fragility of the situation could not have been more clear. In
response, the Department of State, the Army War Plans Division,
and other Washington agencies developed a new national policy that
offered the Latin American countries favorable terms for the purchase of U.S. arms and equipment. President Roosevelt approved the
plan on August 1, 1940, and Ambassador Caffery told the Brazilians
that military assistance was forthcoming.[28]

The new policy created a different mood in Rio de Janeiro. The
value of the German connection diminished as the Brazilians

weighed the now forceful U.S. commitment against the problems of getting German equipment through the British blockade. In September military chiefs agreed among themselves to make available Brazil's resources should the United States become embroiled in the European conflict. Shortly after that decision Góes Monteiro provided Miller with a "secret signed 4-page document regarding Brazil's willingness to cooperate with the United States in hemisphere defense." Although a formal military alliance had yet to be forged, the document effectively ended the Brazilian government's effort to keep Germany and the United States at an equidistance while profiting from both.[29]

Little happened immediately. The realization that England would hold and German preoccupation with consolidating gains seemed to remove the threat to Brazil. Consequently, U.S. officials viewed the Brazilian situation with less urgency. Legal restraints and the inability of U.S. industry to supply matériel also remained as formidable obstacles regardless of the new policy. Even more important was opposition from Secretary of War Henry L. Stimson, who felt military assistance should go to friends actually engaged in combat rather than potential allies not involved in the fighting. At the same time, with German interest and energy focused elsewhere, Brazil maintained its resistance to the placement of U.S. troops on national soil while pressing for aid.[30]

THE AIRPORT DEVELOPMENT PROGRAM

The pace of negotiations slowed, but Brazil–United States relations became more organized and systematized. Joint efforts to eliminate the influence of German and Italian airlines in Brazil (and in all Latin America) exemplified the progress toward closer ties. Much more influential were coordinated endeavors in building air bases in the northeastern bulge. Despite opposition from nationalistic officers, who were wary of U.S. intentions, and from the Department of State, which feared the U.S. military's ideas would damage the Good Neighbor policy, both projects went forward. Differences over assistance and stationing of U.S. troops in Brazilian territory still separated the two countries, but the efforts to supplant the Axis airlines and the air base construction provided important links in the budding relationship.[31]

For the Brazilians the issue of U.S. combat troops on national territory was not subject to negotiation. The elimination of Axis influence and cooperation in constructing air bases, however, were matters in which progress was possible. Efforts to promote U.S. or local ownership of airlines began when war broke out in Europe in 1939, but nothing was accomplished until 1941 when U.S. offers of matériel, financial, and technical assistance persuaded the Brazilians to remove German and Italian influence in airlines such as Vasp and Varig.[32]

Simultaneous with the drive to remove Axis predominance in the airline industry was the move to build air bases capable of handling military aircraft, especially in the Northeast. To link the area with the rest of the country and to the African air route, existing commercial airfields needed refurbishing and new air bases constructed to accommodate military use. To carry out the tasks, the War Department, operating under the Military Appropriations Act of 1940, which allowed the president to authorize secret projects without budget accountability, contracted with Pan American Airports Corporation.[33]

Civilian employees of Pan American carried out negotiations for air base construction, but military diplomacy at the highest level played an important role in obtaining Brazilian agreement, as evidenced by General Marshall's lobbying of Góes Monteiro.[34] It is doubtful, however, that Brazil would have agreed if the project had not been in its interest. The Airport Development Program (ADP) fit both countries' needs and pushed them toward the establishment of a special military relationship. Although still not committed to a U.S. alliance, Brazil undertook joint projects that served national goals, and those goals drove it closer to the United States.

Vargas approved the ADP in February 1941 with full knowledge of the role of the U.S. government. The dynamics of Brazilian politics, however, required cautious action before an authorizing decree could be issued. Potential negative reactions from influential forces in the army and body politic, competitor airlines, and other governments necessitated skillful political maneuvering by Vargas. Support from key military and political leaders allowed Vargas to counter his opponents, and in June an authorizing decree was issued.[35]

Delays hampered the ADP from the beginning, but the major impediments arose in the early stages of its evolution. Poor communications, linguistic differences, bureaucratic roadblocks, a variety of different construction techniques and materials, and lack of trained personnel were problems endemic to an expanding relationship between peoples of disparate cultural traditions and nations in different stages of development.[36] Difficulties aside, the early period gave individuals from both countries valuable experience in working together.

Two of the numerous problems had little to do with the "getting-to-know-each-other" difficulties: the U.S. Army's continued desire to station troops in Brazil and efforts by opponents to bog down the ADP through agitation and sabotage. The latter provided fuel for the U.S. argument that U.S. military personnel were needed to protect the ADP sites. Marshall's concern over the issue was such that he proposed U.S. participation in Brazilian maneuvers in the northeast in mid-August 1941. In part Marshall wanted to send troops because intelligence reports claimed a small elite German air- and seaborne force would soon attempt the seizure of the bulge with the help of fifth columnists, and he wanted U.S. troops in place to repel the expected attack. According to Marshall, ninety-three hundred soldiers and forty-three airplanes could arrive in Brazil in twenty days, and the maneuvers offered the opportunity to begin the process.[37]

The State, War, and Navy Departments were suspicious of the intelligence assessments but agreed to approach the Brazilians. The answer was resoundingly negative; the Brazilians argued that if the United States provided adequate arms, their own military could repulse any attack. Curiously, despite initial cautiousness, U.S. Army planners became indignant over the Brazilian view and protested that some assistance had already been provided. U.S. Navy strategists also forgot naval wariness after German submarines sank the USS *Markin* and the USS *White* in the hemisphere neutral zone.

Navy leaders encouraged Miller to bypass Ambassador Caffery and press his counterparts directly for concessions. Miller had reservations but dutifully sought Brazilian agreement, though he was "embarrassed" by the vehemently negative response he received.[38]

Although the issue of U.S. combat troops was non-negotiable, the Brazilians were pragmatic enough to recognize the need for Americans to operate the African ferry route and to protect ADP personnel. In a compromise agreement the Brazilian government allowed three uniformed but unarmed U.S. Marine companies to provide security at the ADP sites.[39]

The ADP program and the agreement to allow U.S. Marines for security inaugurated the Brazil-U.S. military relationship in a real sense. Efforts by Brazilians and Americans at the highest levels of government to overcome opposition to cooperation paid off for both sides. The United States was able to establish and maintain a military transportation system capable of rapid re-supply to the battlefront, while Brazil received valuable airfields, albeit for U.S. ends. The mutual benefits made the ADP project successful and was one of the key factors that helped the two countries forge regularized military ties later.[40] The question of arms and equipment, however, loomed ever larger and stood in the way of a formal military alliance.

LEND-LEASE

In 1941 there was no certainty the nascent military relationship would develop further. Standing in the way were the cautiousness of many Brazilian military leaders and the inability of the United States to provide arms. Rivalry among the State, Navy, and War Departments for influence over Brazil policy complicated matters even more. As had occurred earlier, however, non-hemisphere events forced budding ties toward another stage despite opposition in Rio de Janeiro and Washington. The end result of those events was a Lend-Lease arrangement between Brazil and the United States.

Under pressure from Nazi overlords the French Vichy government agreed in May 1941 to allow German submarines basing privileges in Dakar, French West Africa. Fearing the worst, the U.S.

military initiated another round of talks on joint defense planning
and the stationing of U.S. troops in Brazil. The latter issue had been
moribund from the start, but the efforts of U.S. negotiator Matthew
B. Ridgeway led to the creation of the Joint Board for the Defense of
Northeast Brazil. Clearly underlined in the "Terms of Agreement"
was Brazil's determination to decide the nature and extent of military cooperation, and U.S. troops in Brazil were not among the
agreed-on items. Nevertheless, U.S. military planners continued to
develop schemes to put troops in Brazil. Under the "Rainbow V"
plan, sixty thousand air and ground personnel would be inserted
around Belém, Natal, and Recife should the need arise.[41]

With the successful prosecution of military diplomacy and the
later development of the war, the Rainbow plan and the Joint Board
for the Defense of Northeast Brazil disappeared. The joint board
accomplished little in its short life but represented another step in
minimizing differences between the two militaries and provided the
basis for the construction of the next stage in evolving ties. World
events in 1941 stimulated the movement toward consolidation of the
relationship, and Lend-Lease offered the means.

Opinion in Brazilian military and diplomatic circles divided over
Lend-Lease. Aranha, Góes Monteiro, and air chief Eduardo Gomes
favored an alliance with the United States, but Eurico Dutra and
other officers and diplomats were troubled by the implied subservi-
ence in Lend-Lease. The split was significant not only because Góes
Monteiro and Dutra were old classmates at the military school in
Porto Alegre, but also because they were the most influential officers
in the politically powerful army. Both recognized that the United
States offered the best opportunity to modernize the military, but
they sat on different sides of the Lend-Lease issue. By late 1941, however, it was clear that there were no other options. On October 1,
1941, Brazil and the United States signed a Lend-Lease agreement.[42]

Under Lend-Lease Brazil was scheduled to receive $100 million
worth of U.S. military equipment. Before much matériel could be
transferred, the United States entered the war, and the two countries
modified the agreement. The modification doubled the amount of
the 1941 deal and provided for the sale of military goods to Brazil at
a sixty-five percent discount. The new arrangement played a large

part in moving the two countries closer; it allayed the fears of Brazilian officers who had earlier argued against an alliance with the United States. Brazil benefited from Lend-Lease more than any other country in the region, receiving almost three-fourths, or $361.4 million, of the matériel sent to Latin America under the program.[43]

The path to the Joint Board for the Defense of Northeast Brazil and the Lend-Lease agreement had not been easy. Progress toward their consummation was slow but steady, as the two countries' interests came more into alignment. The December 7, 1941, Japanese bombing of Pearl Harbor and the entry of the United States into World War II provided the catalyst that hardened military ties. Following the bombing military leaders in Brazil and the United States seemed to be in the grips of hysteria, especially after Germany and Italy declared war on the United States. So great were the fears that the military commander in Recife signaled President Vargas that air and sea attacks could be expected at any moment. Anxiety in Washington and Rio de Janeiro fueled reinvigorated efforts at cooperation.[44]

The apparent threat of an attack on the vulnerable southern flank caused Washington to increase pressure on Brazil for concessions. At the same time, Brazil worried about Axis and Argentine invasions, particularly because a reliable source of arms had yet to be secured. Brazilian and U.S. interests converged in the aftermath of December 7 and the Axis declaration of war on the United States, thereby making close military ties possible. A special relationship emerged in which the United States obtained cooperation in security affairs and Brazil received economic and military assistance. Although not always an easy relationship, the ties forged in World War II made Brazil the premier U.S. ally in Latin America for a number of years.

NOTES

1. According to the U.S. "Quarter-Sphere" hemisphere defense plan, the Panama Canal and Brazil were considered vital because of their strategic locations. See Child, *Unequal Alliance*, 6, 21.

2. Stanley E. Hilton, *Hitler's Secret War in South America: German Military Espionage and Allied Counterespionage in Brazil* (Baton Rouge: Louisiana

State University Press, 1981), 25–26; Moura, *Autonomia na dependência*, 62–66; and John D. Wirth, *The Politics of Brazilian Development, 1930–1954* (Stanford: Stanford University Press, 1970), 20.

3. Lars Shoultz, *Human Rights and United States Policy Toward Latin America* (Princeton: Princeton University Press, 1981), 212; Keith Larry Storrs, *Brazil's Independent Foreign Policy, 1961–1964: Background, Tenets, Linkage to Domestic Politics, and Aftermath* (Ithaca: Cornell University Press, 1973), 120; Theresa Louise Krause, "The Establishment of the United States Army Air Corps Bases in Brazil, 1938–1945" (Ph.D. diss., University of Maryland, 1986), 64; and Joseph Smith, "American Diplomacy and the Naval Mission to Brazil, 1917–1930," *Inter-American Economic Affairs* 25:1 (Summer 1981): 75, 77. Much like later arrangements, establishment of the Naval Mission was difficult because of misunderstandings and opposition from pro-British Brazilian naval officers. See Smith, "American Diplomacy," 78, 81, 83; and Joseph Smith, *Unequal Giants: Diplomatic Relations Between the U.S. and Brazil, 1889–1930* (Pittsburgh: Pittsburgh University Press, 1991), 68.

4. Smith, "American Diplomacy," 89–91; Joseph Smith, "United States Diplomacy Toward Political Revolt in Brazil, 1889–1930," *Inter-American Economic Affairs* 37:2 (Autumn, 1983): 14–15. Although there was a measure of retaliation in the actions, the Vargas administration requested the withdrawal of the French Army Mission along with the U.S. Navy Mission as a means of displaying independence and appeasing nationalist sentiment more than as an expression of displeasure over the U.S. position during the revolt. See Smith, *Unequal Giants*, 71, 92, 95.

5. Abelardo B. Bueno do Prado to Cordell Hull, January 16, 1937; Hull to Prado, February 2, 1937, Department of State, *Foreign Relations of the United States, 1937*, vol. 5, *The American Republics* (Washington, D.C.: GPO, 1954), 375–376 [hereafter all sources from the *Foreign Relations of the United States, the American Republics* will be cited as *FRUS Year*]; and Hull to Caffery, May 12, 1938, *FRUS 1938*, 316–317.

6. José Honório Rodriques, "The Foundation's of Brazil's Foreign Policy," *International Affairs* 38:3 (July 1962): 325; Roger Fontaine, *Brazil and the United States: Toward a Maturing Relationship* (Washington, D.C.: American Enterprise Institute for Policy Research, 1974), 21; McCann, *Brazilian-American Alliance*, 43, 85, 91, 111–113; Marvin Goldwert, *Democracy, Militarism, and Nationalism in Argentina, 1930–1966: An Interpretation* (Austin: University of Texas Press, 1972), 69; David V. Fleischer, "Brazil," in *The Latin American Military Institution*, ed. Robert Wesson (New York: Praeger, 1986), 90; and McCann, "Brazilian Foreign Relations," 11.

7. Fontaine, *Brazil and the U.S.*, 21; McCann, *Brazilian-American Alliance*, 43; and Rodriques, "Foundations of Brazil's Foreign Policy," 325.

8. Alexander Weddell to Secretary of State, August 10, 1937; U.S. Chargé in Brazil (Scotten) to Secretary of State, August 12, 1937; Memo of Conversation Between Secretary of State and British Ambassador (Lindsay), August 12, 1937; British Embassy to U.S. Department of State, September 13, 1937, *FRUS 1937*, 153–157; and Arthur P. Whitaker, *The United States and the Southern Cone: Argentina, Chile, and Uruguay* (Cambridge, Mass.: Harvard University Press, 1976), 376.

9. Frederick M. Nunn, *Yesterday's Soldiers: European Military Professionalism in South America, 1890-1940* (Lincoln: University of Nebraska Press, 1983), 216-217.

10. Hull to Caffery, May 12, 1938; Caffery to Hull, May 19, 1938; and Hull to Caffery, May 20, 1938, *FRUS 1938*, 316-318.

11. Caffery to Hull, May 19, 1938; and Caffery to Hull, May 23, 1938, *FRUS 1938*, 316-318.

12. Caffery to Hull, May 11, 1938; Hull to Caffery, May 20, 1938, *FRUS 1938*, 316-318; Frank D. McCann, "The Brazilian General Staff and Brazil's Military Situation, 1900-1945," *Journal of Inter-American Studies and World Affairs* 25:3 (August, 1983): 310-311; and McCann, "Brazilian Foreign Relations," 9.

13. Lieuwen, *U.S. Policy in Latin America*, 75; and McCann, *Brazilian-American Alliance*, 110.

14. Walter LaFeber, *Inevitable Revolutions: The United States and Central America*, expanded ed. (New York: W. W. Norton, 1984), 82; McCann, *Brazilian-American Alliance*, 7, 110; Moura, *Autonomia na dependência*, 147-148; and Child, *Unequal Alliance*, 17-18.

15. McCann, *Brazilian-American Alliance*, 110 n. 8.

16. Cel. Qema Osny Vasconcelos, *2 Guerra Mundial* (N.p.: Escola de Comando e Estado Maior do Exército, 1969), 52; and McCann, *Brazilian-American Alliance*, 111-112, 119.

17. McCann, *Brazilian-American Alliance*, 117-122, 123-132.

18. Ibid., 124-132. For Brazil's interest in maintaining the German arms supply connection, see Stanley E. Hilton, *Brazil and the Great Powers, 1930-1939: The Politics of Trade Rivalry* (Austin: University of Texas Press, 1975), 181-191.

19. McCann, *Brazilian-American Alliance*, 27, 132-135, n. 31.

20. General Matthew B. Ridgeway, "Conversations with Colonel John M. Blair," December 15, 1971, transcript vol. 1, sess. 2, Senior Officers Debriefing Program, U.S. Army Military Research Collection, U.S. Military History Institute, U.S. Army War College, Carlisle Barracks, Pennsylvania, 42 [hereafter the debriefing program transcripts of any officer will be cited as Officer Name, Oral History, date, page number, USMHI]. Ridgeway was a member of Marshall's staff and the chief Latin American planner in the War Department at the time.

21. Welles to Caffery, May 8, 1940, *FRUS 1940*, 40-42; Moura, *Autonomia na dependência*, 143; and McCann, *Brazilian-American Alliance*, 9, 34.

22. Ibid.

23. Conn and Fairchild, *Framework*, 33, 268-273; and Hilton, *Hitler's Secret War*, 195.

24. Caffery to Hull, May 24, 1940, *FRUS 1940*, 43.

25. Ibid.; Moura, *Autonomia na dependência*, 143; and Nunn, *Yesterday's Soldiers*, 44.

26. Caffery to Hull, June 7, 1940, June 10, 1940, *FRUS 1940*, 45-47. Concern over Brazil's dependence on foreign suppliers for war matériel dated from the

Old Republic and provided the stimulus for the drive for an indigenous arms production base that emerged during the era of Getúlio Vargas. See Stanley E. Hilton, "The Armed Forces and Industrialists in Modern Brazil: The Drive for Military Autonomy (1889–1954)," *Hispanic American Historical Review* 62:4 (November 1982): 629, 633.

27. Caffery to Hull, June 7, 1940, *FRUS 1940*, 46; and McCann, *Brazilian-American Alliance*, 205.

28. "National Policy-Supply of Arms"; and Welles to Caffery, August 2, 1940, *FRUS 1940*, 12–13, 50.

29. Caffery to Hull, September 24, 1940, *FRUS 1940*, 51; and Moura, *Autonomia na dependência*, 143.

30. McCann, *Brazilian-American Alliance*, 208–209.

31. Krause, "Establishment of Brazilian-American Alliance," 83, 89, 91; and McCann, Ibid., 213.

32. Krause, "Establishment," 92–93, 99–102.

33. Conn and Fairchild, *Framework*, 118; and McCann, *Brazilian-American Alliance*, 225– 229.

34. Marshall to Hull, June 12, 1941, RG-59 Records of the Department of State, 810.20 Def/991, NA; and McCann, *Brazilian-American Alliance*, 224–225.

35. Krause, "Establishment," 138–139; and McCann, *Brazilian-American Alliance*, 225–229.

36. Ibid.

37. Dulaney, "Great Power Maneuvering for the Bulge of Brazil: An Episode in Defense," Historical Manuscript Files U.S. Army Military History Center, Washington, D.C., 22–24.

38. Ibid., 27–28.

39. Hilton, *Hitler's Secret War*, 46; and McCann, *Brazilian-American Alliance*, 233–234. Miller also proposed that the Brazilian and U.S. militaries jointly draw up contingency plans for the occupation of Dutch Guiana and the Azores Islands but was rebuffed.

40. The U.S. Army's "Pot of Gold" plan was not discarded but became obsolete with the development of formal military relations.

41. "Terms of Agreement," *FRUS 1941*, 507–509; Conn and Fairchild, *Framework*, 284–291; and McCann, *Brazilian-American Alliance*, 245, 272–273.

42. Terrett, "Great Power Maneuvering," 27; "The Attitude of Brazil Toward the Establishment of Naval and Air Bases by the United States," OSS Research and Analysis Report 154, 1941, cited in Nunn, *Yesterday's Soldiers*, 182; and Peter Flynn, *Brazil: A Political Analysis* (Boulder, Colo.: Westview Press, 1978), 44 nn. 69, 99. Gomes was one of the few young *tenentes* to survive the "Eighteen of the Fort" in the Copacabana revolt in 1922.

43. "Lend-Lease for Brazil (General)," n.d., RG-218, Joint Chiefs of Staff, Military Commissions U.S.-Brazil, Joint Brazil-U.S. Defense Commission, Box 3, BDC 22, NA; David Green, *The Containment of Latin America: A History of the Myths and Realities of the Good Neighbor Policy* (Chicago: Quadrangle Books, 1971), 179; Warren Michael Weis, *Cold Warriors and Coups d'etat:*

Brazilian-American Relations, 1945–1964 (Albuquerque: University of New Mexico Press, 1993), 11; and McCann, *Brazilian-American Alliance*, 267–268.

44. Hilton, *Hitler's Secret War*, 155.

.. 2 ..

Creation of the Special Relationship

When the Brazilian government announced its support of the Allied cause, the need for an arrangement to shore up defenses became more urgent. The United States attempted to supply arms for that purpose but sought concessions at the same time. Negotiations led to a formal alliance and the creation in 1942 of joint commissions to oversee military relations. Adjustment problems in the early stages of the commissions, particularly the JBUSMC, meant continued reliance on personal diplomacy to achieve progress. Once the JBUSMC functioned smoothly, it played a vital role in preparing the Brazilian Expeditionary Force for combat in Europe.

BRAZIL BREAKS RELATIONS WITH GERMANY

On the day following the Pearl Harbor bombing Getúlio Vargas declared Brazil's solidarity with the United States but stopped short of a complete break with the Axis powers. Although Oswaldo Aranha argued for an end to relations, army leaders felt such action would place Brazil in peril. The army was in no position to protect the nation from either a German or an Argentine attack. Minister of War Eurico Dutra claimed that because arms and equipment purchased from Germany could not be delivered and the Americans were unable to supplant the Germans, Brazil's ability to defend itself was questionable.[1]

Assurances from U.S. leaders failed to sway Vargas or military leaders to break relations with Germany. Politics in Rio de Janeiro favored the status quo; Aranha spoke for the Allied connection, while Dutra urged hesitation. Vargas eventually came to believe that Brazil's best opportunity lay with the democracies and sided with his foreign minister. In an address at the final session of the Third Foreign Ministers Conference in Rio de Janeiro on January 28, 1942, Aranha announced that Brazil had severed relations with the Axis powers. Dutra's conspicuous absence from the final session punctuated the military's view and served notice that cooperation with the United States still required tangible forms of assistance.[2]

At first glance Vargas's decision seemed to portend great danger to Brazilian security, for Brazil would surely face German anger without the means to protect itself. Closer examination suggests the decision was shrewd and probably the only one possible if Vargas's dream of a developed and secure Brazil was to become reality. British efforts to isolate the Axis by blockade prevented Brazil from enjoying the benefits of previous economic and military arrangements with Germany and Italy. Moreover, German failure to defeat England and resistance on the North African and Soviet fronts diminished the threat of invasion and ensured that weaponry from the Germans was unavailable. The conditions facing Vargas, coupled with U.S. promises of aid, made the choice easier; neutrality would not lead to security or economic and military assistance. Although the Brazilian decision necessitated a change in the attitude of many in the officer corps, it was probably less onerous than imagined, for pragmatism is a characteristic of Brazilian military and political elites.[3]

The decision to break with the Axis was the most important step in Brazil's move toward a military alliance with the United States. It also forced the United States to act. There was no certainty that Germany would not invade, even though its forces were preoccupied in other areas. The southern defenses were weak; to ensure the security of the approaches through Mexico, the Caribbean, and the Panama Canal, the United States needed Brazilian cooperation. The main barrier to an alliance, however, remained the will and ability of the United States to provide Brazil with assistance.

ARMS AND CONCESSIONS

The key to Brazilian military cooperation was the supply of arms and equipment. If the United States failed to provide aid, Vargas would lose the support of senior officers, thereby spelling the end of previous efforts. Department of State officials were acutely aware of the dangers and of the need to court important military figures, especially regional commanders. In February Undersecretary of State Sumner Welles urged presidential aide Harry Hopkins to exercise his influence to obtain immediate approval from the Munitions Assignment Board of a Brazilian request for spare engine parts. According to Welles, approval of the request was necessary "because of the very helpful effect such approval should have on Brigadeiro Eduardo Gomes, Commander, Fifth Aerial Base, Recife, whose voice may very largely determine the action taken by the Brazilian Government on the request of the War Department for vastly expanded facilities in Brazil with regard to the ferry service via Brazil to Africa and the Far East."[4] Welles's advice was prophetic, for Gomes became a strong supporter of the U.S. connection throughout his lengthy career.

Despite the efforts of Hopkins and Welles, General Amaro Soares Bittencourt, chief of the Brazilian Military Commission, had little to cheer. Bittencourt was in Washington with Finance Minister Artur de Souza Costa to arrange economic and military assistance promised when Brazil broke with Germany. He found that little aid was then available. Low production rates and high demands from Great Britain and the Soviet Union outstripped the U.S. ability to increase or deliver desired war matériel speedily. Bittencourt bitterly observed that "the United States owes an obligation to Brazil." He "was not satisfied with the materiel promised" and requested a definite statement of precisely what would be provided. Bittencourt threatened that "if nothing is received from the United States, the effect upon [Brazilian] public opinion would be disastrous."[5]

Souza Costa dealt with the problem more objectively, but the answers to his queries were the same. After a meeting with U.S. military officials Brazil's finance minister noted that "in regard to the navy—satisfactory; in regard to air—pretty good; in regard to the ground munitions—poor." The realization that the United States was unable to supply Brazil immediately caused Souza Costa to articulate the paniclike fear gripping Brazilians. When informed the equipment for coastal defenses would not be available in the near future, he nervously replied, "Now we will accept anything at all which will help the defense of Brazil." Defense for an expected attack was paramount to Brazil's leaders.[6]

At the same time the Munitions Assignment Board refused Brazilian requests, War Department strategists pressed for concessions. The Army Ferry Command wanted to station additional personnel at ADP bases and to obtain approval for unlimited flights over Brazilian territory. Washington war planners continued to cling to the idea of using U.S. soldiers for Brazil's defense. Parallel to diplomatic efforts to win Brazilian approval, the army made new plans to put U.S. troops in the strategic Northeast. The "Lilac" plan proposed that an initial force of fifteen thousand men, with air support, concentrate around air bases in Belém, Natal, and Recife. Two reinforcing groups of nineteen thousand men each would follow to round out the complement.[7]

The Brazilians were unaware of the Lilac plan and continued to stress a local defense with U.S. weaponry. Bittencourt pleaded Brazil's immediate need of arms and equipment because its break with Germany and its geographic location made his country the candidate for the first attack in the hemisphere. Nevertheless, Washington kept to the position that it was better to send U.S. troops to stem any German attack rather than rely on ill-prepared Brazilian forces.[8] The gulf between the two nations on the issue remained wide and threatened to prevent a formal military alliance, and there was little indication that either side was prepared to relent.

TOWARD A FORMAL ALLIANCE

The U.S. response revealed that many in the army defined diplomacy in a narrow military sense and had yet to grasp the political nature of military relations with Brazil. At a time when the security of the South Atlantic required better communication to resolve differences, U.S. officials ignored Brazilian sensitivity regarding foreign troops on national soil. Oswaldo Aranha recognized that improved dialogue was essential for successful collaboration and astutely suggested the creation of two mixed commissions to oversee military relations.[9] Rather than simply enlarge the U.S. military attaché staff, which could be reduced unilaterally, joint commissions would lock the two militaries into an alliance that would seemingly guarantee Brazil a secure source of war supplies. Before such commissions could be created, however, the Souza Costa mission had to reach agreement with the United States on wider economic and military assistance. And if the Brazilian military was to cooperate, aid would have to be forthcoming. On that issue rested the proposed military alliance.

Allied reverses in Europe and continued fear of invasion drew Brazilian and U.S. national interests together and forced the conclusion of negotiations. In March Welles and Souza Costa signed the Washington Accords. The economic part of the agreement called for large-scale U.S. assistance in the form of loans to develop infrastructure valuable to the war effort. The agreement aimed to increase the output of agricultural products and strategic natural resources. In conjunction with the loans, the United States agreed to provide for the construction of a transportation system to enable the Allies to benefit from the increased production.[10] Concomitantly, other important sectors of the Brazilian economy, such as the steel industry, would be developed.

The section in the accords dealing with military assistance represented a pared-down version of extensive earlier aid requests. During negotiations the Brazilians asked for enough equipment to form and maintain the core of an armored division, as well as small arms, machine guns, ammunition, and guns for anti-aircraft and anti-tank units. Rather than create a new arms supply program, the agreement only expanded the 1941 Lend-Lease arrangement. Under the new deal the United States pledged the transfer of $200 million worth of arms and munitions, including medium and light tanks, a number of anti-aircraft batteries, and a variety of aircraft. Brazil was to pay one-third of the total amount of assistance, and the United States reserved the right to suspend the program should defense needs justify such action. Although the amount was less than desired, the promise of arms and equipment had a salutary effect on Brazilian Army leaders.[11]

At times negotiations were intense, and neither side received all that it wanted, though each achieved its primary objectives at relatively small cost. Brazil received help in modernizing its military and economic infrastructure. The United States obtained approval for a broad expansion of its presence in Brazil that included an increase in the number of maintenance personnel at the ADP sites, use of air and naval bases, and carte blanche permission for U.S. aircraft to pass through Brazilian airspace. The right to station U.S. troops in the Northeast had always been a dead issue, and the accords did not alter matters in that regard. The agreement was of great importance, however, because it established the basis for the May 1942 Political-Military Agreement, which made possible the creation of the Joint Brazil–United States Defense Commission and the Joint Brazil–United States Military Commission, the primary vehicles of the military alliance.[12]

THE 1942 POLITICAL-MILITARY ACCORD

Shortly after the signing of the Washington Accords, the Brazilian Army, Navy, and Air Force chiefs of staff and Foreign Minister Aranha presented the United States with a secret proposal for a defense alliance that went well beyond previous arrangements. Central to the plan was the establishment of two commissions comprising officers from Brazil and the United States to coordinate expanded military relations. The proposal would link the two militaries in a marriage in which the United States supplied the means for Brazil to develop its military capabilities in return for cooperation in the war effort. In addition, the U.S. military was to guarantee Brazil's security from extra- and intracontinental aggression. Under the plan U.S. Army Air Corps and Navy personnel in the country would be under Brazilian command.[13]

War Department reaction was favorable, although certain aspects of the proposal raised questions. Assistant Chief of Staff Dwight D. Eisenhower recommended that the War Department move rapidly to either accept the proposal or offer a counterproposal. Eisenhower objected, however, to the establishment of two mixed military commissions. Not wanting control diffused, the future Allied commander argued that only one commission meeting in Washington was necessary.[14]

Most disturbing to Eisenhower were Articles 9, 16, and 17 of the plan. The first called for U.S. assistance in any "intra-continental campaign," which would oblige the United States to help Brazil if another American republic, particularly Argentina, initiated hostilities. The latter articles were equally troubling because they gave the United States the responsibility for air and sea patrols off the northern coast while placing operational control under Brazilian command. Despite reservations about the military aspects of the plan, Eisenhower was mindful of the need to act while the opportunity existed. He was dubious, however, of including any non-military entities in the negotiations over the proposals. He suggested excluding the Department of State from any negotiations because "to reach [a] suitable defense agreement through the channel of the State Department and via air mail will involve an endless exchange of notes and will require more time than desirable. We should strike now while the iron is hot, even though the advantages to be gained for the present may be more political than military." Strangely, Eisenhower reasoned that army and navy officers currently in Brazil should conduct negotiations under the leadership of Ambassador Jefferson Caffery, which, of course, would involve civilians.[15]

Navy Department objections focused less on Department of State participation than on what the proposal offered. The navy felt the Brazilians demanded much but offered little, especially guaranteed U.S. support without quid pro quo from the Brazilians. Article 16 especially worried the navy, particularly if it meant helping Brazil in a war against Argentina. Navy officials did not reject the plan but wanted modifications before concluding the deal. The navy recognized that any agreement was political and wanted definite political commitments from the Brazilian government for the proposed military commissions to develop a "Basic War Plan" that conformed to U.S. war aims.[16]

Although some officers in the U.S. Army had yet to understand the realities of Brazilian politics, the political nature of a military agreement did not escape many high-ranking officials in the War Department. In a directive to the two army officers assigned to conduct negotiations with the Brazilians, Eisenhower explained that the War Department wished "to conclude an agreement very general in nature, omitting specific details of command, zones of responsibility," and other essentially military matters. What Eisenhower envisioned was an agreement similar to the ABC-1 joint staff planning arrangement the United States had with Great Britain. On the issue of the two commissions Eisenhower changed his mind and concurred with the Brazilian idea of having one body in Washington and another in Rio de Janeiro. Above all, Eisenhower admonished the negotiating officers not to insist on changes that might cause the Brazilians to counter with modifications in the aircraft ferrying operations.[17]

Maintenance of the vital air link to the battlefronts was paramount to the U.S. Joint Chiefs of Staff (JCS), even if it meant accepting the proposal without modifications. The immediate and long-term interests of both countries, especially those of the United States, could best be served by a cooperative spirit at this juncture. Besides, agreements could always be changed to fit objectives as the situation warranted. Now was not the time to raise objections that might spoil negotiations.

While Washington considered the proposal, attempts to establish close personal ties began in earnest. Previous meetings between General Marshall and General Góes Monteiro carried the brunt of early military relations, but the support of regional commanders was crucial for deepening ties. In the important Northeast that meant the cooperation of General Eduardo Gomes, the Brazilian Air Force (FAB) chief of the region. General Robert Olds, head of the U.S. ferrying command, understood the need for Gomes's support and assiduously cultivated his friendship. Olds impressed Gomes with his sincere desire to assist the FAB; the delivery of twelve aircraft also had a salubrious effect on the Brazilian. Gomes returned the support, suggesting an addition to the Political-Military Agreement that expanded the Airport Development Program: "Brazil, in obedience to its continental traditions and to its pledge of solidarity with the U.S. and being aware of the development of international events and the necessities derived from them, will facilitate in the national territory of the Republic, through a direct understanding between the two Governments, the means necessary for normal communications, transportation, and connections between the United States and the different theaters of operations."[18]

The final text of the agreement did not include Gomes's suggestion, but the fact that he made it showed the movement of influential officers toward alignment with the United States. Similarly, Olds's effort indicated the importance the United States placed on developing close relations. The role of personal friendships, however, should not be overrated. National and institutional interests motivated officers such as Gomes and Olds more than personal feelings. While maintenance of the air link provided the motivation for the United States, belief that alliance with the North Americans offered the best chance of modernization undoubtedly disposed many Brazilian officers to accept alignment with the northern giant. Negotiations dealt with issues far removed from personalism.

The U.S. officers charged with conducting negotiations arrived in Brazil in early April 1942, and matters proceeded smoothly because the negotiators did not raise the question of stationing U.S. troops in the Northeast.[19] The two sides reached an understanding quickly, but last-minute U.S. Navy objections nearly derailed the deal. On April 20 at the last meeting prior to the official signing of the agreement, the U.S. naval attaché informed the negotiating officers that the navy did not like the wording of the articles dealing with the maintenance of maritime communications between the two countries and the delivery of Lend-Lease matériel. Of particular concern was Article 2, which absolved the Brazilian Navy of undertaking any operations outside territorial waters, and Article 7, which seemed to ally Brazil and the United States against Argentina.[20]

A spirited discussion ensued between Colonel Kenner F. Hertford of the U.S. Army Latin American Theater and Admiral William O. Spears of the Navy Department. Hertford contended that the agreement in its present form was satisfactory to the War Department and that it was unwise to suggest changes now because negotiations had reached conclusion. Nevertheless, the navy insisted on modifying the text, issuing a veiled threat by suggesting the matter be taken up with the Department of State, which the army wanted to exclude.[21]

Navy tactics angered Hertford. He complained that for two or three weeks he had been discussing the agreement with naval officials and only now had they demanded changes. The navy remained unmoved, and the matter was "being taken pretty high." The army would continue with the final phase of negotiations, but if the Brazilians did not balk at the navy's proposed changes and agreement seemed imminent, the army negotiators were to return home and let the navy representative and Ambassador Caffery conclude the deal.[22] The message to the powerful Brazilian Army leaders would be clear: the U.S. Army was not a party to the proposed changes.

Navy quibbling also provoked Ambassador Caffery's anger. He sent a strongly worded message to the Department of State demanding an explanation for naval recalcitrance. Caffery pointed out that the navy had had a draft of the proposed agreement well before the departure of negotiators to Brazil and should have presented its case before that time.[23]

Pressure from the ambassador and the Department of State failed to deter the navy and threatened to "wreck proceedings" at such a late date but did gain some minor concessions from the navy. The Navy Department agreed to withdraw all objections except those concerning command of naval operations and the supply of war matériel. The navy wanted it clearly stated who was to be in command and that supply would be governed by U.S. needs.[24]

Navy obstinacy forced Ambassador Caffery to present, over his objections, the Brazilians with the proposed modifications. Oswaldo Aranha informed the ambassador that Brazil would not change the agreed-upon draft agreement but shrewdly offered a gentleman's agreement that broke the impasse and served Brazilian purposes. Aranha promised that, regardless of the wording, the Brazilian Navy would operate outside territorial waters in areas designated by the proposed joint military commissions. He added that Brazil understood that supply of war matériel and maintenance of maritime communications would be in relation to the needs and commitments of the United States and its allies. Although the Navy Department preferred a change in text, the assurances placated it enough to rescind all remaining objections.[25]

THE JOINT COMMISSIONS

With navy concerns assuaged, final agreement was reached on May 23 and signed on May 27, 1942. The contents remained the same; the only change was a general tightening of language. The United States pledged to help Brazil develop its military capabilities through organization, training, and supply of arms and equipment, as well as assist in the development of infrastructure relevant to the war effort. To oversee and direct the new military relationship, Article 1 established two joint commissions: the Joint Brazil–United States Defense Commission to be seated in Washington, and the Joint Brazil–United States Military Commission to be located in Rio de Janeiro.[26]

The JBUSDC, which began operations on August 15, 1942, was the locus of high-level military diplomacy during the war. Located in Washington, D.C., from whence financial, material, and technical assistance flowed, the JBUSDC's function was to undertake studies and make recommendations on mutual defense matters. Delegation members consisted of representatives from the various branches of the two nations' armed services. Although the number of members from each country varied, each delegation had only one vote. The Army, Navy, and Air Force Ministries appointed the Brazilian delegation, while the War and Navy Departments selected the U.S. members.[27]

From the beginning, the JBUSDC's composition indicated the importance both countries placed on the relationship. Senior officers from the different branches of the Brazilian and U.S. armed forces sat on the commission. Original Brazilian members included General Estevão Leitão de Carvalho of the army, Admiral Alvaro Rodriques de Vasconcelos of the navy, and General Vasco Alves Secco of the air force. The first U.S. delegation consisted of important officers such as General J. G. Ord, General Kenner F. Hertford, and Colonel (later general) John D. Gillet of the army, and Admiral William O. Spears of the navy.[28]

During the war the JBUSDC had an extra dimension as a facilitator between Brazilian and U.S. companies wishing to undertake war-related enterprises. This role gave the U.S. delegation an element of economic decision making that had implications beyond military matters. One example that illustrates how the mechanism worked was a 1943 request by the Sperry Gyroscope Company to send personnel to train Brazilians in the operation and maintenance of equipment purchased from the company. The line of communication went from Sperry to the Brazilian Air Force delegate, at the time General Alves Secco, who passed the request to General J. G. Ord, chair of the JBUSDC. Ord then approved or disapproved the request and passed his recommendation to the War Department. Once the War Department gave its sanction, communication of the decision went back through the same channels. The commission also recommended the Brazilians coming to the United States for training in private companies where sensitive instrumentation was being developed or manufactured.[29]

Two important facets of the business connection made the JBUSDC a significant actor in Brazil's economic and political life. Commission action could be a negative or a positive force in important areas of Brazilian development. Equally important was the development of close ties between U.S. business executives and politically powerful Brazilian officers made possible by the arrangement. Although no evidence suggests improprieties, the influence of those personal relations in U.S. economic dominance of post-war Brazil cannot be discounted. Given the nature of the U.S. system, Brazilian entrepreneurs did not enjoy the same degree of entrée to economic and political decision-making institutions in the United States. The close contact, however, may have given the Brazilian officers greater confidence in their ability to deal with aspects of development they had not experienced before.

As the senior commission the JBUSDC's first task was to recommend the establishment and functions of the Joint Brazil–United States Military Commission in Rio de Janeiro. Recommendation No. 10 of October 28, 1942, did just that, even though nearly a month passed before the War and Navy Departments gave their approval. Following approval another month went by before the Rio commission began operation. The JBUSMC's role differed from that of its Washington counterpart. As the junior partner the Rio commission had the task of implementing the recommendations and plans prepared by the JBUSDC. The JBUSMC could, however, submit recommendations to the parent commission regarding major changes in operation plans and policies, delivery of military aid, and training. The Rio commission also could review and make recommendations on Brazilian requests for armament and other war matériel. As part of its duties the JBUSMC maintained liaison between and cooperation with U.S. Army and Navy senior commanders in Brazil and the Brazilian chiefs of staff and between local commanders of both countries' armed forces.[30]

As with the JBUSDC, Brazil and the United States thought staffing of the JBUSMC important enough to assign senior officers as delegates. The U.S. Army chief of staff and the chief of naval operations named the U.S. members without specific approval of the president. The chain-of-command reporting, however, was diffuse. In matters of policy and procedure the U.S. Army members answered to the assistant chief of staff, Operations Division of the Joint Chiefs of Staff. The Military Attaché Branch of the Military Intelligence Service had charge of administrative details. Navy delegates reported directly to the Navy Department. The U.S. Navy Mission in Brazil remained intact, but the establishment of the JBUSMC suspended the military and air mission contracts under which army relations had operated since January 1941. In the interest of continuity the officers serving on those missions were among the first U.S. Army delegates to the JBUSMC. Brazilian members were appointed in the same manner as were those on the JBUSDC.[31]

The creation of the JBUSDC and the JBUSMC marked the birth of a formal Brazil–United States military alliance. The new structures provided a systematic means for armed forces interaction and gave breadth to informal military diplomacy. The Joint Board for the Defense of Northeast Brazil disbanded, and its duties passed to the JBUSDC. In addition, a Brazilian purchasing commission separate from the JBUSDC delegation established itself in Washington but negotiated purchases through the JBUSDC. Members of the purchasing commission, however, reported directly to their respective service branch in Brazil rather than to the Brazilian JBUSDC delegates. Although the purchasing commission was a parallel organization, it had a limited role; the JBUSDC was the center of Brazil-U.S. wartime military relations.[32]

EARLY ADJUSTMENTS

Both commissions were operational by early 1943, when they began work in earnest. One of the first recommendations prepared in joint planning sessions in Washington addressed the defense of the Northeast in a way that appeared to signal a change in the Brazilian military's strategic orientation. U.S. military planners believed the recommendation reflected an understanding by the Brazilians of the need to fortify the Northeast and move away from the preoccupation with schemes emphasizing the primacy of defense of the south.[33]

The Americans were wrong. Nothing had changed in Brazilian thinking, and little had been done for ground defense in the Northeast. The U.S. military's failure to understand the Brazilian point of view was due to a lack of knowledge of Brazil's history and intramilitary politics. The Americans thought Minister of War Eurico Dutra's opposition to a Northeast orientation and to the commission's recommendations represented a lukewarm commitment to the Allied cause. Dutra admired much in the German military, but his objections rested on a national view of an Argentine enemy and his personal dislike of the chief Brazilian delegate to the JBUSDC, General Estevão Leitão de Carvalho. As a result, Brazil continued its orientation south, and effective action by the commissions suffered.[34]

U.S. arrogance during the early days of the relationship also hampered cooperative efforts. Unmilitary actions of the U.S. military attaché, General Hayes Kroner, caused widespread belief among JBUSMC members that he was unstable. Kroner remained at his post, however, until the end of the war, when he was relieved and sent home to forced retirement. The chief of the army section of the

JBUSMC, General Roland P. Shugg, also displayed a lack of tact that hurt joint endeavors. Soon after his arrival in Rio de Janeiro Shugg became embroiled in a controversy with the U.S. Embassy and made disparaging remarks to the Brazilians (in addition to violating his orders). He remained only a short time before being reduced to the rank of colonel and sent home in disgrace.[35]

Shugg's replacement, General Charles H. Gerhardt, brought no change in the U.S. manner of dealing with the Brazilians. He disregarded the War Department's conclusion that knowledge of the culture and language of Brazil should be required of U.S. representatives. Instead, Gerhardt made it clear to the Brazilians that he thought it unnecessary for the Americans to speak Portuguese. He also caused dissension by ignoring the advice and recommendations of the U.S. officers on the JBUSMC who were sensitive to the diplomatic skills needed for good relations. The Brazilians responded in kind, often deliberately snubbing Gerhardt. It was, according to the army's chief of the Western Hemisphere Branch, Colonel Godwyn Ordway, a "continual headache" for military leaders concerned with maintaining cordial relations. Gerhardt's conflicts with the JBUSMC and the Brazilians ended when he too was reduced to the rank of colonel and sent back to the United States.[36]

Confusion as to the role each commission played in the alliance blocked progress of joint defense planning. An inspection trip report by two U.S. officers in June 1943 found that unclear roles and responsibilities caused misunderstandings between the JBUSDC and the JBUSMC. Additionally, the report mentioned that "recommendations are apparently not worked out in final form between the Brazilian and American delegates [of the JBUSMC] together before adoption in formal session," which in any case the full U.S. delegation usually did not attend.[37]

Brazilian and U.S. members of the JBUSDC adjusted more rapidly to formalized military relations than did those on the JBUSMC, which in part caused many of the early adjustment problems. Because most of the earlier negotiations took place in Washington, officers engaged in the talks had the opportunity to become accustomed to one another in a U.S. context that made transition to the JBUSDC relatively easy. The situation in Rio de Janeiro was different.

Expansion of ties meant the inclusion of officers who had little or no previous experience working with their foreign counterparts. In replacing the Joint Board for the Defense of Northeast Brazil, the JBUSMC took on a multiregional outlook with wider duties. New individuals came into contact for the first time without benefit of a history to guide personal and professional relations. It is not surprising that problems inherent in the establishment of a joint venture composed of men of diverse cultural and linguistic backgrounds prevented the quick, efficient operation of the commission.

PERSONAL DIPLOMACY

Although the commissions had an inauspicious start, especially the JBUSMC, a modus operandi was worked out among the delegates that allowed the agencies to function reasonably well during the war. Despite the regularization of the relationship, personal diplomacy of senior U.S. officers remained one of the most effective forms of collaboration in the early stages of formal ties. After a time the commissions systematized military relations to the point where personal diplomacy among high-ranking officers became less important.[38] In the process the Brazilian military willingly became dependent on the United States for arms, equipment, and training. Nevertheless, personal ties remained an adjunct in military diplomacy, especially among naval officers.

Naval relations extended back to World War I, when Brazilian Navy officers served aboard U.S. Navy vessels in the South Atlantic. After installation of a mission in Brazil in 1922, the U.S. Navy became an important factor in the development and training of the Brazilian Navy. With an established history, officers of the two navies enjoyed a greater opportunity to form closer relationships than did their army colleagues. Those past links facilitated the efforts of Admiral Jonas H. Ingram, whose personal diplomacy was responsible for the first joint action. His success paved the way for joint army activities.[39]

In the months prior to Pearl Harbor, Ingram, who was the commander of the U.S. South Atlantic Force, skillfully courted important

Brazilian politicians and navy officers in the Northeast to secure basing rights for U.S. ships engaged in convoy escort, interception of enemy shipping, and anti-submarine patrols. His efforts paid high dividends. By early 1942 U.S. navy aircraft were operating from Brazilian bases, and the Brazilians had permitted the establishment of the South Atlantic Wing of the Air Transport Command in Natal and the United States Armed Forces Command South Atlantic in Recife.[40]

Ingram's access to and influence with Brazilian decision makers far exceeded those of U.S. members of the JBUSMC. His relationship with Getúlio Vargas illustrates his impact on military relations. When an early 1942 German submarine campaign did great damage to Brazilian merchant vessels, Vargas embargoed Brazilian shipping, citing the lack of adequate protection. Ingram persuaded Vargas to reverse the order and gained more in the process. Vargas not only lifted the embargo but also placed unofficial command of Brazilian Air and Navy forces in the admiral's hands, calling Ingram his "Sea Lord." More important, Ingram became a personal and confidential adviser to the Brazilian president.[41] Ingram's work bypassed the floundering Joint Board for the Defense of Northeast Brazil and played an important part in expanding ties. After the May agreement and during the early confused operation of the JBUSMC, Ingram's personal diplomacy proved vital to the nascent evolution of military relations.

Interestingly, in a reaction that was to repeat itself in future decades, Washington officials far removed from the scene and with little cultural sensitivity often disapproved of the actions of officers most involved in the practical aspects of the military alliance. Ingram's nemesis was Secretary of State Frank Knox, who denigrated Brazil for giving command of its defenses to a foreigner and opposed that role for the admiral. Knox had no knowledge of Brazilian society, in which personalism was ingrained, of the Brazilians' different view of friendship, or of Brazil's historical attachment to foreigners. Fortunately for military collaboration, subtle pressure from Ambassador Caffery preserved the special place Ingram had in Brazilian defense affairs.[42]

THE BRAZILIAN EXPEDITIONARY FORCE

Brazil declared war on the Axis on August 22, 1942, while the newly created military commission in Rio de Janeiro struggled to plan and implement measures for defense. Immediate problems obviated thought of the participation of Brazilian troops in any plans for the invasion of North Africa or Europe.[43] Brazilian political leaders, however, dreamed of a future in which their country sat with the other powers in world councils. Many argued that in order to achieve that place, Brazil had to do more than provide bases and raw materials. Sharing the dangers of the battlefield in proportion to its ability would guarantee acceptance of Brazil into the inner circle of the world powers.

The idea of an expeditionary force first arose in the heady days following Brazil's declaration of war. In 1941 the United States attempted to obtain cooperation in making contingency plans for the joint occupation of Dutch Guiana and the Azores Islands, but Brazilian military leaders rejected the proposal.[44] Occupation duty was not as attractive as combat in terms of Brazilian "national greatness" (*grandeza*) and the army's institutional prestige. Considerations of the practicality of making a contribution through combat became lost in the emotion of the moment.

The most influential military leaders, Generals Dutra and Góes Monteiro, believed participation in combat would solidify the Brazilian-U.S. alliance and ensure continued military assistance. Their case received support from a group of mid-ranked officers who were pro–United States or had personal reasons for wanting to send forces overseas. Bowing to the desires of the military and the Foreign Ministry, Vargas sanctioned the idea in December 1942.[45] If the United States agreed, Brazilians would actively engage in the greatest upheaval of the twentieth century.

U.S. military personnel in Rio de Janeiro and Washington took a long view and agreed with Vargas, advising that Brazilian participation in combat operations was necessary for the maintenance of good relations. In anticipation, and adding weight to the argument, the JBUSDC issued Recommendation No. 14, which called for a restructuring of the defenses of northern Brazil in a manner that would provide a force "capable of being employed in other operations in collaboration with American forces." In essence the plan would accomplish long-held U.S. desires by directing Brazilian attention away from the south and focusing it on the Northeast. The U.S. General Staff did not favor Brazilian inclusion despite the advice of the JBUSDC and the JBUSMC, for it believed the contribution would have little impact on the war's outcome.[46]

General Staff resistance remained firm until President Roosevelt exercised his powers and acceded to Brazilian wishes. At a late January 1943 meeting with Vargas in Natal Roosevelt promised to supply some of the equipment for a Brazilian expeditionary force. The War Department took its cue from the president and gave its sanction to the inclusion of Brazilian troops in operations abroad.[47] Once the decision had been made, it was the job of the commissions to plan and prepare the Brazilian forces for a combat role. Although the JBUSMC was charged with the task of preparing the Brazilian soldiers, most of the training took place in Italy.

Planning the scope of Brazilian participation in combat rested with the JBUSDC in Washington. General Marshall and the Joint Chiefs of Staff approved a plan by General Leitão de Carvalho that called for the formation of three to four divisions. The plan ran into opposition in Brazil. The Brazilian General Staff, especially Leitão de Carvalho's personal enemy, General Dutra, disagreed with the provisions for training and supplying equipment.[48]

To take advantage of Brazilian troops already in the Northeast, Leitão de Carvalho wanted to create one training center in that region through which each of the three or four divisions would pass. The United States would supply fifty percent of the necessary training equipment, which would be left for each successive division. Dutra had different ideas that were not as efficient but would result in a greater overall amount of assistance from the United States. Dutra envisoned the creation of training centers in three different locations, with the United States providing one-half the equipment for each site. Dutra's scheme required more material aid than the United States was willing to offer. U.S. military leaders rejected the proposal, as did Brazilian members of the JBUSDC.[49] Much as their U.S. colleagues had done regarding the expeditionary force question, the Brazilian delegates opposed their General Staff and won.

The organization of the Brazilian Expeditionary Force cemented the Brazilian military's alliance with and dependence on the United States. The JBUSDC coordinated special training for Brazilian officers at U.S. military schools, and the JBUSMC supervised the training and preparation of the FEB forces in Brazil. Arms and equipment were American, including the boots the FEB troops wore in the Italian campaign. Although original plans called for three divisions, U.S. commitment to a cross-channel invasion left available shipping for only one.[50] Problems associated with adopting new methods, organization, and ideology undoubtedly had an impact on the decision to use only one division as well.

The story of the difficulties in preparing the FEB and of its part in the Italian campaign has been told best elsewhere. Suffice it to say that, despite the obstacles of adjusting to U.S. arms, doctrine, and organization, the participation of a division in combat solidified the special ties between the Brazilian and U.S. militaries. With the onset of World War II Brazilian political and military leaders decided security and national greatness could best be achieved through a partnership with the United States. But before the battles in Italy were over and the victorious Brazilian troops returned home, it became evident that the nature of the relationship was in the process of change.[51]

NOTES

1. Estevão Leitão de Carvalho, *Memórias de um soldado legalista*, vol. 3 (Rio de Janeiro: Biblioteca do Exército Editora, 1964), 437; and Conn and Fairchild, *Framework*, 311.

2. McCann, *Brazilian-American Alliance*, 257.

3. Nelson Werneck Sodré, *História militar do Brasil*, 2 ed., vol. 40 (Rio de Janeiro: Editora Civilização Brasileira S.A., 1968), 284; Frank D. McCann, *A nação armada: Ensaios sobre a história do Exército Brasileiro*, trans. Silvio Robim (Recife: Editora Guararapes, 1982), 140; and Moura, *Autonomia na dependência*, 143.

4. Welles to Hopkins, February 27, 1942, RG-218, JCS Geographic Files, 1942–1945, CCS 400.3295 Brazil (1-9-42), "Lend-Lease Supplies for Brazil," NA.

5. Hopkins to Major General James H. Burns, February 5, 1942; Major General J. H. Burns to General H. S. Aurand, Director of Defense Aid, February 10, 1942; Memorandum of Meeting, February 12, 1942, RG-218, JCS Geographic Files, 1942–1945, CCS 400.3295 Brazil (1-9-42), "Lend-Lease Supplies for Brazil," NA; and Conn and Fairchild, *Framework*, 315–316.

6. Memorandum of Meeting in General J. H. Burns Office, February 17, 1942, RG-218, JCS Geographic Files, 1942–1945, CCS 400.3295 Brazil (1-9-42), "Lend-Lease Supplies for Brazil," NA.

7. Memorandum of Meeting, February 12, 1942, RG-218, JCS Geographic Files, 1942–1945; and Conn and Fairchild, *Framework*, 310.

8. Memorandum of Meeting, February 12, 1942.

9. McCann, *Brazilian-American Alliance*, 261.

10. Ibid.

11. Terrett, "Great Power Maneuvering," 330; and McCann, *Brazilian-American Alliance*, 267–268.

12. McCann, *Brazilian-American Alliance*, 267–269.

13. "Political-Military Agreement Between the United States of Brazil and the United States of America," n.d., RG-218, Records of the JCS, CCS 334 (6-24-45), NA. Despite the command aspect of the plan, Vargas placed control of Brazil's coastal defense under the U.S. admiral Jonas Ingram.

14. Dwight D. Eisenhower to Chief of Staff, March 8, 1942; Eisenhower to Acting Secretary of State, March 20, 1942; and "Political-Military Agreement," n.d., RG-218, Records of the JCS, CCS 334 (6-24-45), NA.

15. Ibid.

16. Navy Comments on Proposed Agreement to Secretary of State, n.d., RG-218, Records of the JCS, CCS 334 (6-24-45), NA.

17. The negotiating officers were Colonels Robert L. Walsh and Henry A. Barber. Eisenhower to Walsh and Barber, April 12, 1942, RG-218, Records of the JCS, CCS 334 (6-24-45), NA; and James F. Ransone, Jr., "The Grand Alliance," in *The Second World War: Europe and the Mediterranean*, ed. Thomas E. Griess (Wayne, N.J.: Avery, 1984), 182.

18. "Presented Personally to Colonel Barber by Brigadeiro Eduardo Gomes, April 14, 1942, in Rio de Janeiro as his [Gomes] suggestion for inclusion in U.S.-Brazil Politico-Military Agreement," RG-218, Records of the JCS, CCS 334 (6-24-45), NA. The FAB became an independent arm of the Brazilian military in 1941.

19. Captain E. E. Brady to Barber and Walsh, April 20, 1942; Admiral F. J. Horne to Secretary of State, April 20, 1942, RG-218, Records of the JCS, CCS 334 (6-24-45), NA. Despite Eisenhower's instructions to Barber and Walsh not to raise the issue, U.S. strategists refused to give up the idea of putting U.S. combat troops in Brazil. The War Department tried to achieve that goal indirectly by giving Barber and Walsh permission to agree to general direction by Brazil of any U.S. forces that might be stationed in the country.

20. The naval attaché was Captain E. E. Brady.

21. Memorandum for the Record, April 25, 1942, RG-218, Records of the JCS, CCS 334 (6-24-45), NA.

22. Transcript of telephone conversation—Hertford with Barber in Rio, April 20, 1942, RG-218, Records of the JCS, CCS 334 (6-24-45), NA.

23. Hertford, Memo for the Record, April 25, 1942, RG-218, Records of the JCS, CCS 334 (6-24-45), NA.

24. Ibid.

25. Caffery to Aranha, May 4, 1942, RG-218, Records of the JCS, CCS 334 (6-24-45), NA.

26. Caffery to Aranha, May 27, 1942, RG-218, Records of the JCS, CCS 334 (6-24-45), NA.

27. "Discussion of the Political-Military Agreement," n.d.; "Status of Joint Brazil-U.S. Defense Commission," Note for the Record, January 4, 1946; Brigadier General Hayes A. Kroner to Assistant Chief of Staff, "Joint Brazilian–United States Military Commission in Rio de Janeiro," November 26, 1942; and JBUSMC, "Recommendations No. 16," October 15, 1945, RG-218, Records of the JCS, CCS 334 (6-24-45), NA.

28. Ibid.

29. Captain Davis O. Harrington to Colonel Armando S. M. Marrariglioia, December 9, 1942; S. W. Bedell (Sperry Corporation) to Colonel Vasco Alves Secco, January 26, 1943; Bedell to Lt. Colonel John D. Gillet, January 27, 1943; Secco to General J. G. Ord, February 10, 1943; Ord to General Thomas T. Handy, February 12, 1943; and Handy to Ord, February 20, 1943, RG-218, Records of the JCS Military Commissions, U.S.-Brazil, Box 2, BDC 2, 3520—Schools Book 2, NA.

30. "Discussion of the Political-Military Agreement," n.d.; and Memo to Lt. Colonel Conner, April 27, 1943, "Missions and Observers," RG-218, Records of the JCS Military Commissions, U.S.-Brazil, Box 3, BDC 5400, NA.

31. General Hayes A. Kroner to Assistant Chief of Staff, G-1, November 26, 1942, RG-218, Records of the JCS, CCS 334 (6-24-45); and Carlos Martins Pereira e Sousa to Cordell Hull, April 21, 1943, RG-218, JCS Central Decimal File, 1948–1950, CCS 300 (9-24-48), NA.

32. "Current Status of the Military Aspects of Brazilian-U.S. Relations," Memorandum for the Secretary of the Army, November 7, 1949, RG-218, Records of the JCS, CCS 091.713 (6-6-47), Sec. 1, NA; and McCann, *Brazilian-American Alliance*, 272–273.

33. Colonel Henry A. Barber to Caffery, April 17, 1942; General J. G. Ord to Chief of Staff, February 12, 1943, RG-218, Records of the JCS Military Commissions, U.S.-Brazil, Box 3, BDC 5400 5410-(1), Conferences and Meetings 1-17, NA.

34. Report of Colonel Joseph G. Hopkins, Plans Division, HG AAF, and Lt. Colonel John D. Gillet, Operations Division, Assistant Secretary of Joint Commissions on Inspection Trip to Brazil, tab G, June 1, 1943, RG-218, JCS Military Commissions, U.S.-Brazil, Box 1, BDC 1300–1350, Visits-1-, 33-6, NA; Estevão Leitão de Carvalho, *A serviço do Brasil no Segunda Guerra Mundial* (Rio de Janeiro: Biblioteca do Exército Editora, 1952), 298–320; and McCann, *Brazilian-American Alliance*, 273–274.

35. "Report of Visit to JBUSMC in RJ and to the Strategic Air Bases in Brazil," August 28, 1946; General S. J. Chamberlin, Director of Intelligence, to General Lauris Norstad, Director P&O, January 29, 1947; Norstad to Chamberlin, January 31, 1947, RG-319, P&O Decimal File, 1946–1948, Box 288, 334 JBUSMC, Cases 15–52, NA; General A. C. Wedemeyer to General William H. H. Morris, Jr., January 20, 1948, RG-319, P&O Decimal File, 1946–1948,

091 Brazil (Sec. I) (Cases 1–), NA; and General Paul Freeman, Oral History, 79–80, USMHI.

36. Ibid.

37. Report of Colonel Joseph G. Hopkins to Lt. Colonel John D. Gillet, June 1, 1943, RG-218, JCS Military Commissions, Box 1, BDC 1300–1350, Visits-1-, 33-6, NA.

38. Close personal relations, however, were developed between Brazilian and U.S. members of the JBUSMC, which assisted bilateral military relations.

39. CIA Intelligence Reports, *Brazil*, SR-17, November 30, 1948 (HST-PSF-260), Harry S. Truman Library, Independence, Missouri [hereafter cited as HST Library].

40. McCann, *Brazilian-American Alliance*, 274–275. For an institutional description of Air Transport Command activities, see Historical Division—Air Transport Command, "History of the South Atlantic Wing of the Air Transport Command," microfilm, NA.

41. McCann, *Brazilian-American Alliance*, 275–277. In calling Ingram his "Sea Lord," Vargas was probably referring, tongue in cheek, to the British admiral Lord Cochrane, who played a minor role in Brazilian independence.

42. Ibid., 295–296.

43. Brazil recognized a state of war with Germany and Italy but not Japan, so the Pacific theater was not then an option.

44. Hilton, *Hitler's Secret War*, 46.

45. McCann, *Brazilian-American Alliance*, 345–346.

46. Colonel Kenner F. Hertford (JBUSDC) to Orme Wilson (State Department Liaison at War Department), January 23, 1943, cited in McCann, *Brazilian-American Alliance*, 349; and Conn and Fairchild, *Framework*, 328.

47. Conn and Fairchild, *Framework*.

48. Leitão de Carvalho, *Serviço do Brasil*, 298–320; and McCann, *Brazilian-American Alliance*, 352–353.

49. McCann, *Brazilian-American Alliance*, 353.

50. CIA Intelligence Reports, *Brazil*, SR-17, November 30, 1948; Vernon Walters, *Silent Missions* (Garden City, N.Y.: Doubleday, 1978), 77; and Sodré, *História militar*, 286. For a listing of some of the modifications the Brazilians had to make, see Marshal João B. Mascarenhas de Morães, *The Brazilian Expeditionary Force by Its Commander*, trans. from 2d ed. (no pub. data).

51. For the best study of the FEB, see McCann, *Brazilian-American Alliance*, 343–377, 403–442. For an institutional explanation of why Brazil allied with the United States, see "O General Dutra com a palavra," *Correio da Noite*, April 3, 1945, 1.

.. 3 ..

Continuity and Change:
Early Post-War Relations

With the end of the war near and the Brazilian-American alliance firmly constructed, few in Rio de Janeiro or Washington thought major changes would ensue. Successful efforts to extend the air base agreement seemed to support that notion. Despite the apparent continuity of the special relationship, an emerging struggle among competing groups in Washington for control of post-war hemisphere defense policy sent a confused message to the Brazilians that caused some unease. Brazilian leaders feared that modernization goals and the flow of military assistance would suffer if the faction that favored a multilateral over a bilateral approach to hemisphere defense prevailed. Implicit in the confused U.S. signals to the Brazilians was that, although some things would remain the same, modifications of the relationship were in the offing.

EXTENSION OF THE AIR BASE AGREEMENT

Included in wartime agreements between Brazil and the United States were promises that U.S. military personnel would withdraw from Brazilian territory once the war was over. In 1944 President Roosevelt and the War Department reversed their positions, deciding that security would be served best with continued use of Brazilian air bases. Favorable reports from U.S. officers in Brazil led the president and Secretary of War Henry L. Stimson to believe that the time was propitious for extending the air base agreement, even though discussions of post-war commercial air rights had already been scheduled. The prevailing attitude was that a military deal would facilitate a commercial one.[1]

The officers who advised Roosevelt and Stimson that the timing was right for an agreement were correct. The Brazilians believed a new arrangement before the end of the war would support their aims by solidifying a post-war alliance. With U.S. assistance, Brazil could develop its economic and military power to the point of making the country the dominant force in South America. That idea motivated Brazilian leaders to do what was necessary to keep aid flowing. As a consequence, negotiations went smoothly, and the two sides reached preliminary agreement swiftly.[2] Brazilian and U.S. interests continued to dovetail.

The main sticking point was whether the joint use of the bases would last five or ten years. The Brazilians accepted the U.S. view that the longer period was best. On June 14, 1944, Vargas and Ambassador Caffery signed a ten-year reciprocal agreement that allowed U.S. military personnel to remain at bases in Natal, Recife, and Belém after the war ended.[3] The agreement seemed a natural progression in the relations of two close friends.

POST-WAR HEMISPHERE DEFENSE

If the air base agreement represented continuity in the relationship, the debate in Washington over the direction of post-war hemisphere defense policy reflected changes on the horizon. As the war entered its final phases, U.S. military planners began examining the role Brazil, and Latin America in general, would play in post-war defense. During the war the U.S. military preferred bilateral over collective security arrangements. A multilateral approach was good only if it made bilateral military cooperation easier. The problem was that the 1942 Rio Conference provided the basis for collective defense through the creation of the Inter-American Defense Board (IADB). Army and navy officers from the United States and the various Latin American countries serving on the board were to recommend measures for a collective hemisphere defense. The concept was unpopular with most U.S. military leaders, who considered the board too unwieldy to act quickly in a crisis and feared such an organization could have its security breached easily. They believed bilateral arrangements prevented such problems.[4]

The military still exerted strong influence on U.S. foreign policy, especially in the Western Hemisphere. Officials of the War and Navy Departments did not like the IADB; they considered it a political-diplomatic organization rather than a military agency. In addition, the military had relative freedom in dealing with the Latin Americans during the war and was reluctant to relinquish control. Department of State officials, however, wanted to regain their prominence in regional policy making and demanded to be consulted before any bilateral staff conversations took place. The military prevailed. Because of military opposition, the IADB played a minor role in wartime and post-war defense relations. Practical military diplomacy remained on a bilateral basis.[5]

BILATERALISM

U.S. military planners sought to re-examine existing arrangements and discuss future hemisphere defense plans through bilateral staff conversations when the war was still a year away from completion. The Brazilian experience was evident in U.S. plans. The Joint Chiefs of Staff wanted to exclude all non-hemisphere military influence and to confirm the role of the U.S. military as the undisputed leader should a future hemisphere defense force be formed. Each Latin American country would have a military commensurate with its capabilities and needs while being friendly and cooperative with the United States. Brazil would serve as the model that demonstrated the value of such a configuration.[6]

The JCS also wanted to maintain access to important air and naval bases in the region, to continue military missions in each Latin American country, and to train foreign officers in U.S. military schools. Most important was a plan to standardize arms to avoid the diversion of U.S. military resources to the region as had occurred during the war and to keep the Latin Americans in the U.S. camp.

High on the JCS list was the preservation of the special relationship with the Brazilian military. The JCS plan was, according to Walter LaFeber, "a textbook example of dependency . . . in the military realm." The objective was to protect the region's resources from foreign powers "through a Latin American military system that was not primarily geared to fight distant wars, but to preserve and protect the resources that North Americans needed to fight a cold, and perhaps hot, war."[7]

To ensure dependence on the United States, the Latin American militaries would be trained in U.S. doctrine under U.S. tables of organization. All the militaries would be equipped with U.S. armament to block any European competition and influence. The enhanced Americanized militaries would ensure domestic stability and "repress subversive influences" while protecting vital strategic resources. To guarantee success, the JCS plan called for placing military training missions in every country; training selected senior, junior, and non-commissioned officers in United States service schools; and providing U.S. arms and equipment to each of the region's militaries. U.S. dominance of the IADB ensured that the multilateral agency would adopt the plan, which it did in October 1945.[8] The U.S. military still preferred bilateral arrangements, but the IADB served the purpose of overall policy goals.

The plan that emerged from staff discussions with the Brazilian military envisaged large-scale arms assistance through a combination of Lend-Lease transfer, sales, and gratis aid as the model for carrying out the ambitious goals. The talks yielded a program that called for the U.S. Navy to transfer two battleships, two light aircraft carriers, fifteen destroyers, nine submarines, and a number of other craft to the Brazilians. The navy would also help the Brazilians build six new naval bases and an arsenal. Under the plan, the U.S. Army sought to equip an active force of 180,000 and a reserve component of twenty-six divisions, as well as assist in the construction of a highway and rail network for military mobility. The Brazilian Air Force would receive help in augmenting its existing inventory to six hundred airplanes and expanding its ground communications facilities to accommodate the larger air force.[9]

The ambitious plan indicated that the U.S. military intended to modernize its Brazilian counterpart, albeit for U.S. purposes, and seemed to confirm to the Brazilians the value of close ties. The project faced strong opposition from Department of State officials, especially the new U.S. ambassador to Brazil, Adolf Berle. He argued that the cost of purchasing and maintaining the equipment was more than Brazil could afford. He believed that with an estimated price tag of $50 million for the navy and $23 million for the air force alone, Brazil would crumble under the weight of the financial burden. Berle also understood that the rapid changes in the technology of warfare meant that arms and equipment provided Brazil would be obsolete when delivered. The fact that the proposed assistance would make the Brazilian military the largest and strongest in Latin America was less worrisome, for Brazil's geographic and demographic size made this logical.[10] Clearly Berle thought of future wars in the conventional sense, with the use of nuclear technology, as did the U.S. military leaders. Apparently neither's imagination could predict the non-conventional evolution of cold war competition.

A shift in the mood in Washington affected the military's bilateralism and arms transfer plans more than did the ambassador's opposition. With the invasion of Normandy in June 1944, the influence of the military on foreign policy diminished, while that of the Department of State increased. The change began when Sumner Welles, the chief exponent of regionalism and Brazil's greatest supporter in Washington, lost a power struggle with Secretary of State Cordell Hull, who favored a policy of internationalism and a collective approach to hemisphere defense. President Roosevelt's death and Harry S. Truman's ascendancy to the presidency weakened military influence further. Truman replaced Roosevelt's tendency to rely on military advice on diplomatic issues by deferring to Department of State judgment.[11]

Truman's reliance on Department of State guidance did not end the struggle over policy or signal a completely new direction. Ironically, the IADB, the agency charged with multilateral defense planning, provided the means for continuation of a bilateral approach to military relations. One of the recommendations of a late-1943 IADB report suggested meetings between the general staffs of the United

States and the Latin American militaries. U.S. military planners recognized opportunity and initiated a series of bilateral conferences with the region's general staffs from mid-1944 to late 1945 to sell the arms standardization program.[12] Policy struggles in Washington failed to deter the U.S. military from pressing ahead with its plans.

THE STRUGGLE OVER POLICY

The divergent views of the Department of State and the military establishment sent confusing messages to the Latin Americans. Perhaps sensing that changes in Washington could have a harmful effect on relations, Brazil declared war on Japan and offered to send troops to the Pacific theater. In making the offer, the Vargas government reiterated its fidelity to economic and military agreements and declared that because the relationship had been "gloriously sealed on the battlefields of Europe, the cooperation of Brazilian and American arms will now make itself felt in this second phase of the combat, with the same confidence and the same fighting spirit."[13]

The Brazilians did not know that the question of their participation in the Pacific war was caught in the middle of a Department of State–military struggle over defense policy. The Department of State felt that Brazil should be given the opportunity to provide a token force to the Pacific, such as an air squadron, for the sake of maintaining good relations and inter-American solidarity. The motive was as purely political as was the Brazilian offer.[14]

The Joint Chiefs of Staff showed little enthusiasm for the idea. Although recognizing the political value of Brazilian participation against Japan, the JCS felt that the outcome of the war was a forgone conclusion with or without Brazil's entry into the fighting. The JCS urged that no political agreement be reached regarding a Brazilian role in combat in the Pacific. Instead, "if the Brazilians raise the matter of a token force, they should be advised to take this up on a military level." The military wanted no interference from the Department of State in the conduct of what it saw as a military affair.[15]

This was not the first time the Department of State and the military clashed over Latin American policy. When the Axis threat assumed greater importance in the late 1930s, the U.S. Army argued for greater U.S. military involvement in the development of the aviation infrastructure in Latin America. The Department of State countered with the argument that any military hand in Latin American aviation would be disastrous for U.S. goodwill efforts. The conflict continued into the late war period over bilateral versus collective security arrangements and standardization of arms. The Department of State's view prevailed at the 1945 Chapultepec Conference in Mexico, where delegates from the Latin American countries and the United States agreed to establish at a later date a hemisphere military staff as a basis for collective security.[16]

The JCS opposed discussion of defense matters at Chapultepec on the grounds that it weakened the role of the military in policy decisions. Just before the conference the JCS developed a position paper recommending that the meeting avoid any military topics, asserting that military objectives could best be gained on a military-to-military basis. In the end neither the Department of State nor the Joint Chiefs of Staff succeeded in achieving all each desired. The collective approach proved ineffectual, and efforts at arms standardization failed.[17]

BRAZIL AND BILATERALISM

The Brazilians disapproved of the collective defense scheme, complaining that a hemisphere military staff as outlined in the Act of Chapultepec was unwieldy and impractical. Instead, they preferred "close bilateral cooperation between the major powers of the hemisphere, with plans for defense and other military matters to be reviewed by the General Staff of the United States." In effect, the Brazilians advocated continuance of U.S. veto authority over bilateral defense plans. Perhaps of more importance to the Brazilians was the fear that collective defense would modify the relationship built during the war and spread U.S. assistance to more countries. Inevitably, that would mean less available aid for Brazil.[18]

The belief that the collective approach would damage close ties was justified. On the same day President Harry Truman announced Japan's surrender, the U.S. Navy proposed the dismantling of the JBUSDC and the JBUSMC, as well as the Joint Mexico–United States Military Commission. Because the Chapultepec resolution called for treating all Latin American countries the same, with defense issues handled through multilateral machinery, the joint commissions seemed unnecessary. The continuation of a joint commission with one country would require the establishment of similar bilateral agencies with all the Latin American republics. Navy officials suggested that the JBUSMC end its operations after implementation of the air base agreement.[19] The navy never agreed fully with the establishment of the commissions because army primacy threatened the privileged position held by the navy since 1922. Bodies such as the JBUSMC restricted navy ability to act unilaterally.

Alarmed that its existence might cease, the Rio commission showed a great adeptness at bureaucratic survival, utilizing the multilateral approach for bilateral ends. In response to the navy proposal, the JBUSMC issued Recommendation No. 16. According to the commission, the functions of the JBUSDC in Washington ended with V-J Day, but the opposite was true of the JBUSMC. Collective defense might apply in other countries but not to the JBUSMC and Brazil because "Brazil's participation in hemisphere defense will require the effective use of United States military equipment and methods adopted by the armed forces of Brazil." The JBUSMC should therefore be the sole agency for coordination between the two nation's military establishments, with exclusive rights to formulate plans for the relationship. The Rio commission also argued that the JBUSDC should remain in place but its role limited to assisting the JBUSMC in specific matters of liaison, procurement, studies, and training.[20]

Although Recommendation No. 16 ignored the fact that the collective defense scheme envisaged the use of U.S. arms and doctrine, it offered a justification for maintaining close bilateral relations within the new multilateral framework. As in previous cases, Brazil's wartime ties with the United States made it the model for the other Latin American countries. The Brazilian military also had no desire to see a diminution of the commission given its dependence on the United States; military organization had been restructured along U.S. lines with the expectation of continual receipt of U.S. arms and equipment. Preservation of the JBUSMC was vital to the foreign policy goal of keeping a special relationship with the United States to achieve great nation status. The Brazilian government approved Recommendation No. 16, as did the War Department and, in an unexplained flip-flop, the Navy Department.[21]

Despite government approval, an astute Góes Monteiro did not like the changes proposed in the recommendation; he believed revitalization of the JBUSDC was more desirable. Góes Monteiro understood that if the Washington commission was deactivated or its role diminished, the Brazilian military would be further distanced from the source of assistance. Such a move would lessen Brazil's chances of acting as a partner with the United States. Instead, Brazil would become a supplicant like most of the Spanish-speaking republics. Unfortunately, some members of the Joint Chiefs of Staff arrogantly interpreted Góes Monteiro's position as a matter of prestige because the Canadian and Mexican joint military commissions were located in Washington.[22]

The JCS members suffered from myopia. Brazilian foreign policy is formulated on the basis of the past and future historical context, but the long-term view is often absent in U.S. policy decisions.[23] Maintaining the JBUSDC was important to the Brazilian idea of a special relationship for national progress. Góes Monteiro obviously took the long view in his efforts to prevent changes in the Washington commission, while the U.S. leaders saw Brazil-U.S. ties as episodic. The end of the war meant the end of a historical moment in which wartime arrangements made in response to immediate needs could be changed because the raison d'être no longer existed.

In the end the JBUSDC was not revitalized, nor was it dismantled. The Washington commission remained in place throughout the duration of the Brazil-U.S. military accord, but its impact on post-war military relations was minimal. The JBUSDC became a reward posting for senior U.S. and Brazilian officers who had faithfully served their institutions. The JBUSMC in Rio de Janeiro kept its original duties and added those of defense planning and the negotiation of bilateral agreements, which previously had been the responsibility of the JBUSDC.[24]

Confused U.S. Post-War Policy

The conflict over a multilateral or bilateral approach to hemisphere defense and Recommendation No. 16 reflected a lack of direction in U.S. policy in the confusion of the post-war world. That confusion made uncertain the role Brazil would play in U.S. world and hemisphere defense plans. The division of wartime allies into two ideological spheres caused an anxiety in U.S. government circles that was manifested in a competition for control of foreign policy that began before the war ended. As a result, policy drifted when direction was needed the most. The commissions, especially the JBUSMC, felt the effects of that drift acutely.[25]

Policy advocates in the early post-war United States argued for their particular positions based on different assumptions about the role Latin America was to play in the new international scheme. One group focused on the USSR and ignored Latin America. Communism appeared to have no foothold in the region, and U.S. economic and military hegemony was taken for granted. For this group the Western Hemisphere had the lowest priority.[26]

Another group struggling for control of U.S. policy making included some members of Congress and the Department of State. Their fears were that purchase of U.S. weapons would divert scarce financial resources needed for economic development and that the weapons could be used in intraregional conflict. The old assertion that Lend-Lease would encourage military dictatorships that used U.S. arms against their own populations continued to be a strong argument for followers of this line. Above all, this group wanted to avoid an arms race among the Latin American countries, especially since the United Nations General Assembly was discussing general disarmament. Department of State officials recognized the special nature of ties with Brazil but opposed large-scale arms transfers. In 1946 the Department of State agreed to the provision of enough equipment for one Brazilian division but refused further arms assistance the next year.[27]

The War and Navy Departments had much narrower views. As the organizations most concerned with preparedness, they wanted to avoid the problems faced in World War II, to keep their wartime pre-eminence in the hemisphere, and to maintain a secure southern flank. During the war scarce resources had been directed to retraining and re-equipping the Latin American militaries, and over one hundred thousand men had been diverted to the region. The military wanted to arm the Latin Americans with surplus equipment for missions of internal security, coastal patrol, and protection of shipping. U.S. forces could then concentrate on conflict areas. The provision of war surplus matériel to Brazil meant the cost would be cheap and the dividends great. As a bonus, military planners thought, the close relations built during the war would continue.[28]

The struggle for dominance among the various interest groups resulted in confused policy that stymied wartime friends. Nowhere was this truer than in Brazil, where great changes had occurred after the war. The military ousted President Getúlio Vargas in a palace coup in late October 1945, and former Minister of War Eurico Dutra (1946–1951) sat in Catete Palace in January 1946. Brazilian loyalty to the United States did not waiver with the coup, although officials were dismayed at the lack of policy direction in Washington. A perceived U.S. failure to respond to Soviet expansionism worried the Brazilians, particularly as they had great expectations that close cooperation would benefit national development.[29] Brazil would continue to support U.S. foreign policy, if it only knew the policy.

The drift in U.S. policy was of particular concern to Brazilian military leaders. At the end of 1945 Colonel José Bina Machado, the head of the president's military household, inquired as to the status of the earlier bilateral staff discussions. Although plans had been worked out jointly, Washington was now conspicuously silent. The Brazilians were unsure of the state of military relations, and the Americans did little to dispel their worries. When the United States assigned a pair of generals to the JBUSMC in December 1945 without prior notification and then withdrew one after receiving ex post facto approval from Rio de Janeiro, military leaders questioned the status of the "partnership." More pointed questions might have been asked had the Brazilians known that the Department of State was admonishing embassy members to give the official line that the relationship remained unchanged and not to discuss the matter until the issue of who controlled policy was resolved in Washington.[30]

Confusion regarding broader relations remained throughout the early post-war period and continued to perplex the Brazilians. During a visit to Brazil by New York mayor Fiorello LaGuardia in January 1946, the new foreign minister, João Neves da Fontoura, reiterated Brazil's support of U.S. policy to Mayor LaGuardia but concluded that "it would be helpful if we knew just what is the policy." Neves da Fontoura and his successor, Raúl Fernandes, reemphasized their concerns by complaining to the new U.S. ambassador, William Pawley, that the United States was not accepting its new responsibilities in ensuring that the Soviets lived up to the commitments made during the war. The Brazilians believed another Munich was in the making and a third world war was inevitable.[31]

With the gradual evolution of the cold war, U.S. military influence in policy making received a boost because U.S. expertise seemed pertinent. The role of Brazil in the new world order, as perceived by the United States, also became more clearly defined as U.S. world policy came into focus. Fundamental changes in defense planning had taken place since the war period. U.S. military strategists relegated Latin America to "Secondary Space." They believed the "Power Belt," or "Primary Space," Northern Hemisphere—the locus of the industrialized states—was where nuclear confrontation would occur. The cold war would be fought in Third World Secondary Space countries, such as in Latin America, whose roles were to be suppliers of important raw materials. Secondary Space countries were to remain locked into spheres of influence of First and Second World countries in a state reminiscent of pre-war colonialism.[32]

BRAZIL AND THE COLD WAR

Bilateral arrangements with a few Latin American nations that contributed directly to the narrowly defined U.S. strategic interests were the keys to cold war military relations in the hemisphere. At the same time, multilaterial machinery could exist as "covers" for the bilateral relationships. U.S. planners viewed military relations with Brazil in this context, and the Brazilians supported the United States under this structure. Brazil's goals remained the same as did those of the United States. The differences in the post-war world were that there was a new enemy and the U.S. response to perceived threats became more complex.

Prior to World War II, Dutra and many in the Brazilian military hierarchy expressed their anti-communist beliefs by word and deed. With Dutra occupying the president's office after the war, Brazil followed the U.S. lead in the cold war anti-communist crusade. His government broke relations with the Soviet Union, closed the Brazilian Communist Party, and backed the U.S. call for a permanent collective security arrangement at the 1947 Inter-American Conference for the Maintenance of Continental Peace and Security in Petrópolis, Brazil. Although the resulting Rio Treaty established the basis for such a system, it did not alter the course of Brazil–United States military relations or the pursuit of other bilateral deals.[33]

Brazilian military leaders praised the U.S. proposal for collective defense in public but in private voiced uncertainty about whether the old relationship would continue in the new framework. To clarify Brazil's position in the U.S. scheme, the chief of the Brazilian Joint General Staff asked the U.S. delegation of the JBUSMC in April 1947 to prepare a detailed study to determine the role and mission of the armed forces in air and coastal defense. Mindful of pending plans for a collective hemisphere defense agreement and expecting the upcoming Bogotá Conference in 1948 to establish the machinery, the U.S. members of the commission developed an entire strategic concept for Brazil. The most important aspect of the study was a call for re-estimation of Brazil's armed forces requirements based on an active role in collective defense under a joint command agency.[34]

The study had two parts: responsibilities Brazil would have in common with other Latin American countries and responsibilities peculiar to Brazil. In common with its Spanish-speaking neighbors, Brazil was to maintain internal order and security, "including suppression of fifth column activity," which came to mean any purported leftist activity. Like the other countries, Brazil would also have to develop necessary communication and transportation facilities, provide and stockpile strategic materials, and resist attack on its territory in accordance with hemisphere defense plans.[35]

Responsibilities peculiar to Brazil were essentially a continuation of its wartime role. According to the study, Brazil was;

1. to provide and maintain adequate facilities in the strategic areas in Northeast Brazil required by hemisphere defense plans;
2. to provide local defense of Brazil's principal ports, centers of industry, and personnel against raiding forces;
3. to protect shipping in vital sea-lanes along the extensive Brazilian coastline;
4. to be prepared to provide from its supplemental manpower expeditionary forces as may be required by hemisphere defense plans;
5. to maintain defense forces available for the general defense of the strategic Northeast area and to employ those forces in that area.

The study added that Brazil needed to modernize its military forces along U.S. lines to carry out the assigned missions. In the event of a direct attack Brazil's primary duty, either on its own or with other hemisphere forces, was to contain the enemy until reinforcements (U.S. troops) could arrive.[36]

The U.S. members of the JBUSMC overstepped their authority in preparing the wide-ranging study and were reprimanded for not obtaining clearance from Washington first. Especially troubling to U.S. military leaders was the reference to a hemisphere command agency. The JCS expected the upcoming Bogotá Conference to establish a permanent hemisphere defense organization but did not want it to have command functions. The JBUSMC's reference implied U.S. acceptance of joint command, which would block unilateral actions by the United States. The JCS directed that until multilateral agreements had been reached on hemisphere defense plans, the U.S. delegation of the Rio commission was to be guided by the assumption that Brazil would maintain armed forces in general for the following purposes:

1. to augment the armed forces of the United Nations in maintaining the security of the western Hemisphere;
2. to maintain internal order and security;
3. to provide local defense against isolated attacks or raids;
4. to protect coastwise shipping;
5. to provide facilities for the use of such U.S. or other American forces as may be required for protection against external aggression.

Most important, Brazil's role was a continuance of World War II defense needs as defined by the United States; Brazilian armed forces were to concentrate on the defense of the Northeast.[37]

Chastised, the U.S. delegation admitted that unguided studies could, on occasion, embarrass the U.S. government or be detrimental to U.S. interests, but delegates nevertheless defended their work. Commission members argued that until the Bogotá Conference changed the situation, "the existing relationship between Brazil and the United States in the JBUSMC should not be disturbed."[38] The episode offers insight into the U.S. military's struggle to come to grips with bilateralism within a collective ideology. It also reflects the closeness of Brazilian and U.S. officers in Rio de Janeiro and the degree to which the Joint Chiefs of Staff viewed, somewhat arrogantly, Brazil's military dependence on the United States. Like Recommendation No. 16, the U.S. delegation's eagerness to fulfill Brazilian wishes showed a strong instinct for institutional survival.

The advent of nuclear weapons and changing worldviews in Washington seemed to relegate Brazil to minor importance, but the unauthorized JBUSMC study had unforeseen results. In June 1948 the U.S. Army expanded the duties of its Brazilian colleagues to include the responsibilities of collecting, evaluating, and disseminating military intelligence required for hemisphere defense, as well as execution of necessary counterintelligence. The army further wanted Brazil to prepare forces for operations outside national borders.[39]

Army leaders recognized that the new duties enlarged Brazil's role in hemisphere defense and ran close to that outlined in the JBUSMC study, but they felt justified in doing so. Expanded responsibilities would keep alive the wartime closeness, which was important because experience with U.S. equipment, methods, and organization gave Brazil a "considerable war potential." Army planners understood that Brazil's lack of adequate transportation and communication systems and poorly developed industries for extracting natural resources were drawbacks but believed familiarity with U.S. arms and procedures made it ideal for supplying forces for offensive operations outside the country. With U.S. assistance, the army claimed, Brazil could provide a "two division corps of approximately 50,000 . . . as an expeditionary force." Moreover, the force could be trained to intervene in neighboring countries "to maintain internal order, which would forestall the necessity for employing U.S. forces for this purposes with the resultant ill-feeling engendered toward the United States."[40]

In effect, the plan proposed that the Brazilian military act as a surrogate for carrying out U.S. policy and seemed to fulfill one of Brazil's long-desired goals. The design offered Brazil the opportunity to play the intermediary role between the United States and Spanish-speaking Latin America for which it had always wished but in a different way than imagined. The scheme demonstrated the value the U.S. Army officials placed on relations with their Portuguese-speaking brothers in arms, given that the Brazilian military was the focal point of U.S. plans to bolster the Latin American militaries as part of anti-communist policy.[41]

MILITARY DIPLOMACY AND INFLUENCE

Because of the role the officer corps played in national politics, the United States saw the Latin American militaries as the most effective ally in securing U.S. pre-eminence in the hemisphere. Collegial relations between U.S. and Latin American officers had greater implications than military contacts normally experienced in countries with strong traditions of civilian government. This was particularly true with the JBUSMC, where Brazilian and U.S. members shared office space. The head of each Brazilian service branch held a cabinet rank, and the U.S. service branch sections of the commission were housed in the appropriate ministry. This arrangement gave the

U.S. delegates a direct line to Brazil's political decision makers that their Brazilian colleagues in the United States lacked. It is little wonder that the Americans believed influence could be exerted through the military connection.[42]

It is logical that liaison was necessary to deal with the vast array of matters associated with the military relationship. The level of entrée in government agencies, however, raises the question of what degree of influence U.S. military representatives exerted and whether ties to U.S. officers reinforced or modified the Brazilian officers' ideologies. To be sure, U.S. political and military leaders had faith in the benign influence of the U.S. military on the actions of politically important Brazilian officers. In a confidential letter to President Truman after the ouster of Vargas, Adolf Berle commented that exposure to the U.S. military impressed the Brazilians with democratic institutions. Berle inferred that the wartime experience had given Brazilian officers a broader view of the world, which impelled them to remove Vargas from office. Paraphrasing Niccolò Machiavelli, Berle exclaimed that like the Italian philosopher's prince, leaders fall when they cling to old responses in new situations. In the post-war world old methods were inadequate, and the Brazilian military's relationship with its North American brother glaringly exposed that fact.[43]

Influence, however, requires more than simple contact with government agencies. Close personal friendships had the potential of swaying important individuals, as it was believed had occurred during World War II. Illustrative of that belief was the claim of General J. G. Ord of the JBUSDC that Cordeiro de Faria's promotion to director of instruction in the War Ministry, which gave him command of all service schools except the Escola de Comando e Estado Maior do Exército (ECEME), came about because it was the wish of the U.S. Army section head of the JBUSMC. After the war U.S. military leaders adhered to a belief in the efficacy of personal ties and sought to foster such relationships. Communiqués to JBUSMC members constantly emphasized the need to project friendship and to inculcate the view that relations with the U.S. military conferred great prestige on Brazilian colleagues.[44]

Close personal ties also had the potential for damaging relations. In mid-1947 the U.S. Air Force delegate on the JBUSMC became embroiled in an internal conflict on defense issues among the Brazilian military ministers by openly supporting the air minister's views. Washington wanted interference by individual U.S. commission members to cease, as it could draw the U.S. delegation as a whole into the controversy. Any ideas should await the JBUSMC plenary session, where U.S. views could be presented and all approaches debated. In that manner potential divisiveness could be diffused and consensus recommendations promulgated. Fortunately, the deft handling of the incident by the chief of the U.S. delegation restored discipline among the U.S. members and smoothed ruffled Brazilian feelings.[45]

If the unfocused U.S. foreign policy during the early post-war period disconcerted the Brazilians, the petty conflicts among the U.S. Army, Navy, and Air Force delegates on the JBUSMC worked against the positive value of close personal ties. Each service section was an independent, autonomous unit, and disputes over jurisdiction were frequent, leading the Brazilians to wonder about the Americans' abilities. As an army member of the commission later remarked, the U.S. delegation "didn't cover ourselves with glory down there" in the first few years after the war.[46]

U.S. military leaders especially wanted the JBUSMC to avoid any actions that could be construed as intelligence gathering. In June 1947 Washington refused a request by the U.S. ambassador to transfer Portuguese-speaking Major Vernon Walters from the attaché's office, where he engaged in intelligence work, to the JBUSMC on the grounds that some Brazilians would interpret the move as "putting the Commission in the Intelligence gathering business." This was to be avoided at all costs because of the potential damage it could do to military relations.[47]

The following year General Albert C. Wedemeyer, director of the Plans and Operations Division, admonished the senior army member of the JBUSMC that "commission personnel must under no circumstances give the impression by word, act or association of engaging in the active collection of, or improper interest in, local intelligence information." Intelligence gathering was the responsibility of the attaché. Commission delegates could learn much; they just were not to seek out intelligence. Moreover, although the attaché often requested and received information from commission members, he was to avoid disclosing the source in either written or oral form.[48]

The line between gathering intelligence and passing on information was a fine one that both sides chose to ignore. The head of the JBUSMC army section, General William H. H. Morris Jr., reported that he constantly reiterated to Brazilian commission members that the U.S. Army delegates were not engaged in intelligence work. The Brazilians knew that army members passed on information but never accused the Americans of improper behavior. Morris went to such great lengths to avoid the appearance of collecting military intelligence that he would not travel in Brazil with the U.S. Army attaché. His efforts became more pronounced after a leftist newspaper accused him of being a spy.[49]

U.S. Army members may have attempted to reassure the Brazilians that they were not gathering intelligence, but the other service branches did not feel the same compunction. The army tried to get the navy and air force to support its approach but met great resistance. The senior navy member of the commission, who was also the head of the U.S. Navy Mission, claimed the mission's contract with the government of Brazil contained a clause that prohibited the collection and dispersal of information concerning the Brazilian Navy. Therefore, the navy had no need to offer constant reassurance. The air force section operated under no such contractual restrictions and refused to make any effort to assure the Brazilians.[50]

MILITARY DEPENDENCE AND ALIENATION

With the end of the war, Brazil entered a period of political crisis associated with the search for national identity. Brazilians recognized that the country had to develop economically, politically, and socially if it was to join the ranks of the world powers, but they disagreed on how best to achieve that goal. The military was not immune to those currents and became alienated as it sought to define its role in national, regional, and world affairs in the post-war world.[51] While searching for identity, the Brazilian military recognized that it had become dependent on the United States.

Evidence of the Brazilian military's dependence on the United States exhibited itself shortly after the end of World War II. In spring 1947 Brazil made a tentative offer to supply instructors to the Bolivian Higher War School, the Escuela Superior de la Guerra. In an act of collegial courtesy that was also meant to ensure that such action was acceptable to the United States, the Brazilian military attaché in La Paz informed the U.S. attaché that if the United States opposed the idea, he would not pursue the subject further.[52]

The War Department objected to the Brazilian plan on the grounds that Article 21 of the U.S.-Bolivian Military Mission Agreement decreed that U.S. doctrine be taught at the war college. Despite assurances from General Philipe M. Rivera, the Bolivian chief of staff, that only U.S. doctrine would be taught and all other foreign military instruction would be excluded, the United States was adamant in its opposition. U.S. military leaders argued that until the arms standardization program could be completed, the best course was for U.S. personnel to become instructors and advisers.[53]

At the time, however, Bolivian restrictions prevented U.S. personnel from acting as tutors, even though French and Spanish instructors were allowed to teach at the school. The U.S. attaché took a novel approach that ensured U.S. dominance and Brazilian military involvement. He suggested that if the Bolivians were unable to remove the restrictions on U.S. instructors, the Brazilians should be encouraged to undertake the job. He reasoned that since Brazil-U.S. military relations were so close and U.S. methods dominated Brazilian thinking, use of Brazilian instructors would be teaching U.S. doctrine secondhand.[54]

A similar incident occurred in July of the same year when Brazil and Paraguay agreed to establish a new Brazilian military mission; a Brazilian cavalry mission had been in Paraguay since 1943. The U.S. Army felt it was more desirable for Americans, rather than Brazilians, to do all the military mission work in Paraguay. Nevertheless, U.S. officials did not oppose the proposition because the Brazil-Paraguay mission contract could not be consummated unless Brazil and the United States reached mutual agreement as per Article 20 of the

U.S.-Paraguay Mission Agreement, which gave the United States veto powers.[55]

The Brazilians rejected U.S. reasoning. National greatness was the objective, even if it clashed with U.S. desires. In October one Brazilian infantry officer and one artillery officer replaced the old cavalry mission. The officers were to teach at the Escuela de Aplicación, a school of great importance in training young Paraguayan officers. Nevertheless, ideals of U.S. dominance persisted. The Paraguayans ignored the U.S. Army Mission when the school was established, which caused Washington to fear that if there was no objection, other Latin American militaries might shake off dependence on the United States. Such a trend would adversely affect the army mission program throughout the region, if not the world.[56]

The U.S. Embassy in Asunción had no objections to Brazilian influence in Paraguay and could not understand army logic. As in the Bolivian case, U.S. doctrine would be taught via the Brazilians, and Latin America was already dependent on the United States for arms and equipment. U.S. influence would be exercised through the Brazilian proxy.[57] Army fears proved to be unfounded, as the embassy had predicted. The Brazilian officers in Paraguay did not diminish U.S. influence any more than they did in Bolivia.

Although the two episodes indicated Brazil's dependence on the United States and its policy decisions followed the U.S. lead, the relationship was not a slavish one. A 1948 Central Intelligence Agency (CIA) report forewarned that, despite reliance on the United States, Brazilian leaders did not hesitate to take independent action in a conflict between cooperation and national sovereignty. As a result, the report warned, the United States should not assume Brazil would make concessions incompatible with its national goals.[58] U.S. decision makers failed to heed the contents of the report, for CIA advice was frequently forgotten over the course of the next decades.

Nevertheless, despite the confusion over U.S. policy and Brazil's post-war defense role, Brazilian leaders reaffirmed full support of the United States in world affairs. The military continued its adoption of U.S. military principles but required assistance in defending its version of democracy during "the most perilous moments Western Civilization has faced so far."[59] The United States wanted to oblige the Brazilians, for the arms standardization program aimed to provide weaponry to its most important ally in the region. As a result, the U.S. military spent much effort in finding the means to arm and train the Brazilians in the post-war period.

NOTES

1. H. L. Stimson to Secretary of State, January 14, 1944, Appendix "A," "U.S. Requirements for Post-War Air Bases in Brazil," RG-218, JCS Geographic Files, 1942–1945, CCS 686.9 Brazil (2-14-44) Sec. 1, NA.

2. Kenneth Callis Lanoue, "An Alliance Shaken: Brazil and the United States, 1945–1950" (Ph.D. diss., Louisiana State University and Agricultural and Mechanical College, 1978), 11-12, 14; and McCann, "Brazilian Foreign Relations in the Twentieth Century," 1, 10.

3. Secretary of State Stettinus to Admiral William D. Leahy, December 20, 1944, RG-218, JCS Geographic Files, 1942–1945, CCS 676.3 Brazil (11-5-44); Leahy to Stettinus, February 24, 1944, RG-218, JCS Geographic Files, 1942–1945, CCS 686.9 Brazil (2-14-44), Sec. 1 "U.S. Requirements for Post-War Air Bases in Brazil"; "Review of Reports on U.S. Military Base Requirements," February 11, 1946, RG-218, JCS Central Decimal File, 1946–1947, CCS 360 (12-9-42), Sec. 14, Appendix "B," 391; and Colonel R. L. Vittrup, GSC, to Department of State, May 28, 1946, RG-319, P&O Division Decimal File, 1946–1948, 686 (Sec. IX) (Cases 36–470), Box 492, NA.

4. Matthew B. Ridgeway Papers, Box 13, Folder "Eyes Only," January 5–September 1, 1949, USMHI; Michael J. Francis, *Attitudes of the United States Government Toward Collective Military Arrangements with Latin America, 1945–1960* (Ann Arbor, Mich.: University Microfilms, 1974), 28; Michael J. Francis, "The United States at Rio, 1942: The Strains of Pan Americanism," *Journal of Latin American Studies* 6:11 (May 1974): 79; and Edwin Lieuwen, *Arms and Politics in Latin America*, rev. ed. (New York: Praeger, 1961), 194.

5. Child, *Unequal Alliance*, 74–77; and Lieuwen, *Arms and Politics*, 194.

6. "Draft of Instructions for Staff Conversations with Military and Naval Representatives of the Other American Republics," July 28, 1944, RG-319, P&O Division Decimal File, 1946–1948, Box 284, 334 JABOAR (Sec. I) (Cases 1–), NA; and Lanoue, "An Alliance Shaken," 55.

7. LaFeber, *Inevitable Revolutions*, 92; and Child, *Unequal Alliance*, 72–73.

8. "Draft Instructions for Staff Conversations," n.d., RG-319, P&O Division Decimal File, 1946–1948, Box 284, 334 JABOAR, NA; Nunn, *Yesterday's Soldiers*, 214–215; and Willard Barber and C. Neale Ronning, *Internal Security and Military Power: Counterinsurgency and Civic Action* (Columbus: Ohio State University Press, 1966), 63–64.

9. Berle to Byrnes, July 26, 1945, July 27, 1945, *FRUS 1945*, 600–620; and Lanoue, "An Alliance Shaken," 56.

10. Ibid.

11. Merwin L. Bohan (U.S. Commissioner, Joint Brazil-U.S. Economic Development Commission, 1952–1953), oral history transcript, June 15, 1974, 20, HST Library [hereafter any oral history will be cited as Name, Oral History, date, page number, location]; Major General Kenner F. Hertford, Oral History, June 17, 1974, 12, HST Library; Francis, *Attitudes of U.S. Government*, 31; and George M. Elsey, "Some White House Recollections," *Diplomatic History* 12:3 (Summer 1988): 360.

12. Child, *Unequal Alliance*, 74.

13. President Vargas to President Truman, Subject—Brazil's Declaration of War on Japan, telegram 6/16/45, Papers of Harry S. Truman, Official Files-80, Box No. 80, HST Library.

14. Joseph C. Grew to Secretary of State, May 23, 1945, RG-218, JCS Combined Chiefs of Staff Decimal File, 1942–1945, CCS 382 (5-21-45), NA.

15. Freeman Matthews to Secretary of State, May 30, 1945, RG-218, JCS Combined Chiefs of Staff Decimal File, 1942–1945, CCS 382 (5-21-45), NA.

16. Storrs, *Brazil's Independent Foreign Policy*, 125; Robert Freeman Smith, ed., *The United States and the Latin American Sphere of Influence*, vol. 2, *Era of Good Neighbors, Cold Warriors, and Hairshirts, 1930–1982* (Malabar, Fla.: Robert E. Krieger, 1983), 25, 30, 34; and Krause, "Establishment," 89.

17. Bohan, Oral History, 13–16; Thomas Mann, Oral History, n.d., 12–13, HST Library; and Child, *Unequal Alliance*, 77.

18. General K. F. Hertford to Chief of Staff, March 13, 1946, RG-319, P&O Decimal File, 1946–1948, 091 Brazil (Sec. I) (Cases 1–), NA.

19. Memo by Vice Admiral A. W. Johnson, August 14, 1945; Admiral E. J. King to Secretary of the Navy James Forrestal, August 24, 1945, RG-218, JCS Combined Chiefs of Staff Decimal File, 1942–1945, CCS 300 (8-35-45), JCS 1485; and Notes of the 64th Meeting of the JBUSMC, August 3, 1945, RG-218, JCS Military Commissions, U.S.-Brazil, 33–29, DDC 1350, Visits, Box 1, NA.

20. Recommendation No. 16 (Rio), October 15, 1945, RG-218, JCS Military Commissions, U.S.-Brazil, 9010 (International Agreements, Political Military Agreements), Box 3, Sec. 1–3, NA.

21. Hertford to Chief of Staff, March 13, 1946, RG-319, P&O Decimal File, 1946–1948, 091 Brazil (Sec. 10) (Cases 1–), Box 59, NA. Early post-war articles in *A Defesa Nacional* extolled the virtues of U.S. organization and power. See Cel. Humberto Martins de Mello, "A restruturação do exército," *A Defesa Nacional* 33:384 (May 1946): 14–15; and Editorial, *A Defesa Nacional* 22:376 (September 1945): 5–8.

22. Hertford to Chief of Staff, March 13, 1946.

23. Ronald M. Schneider, *"Order and Progress": A Political History of Brazil* (Boulder, Colo.: Westview Press, 1991), provides an excellent example of the shortsightedness of U.S. policy makers. See, for example chap. 5.

24. Interview by author with Lt. Colonel Daniel Mason, Military Liaison Office, United States Embassy, June 14, 1985, Brasília, Brazil; and Secretary of the Army to Secretary of Defense, November 7, 1949, Appendix, "Current Status of the Military Aspects of Brazilian-U.S. Relations," RG-218, JCS Central Decimal File, 1948–1950, CCS 091.73 (6-6-47), Sec. 1, NA.

25. General Paul L. Freeman, Oral History, November 29, n.d., USMHI; and Steven S. Kaplan, "U.S. Arms Transfers to Latin America, 1945–1974: Rational Strategy, Bureaucratic Politics, and Executive Parameters," *International Studies Quarterly* 6:11 (December 1975): 407–410.

26. Kaplan, "U.S. Arms Transfers"; and Green, *Containment of Latin America*, 179.

27. Braden to Byrnes, December 16, 1946, *FRUS 1946*, 108–110; and Kaplan, "U.S. Arms Transfers," 407–410.

28. Kaplan, "U.S. Arms Transfers"; and Lanoue, "An Alliance Shaken," 53. Although the War and Navy Departments basically agreed on policy, they objected to the features of the 1947 National Security Act that created the Department of Defense under a civilian head and that created a joint chiefs of staff. See Carl N. Degler, *Affluence and Anxiety, 1945–Present* (Glenview, Ill.: Scott Foresman, 1968), 21–22.

29. Vargas expressed his concerns to the U.S. ambassador about Russian motives before the war ended. See A. A. Berle to Harry S. Truman, June 25, 1945, White House Central Files, State Department Correspondence, 1945–1946, Box 33, Folder 4, CF-33, HST Library; and Pedro Sampio Malan, "Relações econômicas internacionais do Brasil (1945–1964)," in *História geral da civilização brasileira*, vol. 3, *O Brasil repúblicano*, vol. 4, "*Economia e cultura (1930–1964)*, ed. Boris Faustô (São Paulo: DIFEL, 1984), 59.

30. Daniels to Byrnes, December 28, 1945; Byrnes to Daniels, December 31, 1945, *FRUS 1945*, 249–254, 622–623; and Lanoue, "An Alliance Shaken," 59.

31. Mayor LaGuardia to H. S. Truman, "Mission to Dutra's Inauguration," February 13, 1946, Subject Files, Foreign Affairs—Brazil, PSF 171, HST Library; William Pawley to George Marshall, February 6, 1947, William D. Pawley General File-PSF-133, HST Library; and João Henrique, "Speech on U.S.-Brazil Friendship on the Occasion of HST Visit to Chamber," 6–7, Trip Files PSF, August 31–September 20, 1947, Box 103, Folder 2, HST Library. Brazilian fears of a new world war and protestations of friendship can be found in the letters of credence to Truman. For example, see *The Remarks of the Newly Appointed Ambassador of Brazil Maurício Nabuco upon the Occasion of the Presentation of His Letter of Credence*, May 24, 1948, HST Official Files, OF-11, Box 80; and *The Remarks of the Newly Appointed Ambassador of Brazil Senhor Walter Moreira Salles upon the Occasion of the Presentation of His Letter of Credence*, n.d., HST Official Files 10N-11, Misc. OF68, Box 80, HST Library.

32. Child, *Unequal Alliance*, 7; Flynn, *Brazil*, 122; Rollie Poppino, "The Early Cold War Years," *Current History* 56:334 (June 1969): 340; John Lloyd Mecham, *The United States and Inter-American Security, 1889–1960* (Austin: University of Texas Press, 1961), 333; and Craig Neal Andrews, *Foreign Policy and the New American Military* (Beverly Hills, Calif.: Sage, 1974), 5.

33. The Dutra administration broke relations with the Soviet Union over an article in the Moscow magazine *The Literary Gazette* that called the Brazilian government a fascist regime. Alexander DeConde, *A History of American Foreign Policy* (New York: Charles Scribner's Sons, 1963), 719; Fontaine, *Brazil and the United States*, 24; and Storrs, *Brazil's Independent Foreign Policy*, 125. Stephen Rabe argues that in the early cold war years the U.S. military

cooperation in Latin America had less to do with defense than with the preservation of political and economic hegemony. See Stephen Rabe, "Inter-American Military Cooperation, 1944–1951," *World Affairs* 137:2 (Fall 1974): 144. Rabe is correct that political and economic hegemony was important, but so too was security defined in a much broader sense.

34. "The Role of Brazil in a Hemisphere Defense Scheme," Staff Study, U.S. Delegation JBUSMC, June 16, 1947; and Leland P. Lavette, Senior Naval Member, U.S. Delegation JBUSMC to Chief of Naval Operations, June 20, 1947, RG-319, P&O Decimal File, 1946–1948, 381 TS (Sec. V) (Cases 81–90), NA.

35. Ibid.

36. "Role of Brazil in a Hemisphere Defense Scheme."

37. Colonel G. Ordway, Chief, Western Hemisphere Branch, OPS Group Plans & Operations, to U.S. Army Delegation JBUSMC, August 6, 1947, RG-319, P&O Decimal File, 1946–1948, 381 TS (Sec. V) (Cases 81–90), NA.

38. Lt. Colonel Edward L. Austin, Secretary-JBUSMC, to Director, Plans and Operations, September 15, 1947, RG-319, P&O Decimal File, 1946–1948, 381 TS (Sec. V) (Cases 81–90), NA.

39. "Troop Basis for Brazilian Army," Memo for the Record, June 10, 1948, RG-319, P&O Decimal File, 1949–Feb. 1950, 091 Brazil, Box 534 (Sec. 11) (Cases 21–); and Memo for the Record, June 10, 1948, RG-319, P&O Decimal File, 1946–1948, 091 Brazil, Box 59 (Sec. I) (Cases 1–), NA.

40. Ibid. Interestingly, the army's idea of using Brazil as a proxy in hemisphere intervention foreshadowed later U.S. use of Latin American militaries in joint adventures such as the 1965 Dominican Republic intervention.

41. CIA, National Intelligence Estimate, "Conditions and Trends in Latin America Affecting U.S. Security," December 12, 1952, PSF-254, HST Library; John J. Johnson, *The Military and Society in Latin America* (Stanford: Stanford University Press, 1964), 127, 143, 263; Lieuwen, *Arms and Politics*, 196–197, 226; and Gerald K. Haines, *The Americanization of Brazil: A Study of U.S. Cold War Diplomacy in the Third World, 1945–1954* (Wilmington, Del.: SR Books, 1989), 39.

42. CIA, "Conditions and Trends in Latin America"; Admiral Arthur Radford, Chair, JCS, to Secretary of Defense, June 27, 1956, RG-218, JCS Geographic Files 1954–1956, Box 11, CCS 092 Brazil (1-11-49) Sec. 6, NA; John J. Johnson, *Political Change in Latin America: The Emergence of the Middle Sectors* (Stanford: Stanford University Press, 1958), 160–163, 168, 179; Johnson, *Military and Society in Latin America*, 177–223; Samuel Baily, *The United States and the Development of South America, 1945–1975* (New York: New Viewpoints, 1976), 67; and Herbert Goldhamer, *The Foreign Powers in Latin America* (Princeton: Princeton University Press, 1972), 27.

43. Thomas Skidmore is one of the first scholars to raise the question of whether American officers did exert influence. See Thomas E. Skidmore, *Politics in Brazil, 1930–1964: An Experiment in Democracy* (New York: Oxford University Press, 1967), 330; and Berle to Truman, October 30, 1945, White House Central Files, Box 33, Folder 5, HST Library.

44. General J. G. Ord to Chief, American Theater, February 24, 1945, RG-218, JCS Military Commissions, U.S.-Brazil, 33–26, Book 1, Visits, NA. For

examples of communiqués see RG-218, JCS Military Commissions, U.S.-Brazil, Box 1, BDC 3500, NA.

45. General Gordon P. Saville to General Morris, September 30, 1947; and Ordway to Timberman, January 16, 1947, RG-319, P&O Decimal File, 1946–1948, Box 288, 334 JBUSMC, Cases 15–52, NA.

46. General Paul Freeman, Oral History, 79–80.

47. Pawley to Eisenhower, June 17, 1947; Eishenhower to Pawley, June 28, 1947, RG-319, P&O Decimal File, 1946–1948, Box 288, 334, JBUSMC, Cases 15–52. NA.

48. Lt. General A. C. Wedemeyer to Senior U.S. Army Member JBUSMC, May 24, 1948; and Wedemeyer to Major General Edward H. Brooks, Commanding General, U.S. Army Caribbean, May 24, 1948, RG-319, P&O Decimal File, 1946–1948, 091 LATS (Sec. I) (Cases 1–), NA.

49. Major General W.H.H. Morris, Jr., to Director, Plans & Operations, June 17, 1948, RG-319, P&O Decimal File, 1946–1948, 091 LATS (Sec. I) (Cases 1–), NA.

50. Ibid.

51. For an examination of the military's alienation, see Edmundo Campos Coelho, *Em busca de identidade: O exército e a política na sociedade brasileira* (Rio de Janeiro: Forense-Universitária, 1976), 127–152.

52. Colonel Paul W. Steinbeck to U.S. Ambassador, April 2, 1947; Joseph Black to Secretary of State, April 7, 1947; and Colonel G. Ordway to Jack D. Neal, May 7, 1947, RG-319, P&O Decimal File, 1946–1948, P&O 350.1 (Sec. 000) (Case 21), Box 332, NA.

53. Ibid.

54. Steinbeck to U.S. Ambassador, April 2, 1947; Black to Secretary of State, April 7, 1947; and Ordway to Neal, May 7, 1947, RG-319, P&O Decimal File, 1946–1948, P&O 350.1 (Sec. 000) (Case 21), Box 332, NA.

55. Memo for the Record, July 30, 1947, RG-319, P&O Decimal File, 1946–1948 (Army Staff), 091 Brazil (Sec. I) (Cases 1–), Box 59, NA. For an analysis of U.S. involvement in Paraguayan affairs during World War II, see Michael Grow, *The Good Neighbor Policy and Authoritarianism in Paraguay: United States Economic Expansion and Great Power Rivalry in Latin America During World War II* (Lawrence: Regents Press of Kansas, 1981).

56. Colonel G. Ordway to Department of State, October 13, 1947, RG-319, P&O Decimal File, 1946–1948 (Army Staff), 091 Brazil (Sec. I) (Cases 1–), Box 59, NA.

57. U.S. Embassy in Asunción to Secretary of State, January 5, 1948, RG-319, P&O Decimal File, 1946–1948 (Army Staff), 091 Brazil (Sec. I) (Cases 1–), Box 59, NA.

58. CIA Intelligence Reports, *Brazil*, SR-17, November 30, 1948, PSF-260, HST Library.

59. Colonel P. L. Freeman, Jr., to Commanding General, Command and General Staff College, n.d., RG-319, P&O Decimal File, 1946–1948, 091 Brazil (Sec. I) (Cases 1–), Box 59, NA; Memo to General Morris, Chief, U.S. Section— JBUSMC, n.d., RG-319, P&O Decimal File, 1946–1948, Box 288, 334

JBUSMC, Cases 15–52, NA; "Visit of Salvador Cesar Obino, Brazilian Army, January 1947," Willis D. Crittenberger Papers, Box AH, U.S. Army Military History Collection, USMHI; Dutra to Truman, February 4, 1946, OF-80, HST Official Files, Box 80, HST Library; *Remarks of Ambassador Walter Moreira Salles*; and *Remarks of Ambassador Maurício Nabuco.*

.. 4 ..

Post-War Efforts to Arm Brazil

Brazilian military and civilian leaders expected the wartime alliance with the United States and participation in combat to bring development, prosperity, and international status. They believed that Brazil would have a privileged position vis-à-vis its Hispanic neighbors in U.S.–Latin American relations and that wartime economic and military assistance would continue to the benefit of both countries. The October 1945 coup that deposed Getúlio Vargas and the promulgation of the 1946 liberal constitution confirmed Brazil's imitation of the North American model. The 1943 recommendation of large-scale assistance by the Cooke Mission appeared to validate Brazil's adherence to U.S. tutelage. The Brazilians thought that because the only source of capital and arms in the immediate postwar period was its special partner in the hemisphere, the United States would help its friend and oblige requests for aid.[1]

U.S. post-war actions jolted the Brazilians. The Truman administration balked at providing financial aid out of fear that Brazilian demands for U.S. goods would fuel inflation in an already heated U.S. economy. Equally disturbing, especially for nationalists, was U.S. pressure on Brazil to use accumulated gold reserves to finance development and to allow U.S. companies participation in local petroleum exploration. The Brazilian military's post-war reality came in the forms of a lack of legal mechanisms for provision of U.S. arms and equipment and Washington's rapprochement with Argentina. Both conditions threatened to alter the relationship built during the war.[2] Even though the Truman administration budged little on the issue of economic assistance, the U.S. military, with Truman's backing, tried a variety of means to supply Brazil with war matériel.[3]

OBSTACLES TO ARMS ASSISTANCE

For many Brazilians the U.S. position on economic assistance and the problems involved in obtaining military aid belied the special relationship and gave rise to debates among military and political leaders on the direction of post-war relations with the United States. Some questioned the alliance, but Brazil continued to support the United States in the international arena for both ideological and practical reasons. The Dutra government shared an anti-communist outlook with the Truman administration. U.S. efforts to supply the Brazilian military with desired weapons reinforced ideological inclinations. The central role of the military in Brazilian politics was not lost on many U.S. officers who believed a special military relationship was supportive of U.S. post-war security plans.[4]

Defense of the Western Hemisphere was only one part of the post-war security plans drawn up in 1945 by the U.S. Army. The Latin American program not only aimed to reduce the time required to organize the defense of the hemisphere by standardizing the equipment and training of local militaries, but also sought to democratize society. Army officials envisioned a multimillion dollar aid program that integrated the hemisphere's militaries and sparked broad-based development of Latin American society. They believed the region's militaries would act responsibly and that U.S. arms would not be used against their own citizens or those of their neighbors. Such a program, however, relied on the funding of post-war security plans at wartime levels; the military's reach exceeded its grasp. An economy-minded U.S. Congress had little interest in economic or military programs for Latin America in the early post-war period and shunned the region.[5]

The Department of State opposed supplying Brazil, and the other American republics, with U.S. weaponry on the grounds that sophisticated equipment was too expensive to buy and maintain.

With the complexity of armaments increasing rapidly, Brazil could not hope to stay abreast financially or technically. Perhaps more important, military aid ran counter to the "one world" U.N. concept supported by the Department of State. These attitudes hardened when post-war crises in Europe and Asia gobbled up U.S. aid in support of the anti-communist Truman Doctrine of 1947. The dominant view was that Brazil, and Latin America in general, was safe from communist threat.[6]

INDICATIONS OF CHANGE

Despite opposition to assistance, the U.S. military, with the support of President Truman, pressed ahead with the standardization program. From the end of World War II until passage of the 1951 Military Assistance Act, the U.S. military pursued legal and questionable means to supply the Latin Americans with war matériel. As in other cases, the closeness of the American and Brazilian militaries meant Brazil was the model for the supply of U.S. arms, equipment, and training to the region. Because the other Latin American militaries would judge the standardization program by the results in Brazil, the United States made special efforts to accommodate the Brazilian military.

Provision of U.S. arms to Brazil began with the 1941 Lend-Lease Agreement, which was modified in 1942 to reflect the new relationship created by the Political-Military Accord. Under the agreement Brazil received large amounts of military aid at a discount and became the major beneficiary of Lend-Lease in the Western Hemisphere, receiving over $150 million of the $262 million total allocated to Latin America. Before the war ended, however, indications of change caused the Brazilians great anxiety. Especially troublesome was the disposition of war matériel used by the FEB in Italy. The U.S. Army Intelligence Division noted that legal title to Lend-Lease arms and equipment could not pass to Brazil and urged that a solution be found to prevent potential damage to the relationship.[7]

The question of FEB arms and equipment seemed to be a relatively minor problem in bilateral military relations, but the Department of State saw it as an opportunity to reassert dominance in hemisphere policy making. State Department officials resurrected the argument that U.S. arms encouraged Latin American military dictatorships and used the FEB equipment issue as the test case in the debate over the direction of U.S. Latin America policy. Opponents of arms assistance argued that the Brazilians should be allowed to return only with personal arms and equipment that could be hand carried. Such restrictions, they claimed, were necessary because of insufficient space for heavy equipment on the ships designated to transport FEB troops home.[8]

U.S. military officials ignored Department of State arguments and assured the Brazilian delegates of the JBUSDC that the FEB's heavy weapons would be shipped to Brazil. Although the Pacific theater had first priority for excess matériel, Brazil was next in line for transportation of heavy equipment. Brazil would "be able to receive her infantry division fully equipped."[9] In essence U.S. military officials proceeded with confidence that their weight in foreign policy would be the same in the post-war period as it was during wartime.

Brazilian expectations, as well as those of the other Latin American militaries, of extensive U.S. military aid had been raised by U.S. proclamations, but confidence soon waned. As the war drew to a close, planned joint projects were canceled, which eliminated some equipment that had been scheduled for Brazil. In one case not only was a plan to supply aircraft halted, but also the JBUSMC received instructions to repossess matériel already shipped to the Brazilian Air Force.[10] Such actions did not inspire confidence in the United States and gave notice that the special military relationship was to undergo change.

BRAZIL AND ARMS STANDARDIZATION

Despite Brazilian fears, the end of relatively easy access to U.S. equipment did not signal the end of close relations. Similarly, the conclusion of the war in August 1945 and the suspension of Lend-Lease aid were not indications of the end of the U.S. military's interest in Brazil. Instead, the closure of the war and its associated programs meant the legal framework that supported military aid was no longer viable. Until new legislation offered the legal means, other methods of providing Brazil arms and equipment were necessary. As a result, from the end of Lend-Lease to the 1951 Military Assistance Act the U.S. military used existing legal and quasi-legal expedients to arm the Brazilians.

Although countries facing communist threat, such as the Philippines and China under Chiang Kai-shek, received first priority for U.S. military assistance, the Joint Chiefs of Staff believed the Latin American arms standardization program could proceed unhampered. In defense of the program the armed forces chiefs repeated familiar arguments: the program was too important because it would speed mobilization of recipient allies in case of war, it would provide a large reserve pool of troops, and, perhaps most important, it would forestall "other interested nations from furnishing equipment."[11] The arms standardization program gave evidence of Washington's intention to preserve its wartime dominance in the region and reflected a strong element of what Senator J. William Fulbright later called "the arrogance of power."[12]

As in other cases, Brazil became the model for the program and the locus of opposition from U.S. and European interests. Not only was Brazil the closest military ally in the region, but it also was the focus of the major threat to standardization and therefore to U.S. military pre-eminence. The British Navy and Embassy and the Vickers Armstrong Company worked together to pressure the Brazilian Navy into purchasing excess English warships. According to the U.S. Navy Mission in Rio de Janeiro, the Brazilians wanted to modernize the navy with U.S. equipment, but whereas Washington was vague on terms, the British were "down to brass tacks with definite offers hard to refuse." The navy mission complained that competition with England for naval and aircraft sales threatened standardization throughout the region because the British disclosed that the same offer would be extended to Argentina, Chile, and Peru in the near future.[13]

The U.S. Navy Mission report shocked the JCS because discussions with the Brazilians had been conducted on a continual basis for some time. Standardization negotiations began in the last months of the war when the JCS sent General George Brett to Latin America to work out the details. Brett faced great resistance from the U.S. ambassadors in the region, who feared the misuse of U.S. arms was a real possibility. Perhaps most confusing to the Brazilians was Ambassador Adolf Berle's opposition to a Brett-arranged plan that called for Brazil to scrap two outdated battleships and replace them with two Nevada-class cruisers. At the same time Berle protested the Brett scheme, the ambassador was pushing the sale of U.S. military aircraft.[14]

The Brazilians did not know that Berle's resistance was part of a larger struggle between the Department of State and the military over post-war policy in Latin America. The military was dominant during the war, but with peace the Department of State wanted to regain its pre-eminence in policy making. The arms standardization program offered an issue with which the Department of State could test its strength. Undersecretary of State Dean Acheson led the opposition, arguing that

a. the program advocates regionalism at the expense of the United Nations, thereby giving Great Britain and Russia reason to establish spheres of influence in the Middle East and Balkans;

b. providing arms to the Latin American nations encourages a race in armament at a time when disarmament should be emphasized;

c. such arms may be used in disputes between these nations or for the purpose of political upheavals with the countries themselves.

The army answered Acheson's claims with a study that said it would be uneconomical not to equip and train the Latin American militaries now when it was relatively cheap rather than later when an emergency might require large expenditures. Besides, the army contended, the return in good relations and influence would outweigh the costs. The study concluded with the admonition that military assistance, especially in aviation, would assist economic development in the region and thereby offer greater markets for U.S. goods.[15]

President Harry Truman accepted the military position and in May 1947 urged Congress to pass the Inter-American Military Cooperation Act. The bill aimed to legalize equipping the Latin Americans with U.S.-made instruments of war and training military personnel according to North American standards. The effect would be a ready reserve force to supplement the U.S. military. Despite the president's support and a favorable report out of the House of Representatives, Senate and Department of State opposition killed the bill.[16] The failure of the bill provided further indication of a relationship in change and guaranteed that other methods would be employed if arms standardization was to become a reality.

RAPPROCHEMENT WITH ARGENTINA

Brazilian military leaders hoped the Inter-American Military Cooperation Act would be passed quickly and arms supply resumed. The Brazilians, however, opposed U.S. arms assistance to the other Latin American republics, particularly Argentina. General Salvador Cesar Obino, chief of the Armed Forces Joint Staff, argued that, although Brazilian leaders favored hemisphere unity, they did not believe it was currently achievable. Furthermore, the Brazilian military lacked interest in the Inter-American Defense Conference scheduled by the politicians for the following year in Rio de Janeiro. Obino suggested that the meeting be postponed until Brazil improved its armament relative to the Spanish-speaking countries, especially Argentina. As a mainstay of hemisphere defense Brazil should be favored and provided matériel on a unilateral basis. To underscore his point, Obino hinted that the Brazilian military would view arms inspections by the United Nations unfavorably.[17]

Brazilian leaders feared that arms supply to Argentina reflected U.S. attempts at rapprochement with their nation's historic rival. Such a move would place Argentina on an equal footing with Brazil vis-à-vis the United States. The Brazilians worried that Argentina might attack Brazil and felt threatened by U.S. efforts to provide the Argentines with war matériel. The departure of the U.S. ambassador to Argentina in late 1945, Spruille Braden, from the scene only heightened those fears. Argentine-U.S. relations had been strained during the war because Argentina had refused to join the Allies until there was no doubt of the outcome. Tensions reached a high when Braden became the assistant secretary of state. Under Braden's guidance the Department of State put out the infamous *Blue Book*, which accused Juan Perón and leading Argentine officials of aiding the fascist cause during the war. Issued just prior to the 1946 Argentine presidential election, the book was designed to turn voters away from Perón.[18]

The *Blue Book* failed to sway voters, and Perón was elected, which led to Braden's downfall. With his departure from the Department of State and the inception of the anti-communist cold war mentality in 1947, Argentina's Nazi sympathies faded as an obstacle to Argentine-U.S. relations. An early 1947 intelligence report that claimed the Soviet Union had offered training and technology to Argentina helped change Washington's attitude. The report sparked fears that Argentina would accept the offer if the United States failed to provide assistance. Eight months later the Department of Defense dispatched General Willis D. Crittenberger to Buenos Aires to discuss aid with Argentine military leaders. The Department of Defense, however, did not want to alarm the Brazilians and ordered Crittenberger to emphasize publicly that the trip was merely a courtesy call similar to those he made to other Latin American countries.[19]

Crittenberger's visit was more than a gesture and profited Argentina militarily. The Joint Chiefs of Staff approved the transfer of anti-aircraft weaponry in January 1948, but the Argentine price for rapprochement was much greater. The Argentine minister of war, General José Humberto Sosa Molina, traveled to Washington after the April 1948 Bogotá Conference to discuss further military collaboration. Kenneth C. Royall, the secretary of the army, promised Sosa Molina that the United States would sell Argentina a large quantity of arms, ammunition, and other ordnance as surplus property. He also pledged additional places in the U.S. Armed Forces School for Argentine officers.[20]

Argentina's exploration of military ties reflected self-interest, as did Brazil's alliance with the United States. The difference was in the perception of the relationship with the northern giant. Whereas Argentina was wary of attachment, Brazil saw its relations with the

United States as one of a powerful patron with a weaker friend who had proved its worth. Under that assumption the United States had an obligation to support its proven friend rather than an untested new acquaintance.

Self-interest was, of course, present on all sides, for the United States wanted both the Argentines and Brazilians to support its worldview, which was being shaped by the cold war. Argentina's strong post-war economy and geographic location made it an important potential ally despite its historic animosity with current ally Brazil. In the anxious early cold war period U.S. military leaders believed the Straits of Magellan would have strategic importance if war with the Soviets came and the Panama Canal was rendered inoperative. Argentine cooperation was paramount to keep the southern route open should war commence. A military understanding with the Argentines would achieve that goal, as well as win backing in the Organization of American States (OAS) and the United Nations. U.S. military leaders recognized that the Brazilians would view an arrangement with Buenos Aires negatively but thought they could be convinced of the wisdom of gaining Argentine support.[21]

U.S. RESPONSE TO BRAZILIAN FEARS

U.S. military officials were wrong. United States–Argentine rapprochement stunned the Brazilians and helped spur their move to a less emotional and more pragmatic diplomacy. Because of their well-known wariness of Argentina and backing of U.S. initiatives without question at the recent Bogotá Conference, Brazilian military and political leaders did not expect such behavior from their closest friend. The Brazilian delegates to the JBUSDC expressed their concerns at the July 22, 1948, meeting, but the U.S. responses were masterful examples of waffle and deflection.[22]

The U.S. Navy representative observed that the navy had transferred no equipment and that the visit by the Argentine chief of naval operations to Washington was only a routine courtesy call. The army representative, Colonel Paul Freeman, also played down the matter, noting that Brazilian fears obviously stemmed from the visit to the United States by General Sosa Molina. Freeman soothingly pointed out that the amount of military supplies provided was minimal and that the army neither offered industrial or technical assistance nor aided the Argentines in obtaining any machinery for the manufacture of munitions. Freeman admitted, however, that nothing prevented the Argentine government from negotiating directly with U.S. companies for the purchase of such machinery.[23]

Recognizing the weakness of his argument, the army delegate retreated to a reiteration of current U.S. policy and described the overtures to Argentina as part of the collective security program outlined in the Rio Treaty and the Act of Bogotá. Discussions with the Argentines were simply a continuation of the bilateral staff talks held with all Latin American countries, including Brazil, before the end of World War II. The allocation of arms to Argentina was only an effort to prevent that republic from purchasing weapons from non-U.S. sources, which would damage the standardization program. Insisting that the amount of armament offered Argentina was small, Freeman tried to placate the Brazilians by explaining that the recent termination of the Surplus Property Act and the lack of surplus matériel meant that further provision of armament to Argentina was impossible.[24]

Washington did not appreciate the Brazilian view and the degree to which the perceived mistreatment of a faithful friend affected military and political leaders. U.S. members of the JBUSMC, who lived in Brazil, were much more sensitive to the situation than were their Washington counterparts but were nevertheless unable to provide any answers. No one was more attuned to reactions in Brazilian military and political circles than General William Morris, the chief of the U.S. delegation to the JBUSMC. Morris argued against doing so much for Argentina that it offended Brazil, for in his travels throughout the country Brazilian officers asked him "if the United States and Brazil are still as good friends as formerly." The end result, according to Morris, was that Brazilian diplomatic, military, and political leaders were pressing for more equipment from the United States.[25]

Despite appearances, the Joint Chiefs of Staff worried about Brazilian sensitivity regarding overtures to Argentina and the issue of arms supply. The U.S. Army Foreign Liaison Office attempted to deal with the former concern by meticulously arranging courtesies for General Canrobert Pereira da Costa, the Brazilian Army minister, during an early 1949 trip to the United States that were equal to those extended to Sosa Molina. Arming the Brazilians was a more difficult matter. Unless Congress provided new means to supply weaponry, the depletion of surplus stocks made continued shipments of arms and equipment to Brazil impossible. U.S. military leaders feared that such a situation jeopardized the hemisphere defense program and was potentially damaging to U.S. military prestige.[26]

In the interim, however, the U.S. military continued to pursue its standardization program under questionable legal authorization. From 1945 to 1948 the U.S. military relied on the Surplus Property Act to supply arms and equipment to the Latin American armed forces. In 1947 alone the Brazilian Army received enough equipment to outfit an infantry division and a parachute combat team. Concurrently, under "Project Eclipse," as the U.S. forces withdrew from some bases in the Northeast, they turned over to the Brazilians communications and radar equipment and weapons. In fact, the JBUSMC appeared fixated on Eclipse, while elsewhere the cold war took shape.[27]

THE TRANSFER OF INSTALLATIONS AND EQUIPMENT

Withdrawal of U.S. military personnel and transfer of installations became urgent during the transitional period between wartime closeness and the pragmatic friendship that emerged with the cold war. U.S. presence long after the war ended caused many Brazilians to perceive the situation as one of occupation. Riots over the cost of living and working conditions in São Paulo took on anti-American undertones that indicated a growing weariness of foreigners stationed in Brazil. In Recife clashes between U.S. military personnel and the city police reflected increasing estrangement between local officials and the Americans. Nationalists attacked the continued foreign control of bases, and leftists accused the United States of fomenting war with Argentina by establishing military installations in Rio Grande do Sul. An article in the April 1947 issue of the Communist Party organ *Hoje* (São Paulo) entitled "Truman Quer a Nossa Escravização" (Truman Wants Our Enslavement) claimed that the Rio Treaty added military control to the U.S. economic and political domination of Brazil. The following year the *Imprensa Popular* (Rio de Janeiro) contended that the return of the bases to the Brazilian military was an illusion to delude the public. In reality, the article said, the United States still held Brazilian bases.[28]

The articles were partially correct. The United States still occupied military bases in Brazil under the 1944 Strategic Base Agreement, but a reduction in personnel was in progress. The drawdown on personnel, however, was due to declining funds rather than to sensitivity over Brazilian concerns. More money could be spent on maintenance and operation of the sites if less went to personnel costs. Although officers from both countries staffed the JBUSMC, which supervised the base agreement, an overriding U.S. dominance was the popular perception.[29]

Disposition of the Air Transport Command installations was full of potential dangers for military relations. When the Foreign Liquidation Commission (FLC) wanted to offer the bases for sale to the Brazilians at "a fair price," the U.S. delegation of the JBUSMC objected. According to the agreement under which Pan American Airways built the bases for the army, the installations were Brazilian property on loan to the United States. The Brazilians could not be expected to pay for their own property. Any attempt to make them do so would create an unpleasant diplomatic incident and damage military and political relations.[30]

The lack of institutional memory was evident in the debate between the FLC and the JBUSMC. In 1940 President Vargas and General Robert Olds, commanding general of the Air Corps Ferrying Command, made an oral agreement on how the Brazilians would assume post-war control. Nevertheless, the Brazilians had little to say in the final solution to the problem. The FLC, JBUSMC, and South Atlantic Wing of the Air Transport Command ignored the Brazilians and reached a compromise in which fixed installations, building fixtures, and movable property essential to the operation of the bases would be transferred immediately to Brazil. All other property would be considered surplus and sold by the FLC to the Brazilian government or any other interested buyer.[31] The compromise resolved the matter without incident but gave the Brazilians clear indication that post-war relations would be more complex than wartime ties.

Unlike the army, the U.S. Navy was less anxious to relinquish its bases despite pressure to do so. The installation in Rio was particularly obvious and seemed to provide proof of U.S. occupation. To counter Brazilian complaints, Ambassador Adolf Berle recommended the base be closed or reduced to a less visible reminder of U.S. presence. The Navy Department declared that eventually U.S. operation of the base would end, but it refused to be rushed. Navy spokesmen claimed that problems of disposing of surplus property, re-routing shipping, and maintaining the Naval Air Transport Service prohibited fast withdrawal from the base. The navy only relented after Rear Admiral Marshall R. Greer went to Rio de Janeiro for Eurico Dutra's presidential inauguration and reported that the harm of continued U.S. presence at the base outweighed the good.[32]

BRAZILIAN SALE OF SURPLUS PROPERTY

If the solution to the military installations question signified a change in relations, the Brazilian resale of U.S. equipment symbolized the complexity of post-war diplomacy and the desire of the United States to maintain its close ties with Brazil. At the end of the war Brazil purchased Lend-Lease pipeline matériel at a sixty-five percent discount and obtained surplus U.S. arms and wartime installations. Using the Surplus Property Act, the Navy and War Departments sold Brazil numerous aircraft, naval vessels, tank farms, and housing and medical facilities. They also arranged clever swaps. To obtain permission for continued operation of a navy radio station on Rio's Ilha das Cobras, the chief of naval operations, with Department of State concurrence, authorized the free transfer to Brazil of high-frequency radio equipment in Bahia and Belém.[33]

Curiously, while the U.S. military provided arms and equipment in 1947 under the Surplus Property Act, Brazil was selling some of the matériel to the government of Rafael Trujillo in the Dominican Republic. The governments of Cuba and Venezuela feared that Trujillo planned to use the weapons purchased from Brazil to arm exiles for revolutionary purposes in their countries and asked the Brazilians to forgo military sales to the Caribbean nation. When Brazil rejected the requests, saying it had assurances from Trujillo that the arms were only for defense, Cuba and Venezuela urged the United States to intercede with its close friend.[34]

The U.S. government refused to ask Brazil to cancel the arms sales, citing a litany of rationalizations for not intervening. The Truman administration argued that if Brazil did not sell the arms, Trujillo would purchase them elsewhere. Besides, Brazilian sale of U.S. weapons and equipment served the arms standardization program without direct U.S. involvement. In addition, preventing the sale would upset other U.S. plans, especially the seduction of Argentina with surplus weapons. If Washington nullified the Dominican deal, Brazil had grounds to object to U.S. arms sales to Argentina.[35]

Even the Department of State, which opposed arms standardization, endorsed the sale. The department reasoned that attempts to veto the sale would weaken Brazil's civilian government vis-à-vis the military and impair the influence of pro-American foreign minister Raúl Fernandes because senior Brazilian officers who were secretly profiting from the deal would resent U.S. interference.[36] Somewhat hypocritically, the Department of State's position contradicted its earlier concern that U.S. weapons would be used in intraregional warfare or against a Latin American country's own population. Despite its rhetoric, the Department of State recognized the importance of maintaining the friendship of Brazil's military leaders.

Perhaps more telling, the Truman administration did not want to antagonize influential officers in hope of garnering their support for a national petroleum law that satisfied U.S. interests. The desire to prevent passage of nationalistic petroleum legislation was so strong that the Department of State pressed U.S. members of the JBUSMC to lobby their Brazilian colleagues for U.S. participation in the development of Brazil's oil industry. It is uncertain to what degree the U.S.

officers on the JBUSMC did so, but whatever effort was expended to such an end came to nothing. Many, if not most, Brazilian senior officers and politicians strongly favored legislation that excluded U.S. entry in the development of Brazilian petroleum.[37]

CONTINUED EFFORTS TO ARM BRAZIL

Neither the refusal to allow U.S. participation in national oil development nor the termination of the Surplus Property Act on July 1, 1948, marked the end of the U.S. military's efforts to send arms south. As soon as the Surplus Property Act expired, the military resorted to the obscure American Republics Act of 1920 to continue supplying matériel to Brazil. The Logistics Division of the Department of the Army, however, determined that the use of the 1920 act as authority for transferring arms involved "such broad interpretation of legislation, and such loose application of logistical criteria in determining availability of materials, that it places the D/A in an unjustifiable position and one which was never intended by law." Fearing that continued use of the act jeopardized chances for future arms assistance legislation, the Department of the Army suspended action on Brazilian requests for matériel.[38]

The amount of arms and equipment transferred under the 1920 act was small, but creative use of existing legislation showed the lengths to which the U.S. military went to maintain ties with the Brazilian military. Nevertheless, suspension of use of the act meant Brazilian requests for diesel engines for tanks, manufacturing data for ammunition, caterpillar tractors for the air force, ammunition, and demolition explosives were shelved for the moment. Despite the setback, U.S. military officials continued to "endeavor to find ways and means to satisfy the more urgent requests of the Brazilian Army" but made clear to the Brazilians that the Pentagon had no legal authority to continue military assistance until Congress passed the Military Assistance Program (MAP).[39]

The message to the Brazilian military was vivid and may have had other motives. The suspension of arms transfers might prod the Brazilian government into adding its voice to those attempting to persuade the U.S. Congress to allow renewal of large-scale military assistance. Certainly the assertion that the army would try "to find ways and means" to provide matériel suggests that extra-legal methods were not out of the question. Nevertheless, the U.S. military pinned its hopes for the standardization program on the passage of legal machinery. In 1949 those hopes rested on the Mutual Defense Assistance Act.

The Latin Americans resented not receiving assistance they considered their due for past friendship, especially given that the United States was funneling large amounts of economic and military aid to Europe. These feelings were particularly strong in Brazil and became a major concern of the JBUSMC. In an early 1947 joint meeting of the commission following the second defeat of the Inter-American Military Cooperation Act, General Byron Gates urged the Brazilian military to continue its close cooperation so as not to adversely affect defense plans as the pendulum swung back toward tight national economies and attendant world disarmament.[40]

The problem became acute after the stormy Bogotá Conference in April 1948, when the Latin Americans learned that large-scale U.S. aid was not forthcoming. General Omar Bradley feared that the Latin American republics would turn to other sources for military assistance as a result. Such action, he warned, would hurt the personal relations that U.S. military personnel had built during the war. The situation was delicate and required tact and intelligence by officers assigned to the various "missions to maintain their favorable status and convince the local military that we have not lost our desire for hemisphere solidarity and military collaboration."[41] U.S. military pre-eminence in the region seemed to be slipping away for want of legal means to provide arms.

The Truman administration and the military did not give up and in 1949 presented to Congress the Mutual Defense Assistance Act. Their hopes were fulfilled only partially. Congress passed the act but allocated no funds for Latin America; arms could be transferred only by sale. North Atlantic Treaty Organization (NATO) countries could receive comprehensive military aid to contain the communist threat in Europe, but Latin America was deemed safe. One high-ranking U.S. officer lamented a "tendency on the part of our policy-makers to de-emphasize the importance of Latin American countries."[42] To obtain hemisphere solidarity, the United States had to give tangible evidence of its determination to implement the Bogotá agreements; the Mutual Defense Assistance Act failed to provide the means. The only value of the act's passage for Latin America was that it kept the hemisphere military program alive legally, though on a cash-and-carry basis.

MILITARY TRAINING ASSISTANCE

Events in the Far and Near East soon had a sobering effect on Congress, but in 1949 there appeared to be little need of arms assistance to Latin America. Training Latin American officers, however, was legal and less expensive. In grouping countries as to the desirability of training their military personnel, the Department of State and the Pentagon agreed that U.S. national interests placed Brazil in Group I. Brazil was one of the "nations whose interests appear at this time to be most closely allied to the U.S. national interest or which for other reasons should be granted the highest priority of training assistance." Mexico and Venezuela were the only other Latin American countries in the same category. Interestingly, Argentina, Brazil's nemesis, received the lowest-priority Group III status.[43]

Since the 1942 Military-Political Accords, Brazilian military personnel had been trained at U.S. service schools and at bases in Brazil. Many officers who were to play leading roles in Brazil's political future, such as Eduardo Gomes, Humberto de Alencar Castello Branco, and Ernesto Geisel, attended U.S. service schools. Both Brazilian and U.S. authorities carefully screened officers before accepting them for training, with their politics receiving special scrutiny.[44] Any officer suspected of leftist sympathies was automatically excluded.

If the political bent of Brazilian candidates for training was of concern, the quality and rank of U.S. training personnel sent to Brazil worried the JBUSDC. In evaluating the various training units, the commission noted that the quality of air personnel was "rather poor." Cognizant of the importance of rank, and the need to gain respect, the JBUSDC recommended that U.S. enlisted men be of the same rank, or higher, as the Brazilian soldiers being trained. Better screening and briefing would familiarize the U.S. personnel with training problems particular to the Brazilian military. The aim was to ensure that the trainers had proper abilities and personal characteristics. The JBUSDC was especially concerned that U.S. personnel understood that the language of Brazil was Portuguese, not Spanish.[45]

JBUSDC concerns stemmed from earlier problems caused by culture shock and by the arrogance of some U.S. officers in Washington and Brazil. In 1948 General Albert C. Wedemeyer complained of the difficulties of making his brother officers understand the necessity of having U.S. personnel assigned to the region who possessed a knowledge of the temperament of the Latin American officers with whom they would work. Assistant Secretary of Defense H. Struve Hensel echoed the complaint several years later when speaking of the Military Assistance Advisory Groups (MAAG). Hensel lamented that it was difficult to find officers with skills in international and political-military affairs to serve in important locations.[46]

The JBUSDC displayed an understanding of Brazilian culture not always shared by other U.S. officers. Although most reports commented favorably on the Brazilians' progress, the analyses were not uniform. Some criticized the Brazilians' use of U.S. matériel, complaining that the equipment for civic action programs sat idle in warehouses. Draftees returned home when money in the Brazilian budget ran out, and the equipment remained unused until another group came the next year. Consequently, work centered on constant training cycles rather than on practical use of the equipment by trained troops.[47]

Despite criticisms, the U.S. military favored educating Brazilian military personnel. Enlisted men learned to use U.S. equipment under U.S. standards and officers were indoctrinated in U.S. organization and thought. Once convinced of the value of the American way, the politically important officer corps would be a powerful counterweight to nationalist and leftist tendencies within military and political circles. In this line of thinking, training and education were tools for maintaining influence, especially when applied at advanced levels in a war college.

The major problem, however, was that training alone was not enough. The lack of legal means to provide arms assistance still hampered the standardization program. The perception was that U.S. influence would erode unless a way was found to carry out the project. Another problem was that U.S. views were predicated on the mistaken belief that Brazilian officers would be content to accept the U.S. definition of their role in the relationship. The negotiations for U.S. assistance in the establishment of the Escola Superior de Guerra provided an example of this proposition and of the Brazilian rejection of a permanent junior place on the board of hemispheric military directors.

NOTES

1. Weis, *Cold Warriors,* 24; and Malan, "Relações econômicas," 59–60. The Cooke Mission, named after its chief, Morris Llewellyn Cooke, grew out of the 1942 Washington accords. The mission examined the Brazilian economy and made recommendations for developing import substitution, raw materials production, and the transportation system with U.S. aid to create conditions for expanding industrialization. McCann, *Brazilian-American Alliance,* 381–388. For a description of the mission chief's experiences, see Morris L. Cooke, *Brazil on the March: A Study in International Cooperation* (New York: McGraw and Hill, 1944).

2. Weis, *Cold Warriors,* 24–26; and Malan, "Relações econômicas," 62–66. Vargas had worried that foreign participation in petroleum exploration would undermine national sovereignty; in 1945 he promulgated a decree limiting foreign companies to marketing. Eurico Dutra repealed the decree in 1946, but the Brazilian Congress refused to pass enabling legislation. The result was the creation of the state-owned Petrobras.

3. For a good analysis of the U.S. efforts to arm Latin America in the early post-war period, see Chester J. Pach, Jr., *Arming the Free World: The Origins of the United States Military Assistance Program, 1945–1950* (Chapel Hill: University of North Carolina Press, 1991), chap. 2.

4. Weis, *Cold Warriors,* 18–20. David Green correctly suggests that the supply of hardware to Latin American militaries supported an anti-revolutionary or anti-subversive bent in U.S. post-war economic and political policies, especially in the late 1950s and 1960s. Preventing communist revolutions in the hemisphere was an integral part of overall U.S. security defense. See Green, *Containment of Latin America,* 182.

5. "Military-Political Cooperation with the Other American Republics," June 24, 1946, RG-319, P&O Decimal File, 1946–1948, 091 LA (Sec. I) (Cases 1–15); Briefs for Commanders Conference in Memorandum for General Norstad, January 18, 1947, RG-319, P&O Decimal File, 1946–1948, 337 TS (Sec. I) (Cases 2–24), NA; and General Kenner F. Hertford, Oral History, 45–46. Hertford's recollection of events occurred long after the promulgation of

the doctrine of security and development. To accept his contention that the U.S. Army program foresaw broad development, with the Latin American militaries playing a democratic role, is to accept the idea that the U.S. military was thinking along security and development lines immediately after the war and before the inception of the cold war.

6. Dean Acheson, *Present at the Creation: My Years in the State Department* (New York: W. W. Norton, 1969), 217–235; Mann, Oral History, 75; Bohan, Oral History, 16; DeConde, *History of American Foreign Policy*, 722; and Poppino, "Early Cold War Years," 340–341.

7. "Lend-Lease for Brazil (General)," n.d., RG-218, JCS Military Commissions, U.S.-Brazil; Major John W. Connoly, Jr., to Lt. Colonel Winant Johnson, September 15, 1944, RG-218, JCS Military Commissions, U.S.-Brazil, BDC 1300–1350, Visits-1, Box 33-24; Major Joaquim Ribeiro Monteiro to Colonel Stenio Lima, Chief, Brazilian Delegation—JBUSMC, October 17, 1944, RG-218, JCS Military Commissions, U.S.-Brazil, BDC 3500–3520, Schools Book-1, Box 33-24, NA; and Green, *Containment of Latin America*, 179.

8. Ibid.

9. Monteiro to Lima, October 17, 1944; and McCann, *Brazilian-American Alliance*, 439.

10. Monteiro to Lima, October 17, 1944; and D. R. Patrick to Chair, JBUSDC, June 6, 1945, RG-218, JCS Military Commissions, U.S.-Brazil, BDC 3500–3520, Schools Book 1, 2, 4, Boxes 1, 2, NA; and Pach, *Arming the Free World*, 41.

11. A. S. Peterson, JBUSMC, to J. G. Ord, JBUSDC, September 26, 1945, Escola Technica [*sic*] de Aviação-4-, RG-218, JCS Military Commissions, U.S.-Brazil, BDC 3500–3520, Schools Book; "Desirability and Priority of Providing U.S. Military Supplies and Equipment to Foreign Nations," December 11, 1945; and Appendix "B," Memorandum for the State-War-Navy Coordinating Committee, December 11, 1945, RG-218, JCS Combined Chiefs of Staff Decimal File, 1942–1945, CCS 400.3 (10-20-45), NA.

12. See J. William Fulbright, *The Arrogance of Power* (New York: Random House, 1966).

13. "Desirability and Priority of Providing U.S. Military Supplies and Equipment to Foreign Nations"; and McCann, *Brazilian-American Alliance*, 455–456.

14. Minutes of the Joint Advisory Board on American Republics, June 5, 1945, RG-319, P&O Decimal File, 1946–1948, 334 JABOAR (Sec. I) (Cases 1–), Box 284, NA; Green, *Containment of Latin America*, 181–182; and McCann, *Brazilian-American Alliance*.

15. "Military-Political Cooperation with the Other American Republics," June 24, 1946, RG-319, P&O Decimal File, 1946–1948, NA; and Lieuwen, *Arms and Politics*, 197.

16. "Briefs for Commanders Conference in Memorandum for General Norstad," January 18, 1948, RG-319, P&O Decimal File, 1946–1948, 337 TS (Sec. I) (Cases 2–24), NA; and "Military-Political Cooperation with the Other American Republics."

17. Memorandum of Conversation by the Chief of the Division of Brazilian Affairs (Braddock), December 10, 1946, *FRUS 1946*, 460; and Notes of Con-

ference Between General Obino (Brazil) and General Eisenhower at 0930, December 4, 1946, RG-319, P&O Decimal File, 1946–1948, Entry 154, Box 73, P&O Top Secret, P&O 337 TS (Sec. I) (Case 14), NA.

18. Donald Hodges, *Argentina, 1943–1976: The National Revolution and Resistance* (Albuquerque: University of New Mexico Press, 1976), 12; and Whitaker, *United States and the Southern Cone*, 215. Perón responded with the *Blue and White Book* (blue and white are the colors of the Argentine flag), which raised the specter of Yankee imperialism.

19. Memorandum to U.S. Army Representative—UN Military Staff Committee, 140, March 24, 1947, Intelligence Review 56, 2; and Department of Defense to Crittenberger, November 18, 1947, Willis D. Crittenberger Papers, Box B, File U.N.M.S.C.—IADB, V. I, 1944–June 1948, USMHI.

20. Memorandum of Omar Bradley, Subject: Possible Discussions with the Argentine Minister of War, May 14, 1948, RG-218, JCS Central Decimal File, 1946–1947, CCS 091.73 (6-6-47), Sec. I, NA [although this document is dated 1948, it has been placed, perhaps by accident, in the file dated 1946–1947]; and Royall to Molina, June 4, 1948, *FRUS 1948*, 322.

21. Royall to Molina, June 4, 1948; and Ridgeway to Bradley, July 28, 1949, Box 13, Official Papers Folder, Matthew B. Ridgeway Papers, USMHI.

22. General T. S. Timberman, Chief—Operations Group P&O, to Director, P&O General Staff—U.S. Army, July 22, 1948, RG-319, P&O Decimal File, 1946–1948, 334 Joint Brazil-U.S. Defense Commission (Sec. I) (Cases 1–), Box 284, NA; and Ridgeway, Oral History, 10–12.

23. Timberman to Director, P&O Division, July 22, 1948.

24. Ibid.

25. General W.H.H. Morris to General Omar Bradley, n.d., RG-319, P&O Decimal File, 1946–1948, 091 Brazil (Sec. I) (Cases 1–), Box 59, NA.

26. Colonel Frances J. Graling—Foreign Liaison Officer, to Chief of Protocol, Department of State, March 21, 1949, White House Central Files, State Department Correspondence, Box 35, Folder 16, HST Library; and Bradley to Morris, July 14, 1949, RG-319, P & O Decimal File, 1946–1948, 091 Brazil (Sec. I) (Cases 1–), Box 59, NA.

27. General Gordon P. Saville to Chief of Staff, U.S. Army, February 28, 1947, RG-319, P&O Decimal File, 1946–1948, JBUSMC, Box 288; Major General W. O. Felder, Logistics, to Plans & Operations, July 5, 1949, RG-319, P&O Decimal File, 1949–February 1950, 091 Brazil, Box 534, NA; Hertford, Oral History, 33–34; and Ridgeway, Oral History, 12–13.

28. "Truman quer a nossa escravização," *Hoje*, April 26, 1947, 1; "Ainda as nossa bases são ocupada," *Imprensa Popular*, March 28, 1948; Frank L. Kluckhohn, "Brazilians Cooler to U.S. Occupation," *New York Times*, January 5, 1946, 4. For the atmosphere in São Paulo, see Joel W. Wolfe, "The Rise of Brazil's Industrial Working Class: Community, Work, and Politics in São Paulo, 1900–1955" (Ph.D. diss., University of Wisconsin, 1990), chap. 6.

29. Philip O. Chalmers, Chief of the Division of Brazilian Affairs, to W. O. Briggs, Director of the Office of American Republic Affairs, January 7, 1946; Byrnes to Paul C. Daniels, Chargé d'Affaires—Rio, March 1, 1946; Daniels to Secretary of State, April 2, 1946, *FRUS 1946*, 428–429, 439, 441–442.

30. Daniels to Byrnes, January 4, 1946, *FRUS 1946*, 426–427. For an examination of the development of the air corp bases, see Krause, "Establishment."

31. Memorandum by Adolf A. Berle, January 24, 1946; Daniels to Secretary of State, February 27, 1946, *FRUS 1946*, 431, 436–437.

32. Chalmers to Briggs, January 7, 1946; Byrnes to Forrestal, February 9, 1946, *FRUS 1946*, 428–429, 435–436. On April 25, 1946, the Navy Department ordered the end of its occupation of the base.

33. Spruille Braden to Berle, February 7, 1946; Secretary of State to Daniels, April 12, 1946; Secretary of War Robert P. Patterson to Secretary of State, April 20, 1946; Dean Acheson to Harry Truman, May 14, 1946; Carlos Martins Pereira e Sousa to Secretary of State, June 28, 1946; Pawley to Acting Minister of Foreign Affairs Leão Gracie, September 16, 1946; Assistant Secretary of State to Secretary of War, October 7, 1946, *FRUS 1946*, 434–435, 443–445, 447, 450, 455. The Brazilians allowed the United States to maintain and utilize the radio station for three additional months in return for equipment in Bahia and Belém.

34. Memo of Conversation by Mr. Richard H. Post of the Division of North and West Coast Affairs, December 15, 1947; and David Key to Secretary of State, December 15, 1947, *FRUS 1947*, 131–144.

35. Ibid.

36. Memo of Conversation by Richard H. Post, December 15, 1947, *FRUS 1947*, 131–144.

37. Secretary of State to Chargé in Brazil, February 14, 1948, *FRUS 1948*, 357.

38. "Military Assistance for Brazil," enclosure in Memorandum for the Director of Logistics Division from Ray T. Maddocks, Major General, Director, P&O, March 30, 1949; and Major General Felder to P&O, July 5, 1949, RG-319, P&O Decimal File, 1949–February 1950, 091 Brazil, Box 534, NA. The National Security Act of 1947 brought the old Navy and War Departments under a single civilian head through the creation of the Department of Defense.

39. Maddocks to Director, P&O, March 30, 1949; and Ridgeway, Oral History, vol. 2, sess. January 2, 6, 1972, 4.

40. Minutes of JBUSMC 75th Meeting, February 3, 1947, RG-319, P&O Decimal File, 1946–1948, 334 Cases 15–52, Box 288, NA; and Paul C. Daniels, Oral History, 34, 36, HST Library.

41. Bradley to Ridgeway, July 5, 1948, Matthew B. Ridgeway Papers, Box 13—Caribbean Defense Command Official Papers, May–December 1948, Tab "5," USMHI. Maintaining favorable personal relations was not an easy task. Arrogant U.S. officers assigned to the JBUSMC and to the military attaché's office did not help matters during the war and early post-war period. See chap. 2.

42. A. C. Wedemeyer to Ridgeway, August 1, 1949, Matthew B. Ridgeway Papers, Box 13, Caribbean Defense Command "Eyes Only" Correspondence, January 5–September 11, 1949, USMHI; and Freeman to Ridgeway, April 8, 1949, RG-319, P&O Decimal File, 1949–February 1950, Box 550, 091 LA (Sec. I) (Cases 1–20), NA.

43. SWNCC, "Training of Foreign Nationals at U.S. Service Schools," March 24, 1947, RG-218, JCS Central Decimal File, 1946–1947, CCS 353 (531-43), Sec. 3, 40; "Training Foreign Nationals at U.S. Service Schools," Report by the Joint Strategic Plans Committee to the JCS, August 12, 1949, annex to Appendix "A" to enclosure "A," RG-218, JCS Central Decimal File, 1948–1950, CCS 353 (5-31-43), Sec. 6, 566–567; Adjutant General to Commandant, AAF Special Staff School, June 7, 1946, RG-218, JCS Military Commissions, U.S.-Brazil, BOC 1300–1350, Visits-1-, BDC 3500–3520, Schools Book-1, 15-8; and Memorandum for the Record, October 9, 1946, RG-319, P&O Decimal File, 1946–1948, 350.2 (Sec. I) (Cases 1–20), Box 332, NA.

44. Memorandum for the Record, October 9, 1946.

45. JBUSDC to AC/AS-5, Western Hemisphere Branch (Major Chairsell, Pentagon), October 9, 1945, RG-218, JCS Military Commissions, U.S.-Brazil, BDC 3500–3520, Schools Book-2, 16-1, Box 2, NA.

46. Wedemeyer to Ridgeway, January 16, 1948, Ridgeway Papers, Box 10, USMHI; and Hensel to Assistant Secretary of the Army, Assistant Secretary of the Air Force, and Assistant Secretary of the Navy, May 26, 1955, RG-218, JCS Central Decimal File, 1954–1956, CCS 092 (8-22-46), (2) Sec. 12, NA.

47. Lt. General Arthur G. Trudeau, Oral History, 1971, 255, USMHI.

.. 5 ..

The Escola Superior de Guerra

The advent of the atomic bomb and the cold war symbolized the complexity of the post–World War II world and signaled a change in Brazil–United States relations. Internal and international pressures strained ties, as the U.S. commitment to an anti-communist ideology often clashed with Brazil's desire to achieve greatness with U.S. assistance. Military relations remained special, but the post-war environment required that both sides make adjustments. Military statecraft between the two nations assumed more intricate and pragmatic forms. The role of the U.S. military in the creation and operation of the Escola Superior de Guerra, Brazil's National War School, reflected the evolutionary process of change in the relationship.

The Brazilians wanted U.S. assistance in creating the school to be coordinated by the JBUSMC, which meant the United States would bear most of the costs. The U.S. military objected to such an arrangement but not to assisting in the establishment of the school. Washington recognized that the ESG, as well as the Escola de Comando e Estado Maior do Exército (Army Command and High Staff School), would be the most important doctrinal and clique-forming institutions in Brazil and therefore could serve U.S. ends.[1] The U.S. connection ensured that U.S. influence pervaded military thinking taught at the schools, but in a Brazilian context. The negotiations for U.S. assistance in creating the ESG, however, brought home the fact that the situation had changed and difficult adjustments had to be made to keep the relationship alive.

The Informal Brazilian Request

The question of U.S. assistance in creating the ESG first arose during late 1946 discussions between General Dwight D. Eisenhower and General Salvador Cesar Obino, Brazil's chief of the Armed Forces Staff. Obino wanted active-duty U.S. officers from each of the military branches to direct the creation of the school and a three- or four-star army general to act as the school's commandant or chief adviser.[2] The request for U.S. officers to organize and command the school grew out of the desire of important Brazilian officers, who had close ties to the U.S. military, to reorganize military education to conform to the North American model.[3] Educating officers along the lines of Brazil's closest ally was an important step on the path to national greatness.

The United States quickly agreed, for the request dovetailed with the post-war anti-communist policy of confirming the pre-eminent role of the U.S. military in hemisphere defense and bolstering the Latin American militaries because of their influence in national politics. Given Brazil's strategic geographic location and familiarity with U.S. doctrine and methods, its military was to be the focal point of that policy in the region. Some military and political leaders in Washington even believed in a benign influence of the U.S. military on the actions of the politically important Brazilian officer corps.[4]

The negotiations for U.S. assistance in establishing the ESG, however, served notice to the Brazilians that U.S. largesse and ease in dealing with military matters were over. The Brazilians wanted the active-duty U.S. officers charged with the task to operate under the aegis of the Joint Brazil–United States Military Commission, the primary vehicle for joint military projects since 1942. Such an arrangement would make the officers part of regular bilateral military structures, thereby freeing Brazil of any additional financial burdens for their services and avoiding the need to negotiate a separate agreement.[5]

THE U.S. MILITARY'S RESPONSE

Washington's response shocked Brazilian leaders. U.S. military leaders agreed to help establish the ESG but balked at Brazilian proposals. Rather than use active or reserve officers, the War Department wished to use retired personnel. More important, despite Eisenhower's desire to operate under the JBUSMC umbrella, U.S. law required that the officers form a military mission separate from the Rio commission. Not only was a new contractual agreement necessary, but also U.S. military leaders proposed a high annual salary of $12,000 for each officer to be paid by Brazil rather than the United States and refused to allow the officers to do more than act as advisers to the school. In addition, the Americans recommended that instead of creating an institution that mirrored the U.S. model, the ESG combine the purposes of the U.S. Armed Forces Staff College, National War College, and Industrial College.[6]

BRAZILIAN DISMAY OVER THE U.S. RESPONSE

Obino "was flabbergasted" when he learned Brazil would have to pay the U.S. officers under a separate agreement and that they would act only as advisers. His expectation was that the wartime manner of the relationship would continue. Besides, using Americans to head the school had the precedent of French officers directing the Escola de Estado Maior do Exército (later called the Escola de Comando e Estado Maior do Exército) and the Escola de Aperfeiçoamento after the arrival of the French Military Mission in 1919.[7]

Equally shocked was Brigadier General Henrique Teixeira Lott, Brazil's military attaché and delegate to the Inter-American Defense Board. Lott had little clue of the U.S. position even though he was in the midst of discussing the project with U.S. military chiefs. The U.S. position forced the stunned Brazilians, who expected quick action on the request for assistance, to develop a new strategy and stalled negotiations for the ESG Mission as the Brazilians sought to lessen the onerous financial arrangements demanded by the United States.[8]

AMERICAN INTER-SERVICE RIVALRY

Lott's dismay would have been greater had he known of the inter-service struggle among the U.S. military regarding the project. A dominant Brazilian Army ensured that the Escola Superior de Guerra proposal received the support of the other services. But among the U.S. armed forces, the navy and army fought for pre-eminence, while the air force sought to create a niche for itself. Army leaders often complained of navy intransigence; while the army and air force agreed with the Brazilian proposal and began making plans for the school, the navy dragged its feet.[9]

To appease the navy, the army suggested that no commitments be made regarding provision of a planning team to develop curriculum and instructional materials. Despite a desire for speed, U.S. officials informed the Brazilians that time was required to lay the groundwork for a joint war school of the scope and size envisioned and that such a school could not become operational until at least 1948.[10]

Finally understanding that the United States was refusing to include the project as part of the JBUSMC, the Brazilians abandoned the informal approach and turned to formal diplomatic channels. On June 18, 1947, Ambassador Carlos Martins Pereira e Sousa presented the secretary of state with a formal request for U.S. assistance in establishing the school.[11] Six months had passed since the Eisenhower-Obino meeting. The relative ease with which such matters had been dealt with during the war was a thing of the past. The discussions and ensuing contract negotiations showed a military relationship adjusting to the exigencies of a new world.

NEGOTIATIONS FOR U.S. ASSISTANCE

Contract negotiations began in earnest with Brazil's official request. The Brazilians reluctantly accepted the U.S. plan to create a mission separate from the JBUSMC but balked at some of the provisions considered financially excessive. In October 1947 Lott relayed word that his government wanted to make modifications to a draft agreement, most of which were minor. Lott asked that Brazil be exempted from the obligation of providing such high compensation for the retired officers and their active-duty assistants. Besides lowering the annual $12,000 salary per officer, Brazil did not want to pay for the transportation of the mission's families, household goods, and automobiles to Rio de Janeiro.[12]

The Americans insisted, arguing that U.S. agreements with other Latin American countries contained the same financial provisions. The Americans argued that the retired officers would be volunteers and would not be attracted to the project without additional compensation because their retirement pay was low. U.S. negotiators believed that because Brazil had benefited from the JBUSMC at no cost since 1942, it should assume all the costs of the mission.[13]

The U.S. Navy was the most inflexible and haughty, leaving no room for compromise. The navy contended that either Brazil assume all financial obligations specified in the draft contract or that the United States withdraw from the project. Army members of the JBUSMC noted that because the navy had a long-standing mission in Brazil, it was not interested in a combined service effort; the navy preferred that each service establish a separate mission.[14] The navy attitude stemmed from self-interest rather than national interest. A joint effort could eventually weaken the justification for the naval mission, but separate missions ensured its continuance.

This was not the first time the navy had attempted to block contract negotiations. In August the chief of naval operations informed the navy member of the JBUSMC that the navy wanted naval and marine officers assigned to the ESG mission, one for surface and one each for the naval and marine air arms. Although the air force and army would have only one officer each, such a configuration would "insure familiarity with the U.S. Naval concepts." The Brazilians pointed out that the navy's position required more personnel, which meant greater expense for Brazil. The increased cost was trivial by U.S. standards but represented a substantial burden for Brazil.[15]

Faced with the U.S. refusal to compromise and the self-interested behavior of the U.S. Navy, Brazilian military leaders were forced to re-evaluate their position. Brazil no longer wanted three generals or admirals but only one general with assistants. The general should be a ground officer who would advise a Brazilian director of the school and be assisted by an army colonel, an air force general, and a navy captain.[16]

U.S. Army officials favored the new Brazilian proposals, viewing the arrangement as preferable to the navy idea of separate missions. Nevertheless, it took three months of discussions among the U.S. armed service branches before they agreed to accept the Brazilian plan. The Americans added, however, that they wanted the chief U.S. adviser to be a retired senior officer who would serve under a three-year non-renewable contract and that the position be rotated among the three service branches.[17]

Another four months of negotiations between U.S. and Brazilian members of the JBUSMC elapsed before final accommodation. In July 1948 both parties agreed that there would be two contracts: an individual one providing for a retired army general to command the mission and a broad general contract covering three active-duty officers and three enlisted men representing each U.S. service branch. Brazil also agreed to accept the financial obligations as outlined in earlier discussions.[18]

Signing of the general contract took place on July 29, 1948, but another surprising development arose before signatures could be affixed to the individual contract. Perhaps recoiling from the financial burden of the deal and seeing other benefits, Brazil informed U.S. officials on August 10 that it no longer wished to conclude the individual contract for a retired senior officer but would implement the already signed general contract.[19] The maneuver allowed Brazil to reduce costs and raise the importance of the mission at the same time. In Brazil's view retired officers had completed their careers and had diminishing influence on military affairs, whereas active officers were at their peak or in ascendancy. After serving in Rio de Janeiro, such men might well influence future U.S. military policy to Brazil's benefit.

EARLY DIFFICULTIES

Once final agreement had been reached and the personnel assigned, the ESG Military Mission found the transitional planning as difficult as the negotiation phase. Although poised to begin work rapidly, the mission spent three unproductive weeks before it was able to meet with General Obino and General Oswaldo Cordeiro de Farias, the former *tenente* and ex-FEB officer appointed to command the school. Interim conferences with members of the Brazilian Joint General Staff yielded little. Without the consent of Obino and Cordeiro de Farias, the General Staff was in no position to accept or act on any of the mission's recommendations.[20]

Physical problems hampered the missions's ability to function as well. On arriving in Rio de Janeiro, mission members found the building designated to house the school still occupied. As a result, officers of the mission received desk space in the General Staff building, while their enlisted assistants were given a room with little furniture and no office equipment in the school building.[21]

CURRICULUM DEVELOPMENT

Despite the inauspicious start, the mission quickly developed a course of study that on the surface reflected a liberal democratic approach to learning. The proposed curriculum called for an examination of all ideologies and guest lectures by individuals of various political and religious persuasions. Information of national and international importance would be presented on a continual basis throughout the period of instruction, and experts on special topics were to be utilized.[22]

Although the curriculum appeared to embrace a broad methodology, the underlying theme espoused anti-communism and elitism. Juxtaposed with the seemingly liberal approach was a structure that by its nature meant a select few would have access to knowledge unavailable to most Brazilians. It is not surprising that the civilians and military officers who attended ESG courses considered themselves an elite uniquely qualified to solve national problems.[23]

Hoping to open the school to students by January 1950, the ESG mission planned to provide faculty and staff a sixteen-week preparatory course at the Fortaleza de São João in the Rio district of Urca. Plans called for a new school to be built at Praia Vermelha within two years. Interestingly, the Americans and Brazilians began planning the school curricula and structural makeup of the institution long before the Brazilian Congress voted to provide funds for the project.[24]

The U.S. officers assigned to the ESG intended the sixteen-week preliminary course to prepare faculty and staff for their teaching and administrative duties. The goal proved unreachable. The U.S. members of the JBUSMC correctly predicted that the three mission officers would be unable to develop the preparatory course lectures in such a short time. Bowing to reality, the ESG mission officers created a truncated course that lasted eight weeks and began on September 1, 1949. The course for the first ESG group began the following year on January 1, 1950. The year-long ESG course comprised four parts in which eight weeks were devoted to doctrine, twenty-two weeks to issues, and ten weeks to problem solving. A three-week tour of U.S. military facilities, at U.S. expense, and tours of Brazil rounded out the course. Spread throughout the year were nine weeks of vacation.[25]

The ESG and U.S. Influence

Arriving at the point of opening the Escola Superior de Guerra had not been a simple process. Nearly four years passed between the Eisenhower-Obino discussion and the beginning of the first regular course in January 1950. Acceptance of the U.S. position in negotiations for assistance in creating the ESG marked the subtle nature of change and indicated the manner in which post-war military relations were to be conducted. During the war economics came second to the goal of victory. In the resource-poor post-war era economics, as well as national and internal institutional interests, assumed greater importance. The brotherhood of arms was no longer simple, nor was it equal.

The preponderance of U.S. doctrine at the ESG also reflected a change in the relationship. The privileged position of the U.S. armed forces in Brazil's military development ensured the special place of the United States in Brazilian affairs. The influence of the ESG, and the U.S. presence at the school, had a profound effect on Brazilian democracy. Indeed, U.S. documents, books, and knowledge provided much of the theoretical basis of the national security and development policies adopted by the military-civilian alliance formed in the ESG classroom. As a result, in 1964 the Brazilian military and its civilian allies were "alert and prepared to act at the opportune moment against the communization of the country, thanks to the training received at the different military schools."[26]

The impact of the Escola Superior de Guerra in developing national objectives and inculcating the military elite with a belief in its ability to build the nation cannot be overestimated. The United States must share some of the responsibility for that belief because Americans set the tone for the future role of the Brazilian officer. In a 1946 talk at the ECEME, Dwight D. Eisenhower said that in the post-war era it was not enough for an officer to have only a military education. A knowledge of economics, psychology, and methods of dealing with non-military people was as important as the martial arts.[27]

Roger Hilsman contends that the purpose of training U.S. officers in economic and political matters at the various service schools is to provide the officer with an understanding of the context in which military advice is judged. This knowledge is supposed to give the officer the skills necessary to adapt effective military means to the political requirements of civilian authority. Eisenhower's speech indicated that the United States believed the ESG would offer similar training. With a U.S. mission providing valuable advice, the ESG would be a national think tank in which civilian and military elites, and the U.S. military, exchanged geopolitical and strategic ideas.[28]

Command of the ESG certainly bore the U.S. imprint. The first commandant of the school was former FEB artillery commander General Oswaldo Cordeiro de Farias. Moreover, many of the first faculty and staff members were ex-*Febianos* who had experience dealing with Americans. Following the ideological bent of the staff, the ESG taught its students the concept of interdependence with the United States and emphasized Brazil's place in the anti-communist crusade, as well as the dangers of "excessive nationalism."[29]

THE DOCTRINE OF NATIONAL SECURITY

The role of the U.S. military in promulgation of the doctrine taught at the ESG was important but should not overshadow the contribution of Brazilian thinking. Anti-communism and cooperation with the United States were dominant themes at the ESG, and at the ECEME, but Brazilian officers developed many of the principles that shaped future actions by the military. In a pamphlet entitled "Princípios Fundamentais da Escola Superior de Guerra," Lieutenant Colonel Idálio Sardenberg, one of the school's first staff members, articulated the basic principles of national security and development. Sardenberg argued that the United States National War College provided the model for the ESG, but with an important difference. Unlike the Brazilian system, the U.S. education system trained the masses, which allowed the U.S. War College to focus on war rather than on national infrastructure and society. Brazil's poorly developed education system meant that the ESG's "primary task would be to form elites for the solution of the country's problems in time of peace." From this consideration came the principles of national security and development.[30]

The doctrine taught at the ESG evolved in four phases. From 1949 to 1952, the first phase, themes were isolated and subdivided into national, international, and military matters. In the second phase, from 1953 to 1967, the doctrine of security and theory combined to make up the material of most of the courses. In 1953 the commandant, General Juarez Távora, developed the ideas of the security doctrine for Brazil in a speech entitled "The Politics and Strategy of National Security: Conceptions and Interrelationships." The concept of development joined security to form the core of coursework in the third phase, from 1968 to 1973. In 1973 the regulation "Formulation of the National Politics of Security and Development" entered into force to codify the doctrine. The final phase, after 1973, continued the third phase but added a student problem-solving component.[31]

Some observers argue that the Escola Superior de Guerra was an agent for diffusing U.S. military doctrines and for formulating policies that served the interests of the multinational companies and their Brazilian associates. Brazil's modern geopolitical thought, however, antedates the formulation of national security and development doctrine. Brazilian geopoliticians point to Everado Backheuser in the late 1920s as the father of Brazil's modern geopolitical thinking; he stressed alignment with the Western capitalist democracies. In the 1930s and 1940s Mario Travassos was the leading proponent of the Brazilian view of the world.[32]

Travassos, who participated in the FEB, influenced many students at the ECEME. Among those were Carlos de Meira Mattos and Golbery do Couto e Silva, whose ideas of Brazil as a great power with a role in the defense of Western culture and alignment with the United States against communism became dominant among military thinkers in the 1950s through the 1970s. Nevertheless, the doctrine taught at the ESG had little influence on government decisions until the 1964 coup. The coup brought forward the idea of security and development, which had been evolving during the 1949–1964 period, because many of the officers involved in the overthrow of President João Goulart and in the subsequent military governments had participated in the formulation of doctrine while at the ESG as instructors or students. With the coup it was natural for General Humberto de Alencar Castello Branco and his principal advisers, such as Golbery do Couto e Silva, Juarez Távora, Cordeiro de Farias, and Ernesto Geisel, to utilize the doctrine to govern the country.[33]

The evolution of the security and development doctrine was a lengthy process. General Tristão de Alencar Araripe enunciated the concepts at the ESG and ECEME as early as 1950. In an article in the military journal *A Defesa Nacional*, Araripe declared that "a nation, organizing itself for war, is also preparing itself for a better life." After 1964 various articles in *A Defesa Nacional* and the *Revista do Clube Militar* and in books by Brazilian officers justified the coup and promoted the doctrine and the army's role in nation building. Particularly vocal was the minister of war, General Aurélio de Lyra Tavares, who asserted that the doctrine and the army's anti-communism permitted the country to progress. Other officers praised the ESG as the laboratory of ideas that inspired the doctrine.[34] Clearly evident in their proclamations was the nineteenth-century positivism motto "Order and Progress," which adorns the Brazilian flag.

The Escola de Comando e Estado Maior do Exército

The post-1964 governments drew inspiration from the intellectual preparation of the ESG, but it would be a mistake to ignore the importance of the Escola de Comando e Estado Maior do Exército. A French military mission helped reshape the ECEME's predecessor, the Escola de Estado Maior, in 1919–1930, which set the pattern of the Brazilian Army officer's education. Unlike the ESG, whose military students were colonels and generals, ECEME students were majors and lieutenant colonels who undertook a three-year course that indoctrinated them in military thought.[35] The ECEME was therefore an important element in the diffusion of doctrine that for some continued at the ESG.

After the Allied victory in World War II the ECEME naturally adopted the positions espoused by the United States. Over time, however, U.S. doctrine failed to correspond to Brazil's economic, political, and social realities, which led to a rejection of the U.S. model in ECEME courses. The change began at the end of 1955, when Brigadier General Humberto de Alencar Castello Branco assumed command of the school. The ESG still mimicked U.S. concepts and principles, but at the ECEME Castello Branco introduced thinking adapted to the Brazilian environment.[36]

Castello Branco's efforts to create a doctrine that emphasized the Brazilian character suffered a setback with the introduction of nuclear tactics in ECEME courses in 1956. Since the United States was the Western democracies' nuclear arms leader and the Brazilian officers knew little of atomic technology, the ECEME followed the U.S. lead. The new course that stressed the strategic use of nuclear weapons created what Brazilian observers called a "nuclear psychosis" at the school. Nuclear warfare had little to do with the Brazilian reality, however, and the move toward a purely Brazilian approach soon continued.[37]

With the success of Fidel Castro in Cuba and the export of revolution to South America in the 1960s, the study of guerrilla warfare in the ECEME curriculum grew in importance and blended with the concepts of security and development. Although this aspect of the program of study began in 1961, it received impetus in 1962 when General Jurandir de Bizarria Mamede assumed command of the school. Mamede stressed national development because he believed one of the reasons people resorted to revolution was underdevelopment. Thus, the study of economics, politics, and society translated into a belief that "security is equal to development," which the army officer corps used to justify interference in national politics. The program included a special series of anti-communist lectures instituted earlier by Castello Branco that accented the lessons of "revolutionary wars" throughout the world. The lessons presumably would help the military avert similar occurrences in Brazil.[38]

Under the guidance of General João Bina Machado, commandant of the ECEME from 1964 to 1966, internal security became the most important aspect of the curriculum. Bina Machado instituted areas of instruction aimed at preventing activity that might lead to insurrection and at developing strategy for combating guerrillas. By 1966 ECEME coursework included 351 hours of internal security and irregular warfare study but only 24 hours of study devoted to conventional war. Heavy emphasis was placed on the application of lessons learned in the Brazilian context.[39]

Testimony on the efficacy of ECEME indoctrination came after the military ousted João Goulart. In 1967 the Comissão de Relações Públicas do Exército (Army Public Relations Commission) proudly quoted an unnamed minister in the Goulart government as saying, "From the ECEME came not only the present President of the Republic. From the ECEME arose all the revolutionary command. From the ECEME arose the plans of action. From the ECEME you have to owe the emergence of all the philosophy of the revolutionary movement." The comissão went on to announce that those words gave "a measure of the participation of the Escola da Praia Vermelha in the Democratic Revolution."[40]

The Brazilian military intellectuals who gravitated to the ECEME and the ESG influenced the thinking of a significant portion of the officer corps.[41] It is questionable whether the ESG and ECEME were as sinister an agent as some claim or that the doctrine taught at the schools was as purely Brazilian as others argue. Adoption of U.S. doctrine and the U.S. role at the ESG, and at other service schools such as the airborne school, ensured similarities. Furthermore, guerrilla warfare and civic action were part of the U.S. military repertoire by 1962. Nevertheless, as Peter Flynn notes, the Brazilians adapted the methods of their ally to their own situation.[42]

Military involvement in national politics owed much to the *tenentes* of the 1920s and 1930s. The *tenente* movement began in 1922 as a political protest by young army officers against perceived corruption and the besmirching of army honor. Its high point came with the success of the 1930 revolution that put Getúlio Vargas into the presidency. The *tenentes* helped mold much of the post-revolution state. Many also served in the FEB and supported close ties with the United States. Their influence shaped post-war Brazilian society and military policy, including the content of instruction at the various military schools.[43] There is little wonder that the doctrine taught at Brazil's service schools mirrored that of the United States.

CHANGES IN U.S. INVOLVEMENT

Disillusionment on both sides over the value of the military relationship became clear in the closing years of the 1950s. U.S. weight remained heavy at the ESG throughout the decade, but increasingly contentious relations colored the U.S. presence. At the end of the 1950s U.S. participation at the school came under scrutiny as a perceived lack of U.S. assistance and the rise of Brazilian nationalism led some to question the value of close military ties.[44] The 1959 passage of the Mansfield Amendment, an attempt by the U.S. Congress to hold down military assistance costs while emphasizing economic objectives, reflected another change in the relationship. According to the legislation, military missions could no longer receive direct payment from foreign governments. Instead, countries like Brazil had to make lump payments to the U.S. government, which would then disperse salaries.[45]

Soon after passage of the amendment the Brazilians indicated a desire to terminate by 1960 the ESG Mission structure, citing economic reasons. Under the existing arrangement a U.S. officer lectured and an enlisted man provided staff liaison.[46] Although economy may have been a reason for the decision, other issues were involved. The military was unhappy with assistance negotiations and the focus on economic over military aid. At the same time, a more independent foreign policy that stressed distancing from the United States had the support of many important officers.[47] Changing the role of the United States in the ESG would send a message of displeasure, as well as represent a manifestation of Brazilian independence.

Brazilian politicians added their discontent over the U.S. role at the ESG. During a May 25, 1959, lecture at the school Deputy Aurélio Vianna, a member of the Brazilian Socialist Party from Alagoas and a student at the ESG, questioned the presence of an American officer when sensitive subjects were discussed. The commandant of the school, General Arthur Hesckett-Hall, argued that as a member of the ESG staff the U.S. officer was entitled to remain. Vianna disagreed and left the school to carry the issue to the floor of the Chamber of Deputies.[48]

Vianna had reason to be suspicious, although he was unaware of how much so. In a note to the U.S. chargé in Rio de Janeiro the Department of State's chief of the Office of South American Affairs, William T. Briggs, explained that State and military officials wanted greater care in staffing the ESG mission with an "eye to the more complete development of the intelligence possibilities inherent in the job." Briggs and the military also wanted more "lectures of opportunity" for U.S. officers as a means of increasing contact with the school's students and faculty.[49] A belief in the ability to influence the politically important Brazilian officer corps and influential civilians remained a strong component of U.S. anti-communist strategy.

Debate over the U.S. presence at the ESG raged in the Chamber of Deputies into July, when the current U.S. officer's term of duty expired. The whole episode became an issue between opposing political groups in Brazil, as well as a point of military honor. Although the U.S. officer's term of duty was scheduled to expire before the expected termination of the ESG mission agreement in

1960, Hesckett-Hall wanted him to remain at the school until then in order to avoid the appointment of another officer for such a short period of time. Washington readily agreed, for it was loathe to forgo consistent entrée to the school.[50]

Vianna, supported by Rio Grande do Sul deputy Rui Ramos of the Brazilian Labor Party (PTB), argued that because the current officer's term expired in July, any agreement for the soldier to remain until 1960 was invalid. The Chamber of Deputies' powerful Executive Committee agreed with their contention and announced that no deputies would attend the ESG until the issue was settled. Strong opposition to the Executive Committee's announcement arose from powerful conservatives Carlos Lacerda (of the National Democratic Union, or UDN) and Majority Leader Armando Falção (Social Democratic Party, or PSD), who feared precipitous action could damage relations with the United States and, perhaps more important, embarrass the well-liked Hesckett-Hall.[51]

With the issue promising to create even more acrimonious debate, the feuding deputies reached a short-term compromise solution. Given that Hesckett-Hall was soon due to become the chief of the Armed Forces General Staff, the opposing sides agreed to postpone execution of the Executive Committee's decision until the popular general left the school. Postponement, however, became long term as chaotic Brazilian politics and U.S. efforts to salvage the situation rendered opposition and the Executive Committee decision inconsequential.[52]

Alarmed that debate would lead to the complete removal of the U.S. presence at the ESG, the American members of the Joint Brazil–United States Military Commission urged the reconfiguration of the mission to make it palatable to the Brazilians. Instead of continuing a teaching role for U.S. officers at the school, the commission delegates suggested that the United States alter the ESG Mission's role to one of liaison and make it part of the Military Assistance Advisory Group. The incentive for the Brazilians to accept the plan was financial, for the cost of MAAGs was borne by the United States.[53]

Apparently the Americans did not notice that their proposal adopted the Brazilian position in the 1949 negotiations regarding the ESG Mission. The difference was that in 1949 the Brazilians had

had little bargaining power. By 1959 Brazilian military and political development was making the U.S. connection less important, if not less desirable. The United States was now the supplicant.

In a rare show of unanimity both the State and Defense Departments agreed that the JBUSMC plan had merit. The United States would not oppose letting the mission agreement expire at the end of the current officer's tour in 1960 as long as U.S. personnel remained at the school under the MAAG. The Brazilians accepted the proposal as well, for it also met their objectives. A liaison officer had a less intimate role in the school than did a staff member and cost Brazil nothing. At the same time, the U.S. connection could be maintained.[54]

In reaching an accommodation on the issue, Brazil again became the model for implementation of U.S. policy. The MAAG agreement with Brazil was the first of thirty-eight reached with other countries in which foreign governments were relieved of the expense of supporting U.S. military advisers. In the case of Brazil it meant that from 1960 until the end of formal military relations in 1977 a U.S. officer on the JBUSMC acted as the liaison to the ESG as part of the MAAG. U.S. presence continued, but in a muted, less influential form.[55]

The negotiations for U.S. assistance in the creation of the Escola Superior de Guerra and the evolving U.S. presence at the school were part of a continual process of adjustment to national and international realities after World War II. U.S. influence dominated the curriculum because Brazilian military leaders believed in the correctness of U.S. doctrine and accepted tutelage as the price of military development. The relationship was not one of total adherence to a U.S. master, however, because the Brazilians placed their own imprint on doctrine taught at their military schools.

Over time Brazil's military and political development allowed a distancing from U.S. dominance without severing the close connection. Changes in the structure of the U.S. presence at the ESG reflected the growing maturity and confidence of the Brazilian military. Maturation and the changing priorities of both nations guaranteed that Brazil-U.S. military relations would continue to become more and more complex. Nevertheless, the U.S. role in the birth and growth of the ESG gained basic objectives for both Brazil and the United States. Brazil received help in building an institution important to its military development, and the United States secured a prominent place in the Brazilian military and, as a result, political affairs. U.S. requests for Brazilian troops in the Korean War confirmed that the relationship continued to adjust to ever-changing national and international requirements.

NOTES

1.   Two works that examine the importance of the ESG in Brazilian political life are Ronald M. Schneider, *The Political System of Brazil: Emergence of a "Modernizing" Authoritarian Regime, 1964–1970* (New York: Columbia University Press, 1971); and Alfred Stepan, *The Military in Politics: Changing Patterns in Brazil* (Princeton: Princeton University Press, 1971). For a good study of how the two schools assist clique formation, see Frank D. McCann, "The Military," in *Modern Brazil: Elites and Masses in Historical Perspective,* ed. Michael L. Conniff and Frank D. McCann (Lincoln: University of Nebraska Press, 1989), 49–54. For the role of Cordeiro de Farias in establishing the ESG, see General Oswaldo Cordeiro de Farias, Aspasia Camargo, and Wilder de Góes, *Meio seculo de combate: Dialógo com Cordeiro de Farias* (Rio de Janeiro: Editora Nova Fronteira, 1981), 412–418.

2.   "Notes of Conference Between General Obino (Brazil) and General Eisenhower at 0930," December 4, 1946, RG-319, P&O Decimal File, 1946–1948, Entry 154, Box 73, Sec. I, Case 14; Colonel Godwyn Ordway to U.S. Army Member, Ground Section—JBUSMC, March 18, 1947, RG-319, P&O Decimal File, 1946–1948, Box 332 (Sec. III) (Cases 21–); and Colonel Paul L. Freeman, Jr., to Major General C. L. Mullins, Jr.—JBUSMC, January 13, 1950, RG-319, P&O Decimal File, 1949–February 1950, Entry 154, Box 200, 334 JBUSMC TS (Sec. I) (Cases 1–), NA.

3.   Ruth Leacock, *Requiem for Revolution: The United States and Brazil, 1961–1969* (Kent, Ohio: Kent State University Press, 1990), 182–183; Antônio de Arruda, *ESG: História de sua doutrina* (São Paulo: Editores GRD, 1980), 1–9; Cordeiro de Farias et al., *Meio seculo,* 412–418; Stepan, *Military in Politics,* 174–183; and Schneider, *Political System of Brazil,* 250–252. Cordeiro de Farias participated in the Brazilian Expeditionary Force that fought with the U.S. Army in Italy in World War II.

4.   "Draft of Instruction for Staff Conversations with Military and Naval Representatives of Other American Republics, July 28, 1944," RG-319, P&O Decimal File, 1946–1948, Box 284, 334 JABOAR (Sec. I) (Cases 1–), NA; CIA, National Intelligence Estimate, "Conditions and Trends in Latin America Affecting U.S. Security," December 12, 1952, President's Secretary's File (PSF)-254; and Berle to Truman, October 30, 1945, White House Central Files, Box 33, Folder 5, HST Library. In a letter to Truman Adolf Berle praised the army coup that overthrew President Getúlio Vargas and unknowingly foreshadowed

the concept of the military as a nation builder, which later became a dominate theme at the ESG. A number of works address U.S. policy toward and beliefs about the Latin American and Brazilian officer corps and the role of officers in national politics. See, for example, Johnson, *Military and Society*, 127, 143, 263; Lieuwen, *Arms and Politics*, 196–197, 226; Haines, *Americanization of Brazil*, 39; Skidmore, *Politics in Brazil*, 330; and Wilfred A. Bacchus, *Mission in Mufti: Brazil's Military Regimes, 1964–1985* (New York: Greenwood Press, 1990), 17–39.

5. Colonel Godwyn Ordway to General Henrique Lott, October 7, 1947, RG-319, P&O Decimal File, 1946–1948, Box 332 (Sec. II) (Case 20 only) (Sub-Nos 1), NA. Obino revised his proposal in February 1947, requesting three to six reserve or retired officers to organize, guide, and direct the projected school under commission auspices. See Gen. C. H. Gerhardt, JBUSMC, to Director, Plans & Operations, February 28, 1947, RG-319, P&O Decimal File, 1946–1948, Box 332 (Sec. III) (Cases 21–), NA.

6. Eisenhower to Gerhardt, January 16, 1947, Charles H. Gerhardt Papers, Folder 2, USMHI; Gerhardt to Director, P&O, February 25, 1947, RG-319, P&O Decimal File, 1946–1948, Box 332 (Sec. III) (Cases 21–); Ordway to U.S. Army Member, Ground Section—JBUSMC, March 18, 1947; Brig. Gen. Gordon P. Saville, U.S. Army Member, Air Section—JBUSMC, to Commanding General, Army Air Forces, March 11, 1947, RG-319, P&O Decimal File 1946–1948, Box 332 (Sec. II) (Cases 20–) (Sub-Nos 1–), NA; and Stepan, *Military in Politics*, 175–178.

7. Freeman to Mullins, January 13, 1950, RG-319, P&O Decimal File, 1949–February 1950, Entry 154, Box 200, 334 JBUSMC TS (Sec. I) (Case 1), NA; and Stepan, *Military in Politics*, 175–178.

8. Brig. Gen. Henrique Baptista Duffles Teixeira Lott to Foreign Liaison Officer, February 12, 1947, RG-319, P&O Decimal File, 1946–1948, Box 332 (Sec. II) (Case 20 only) (Sub-Nos 1), NA; Comissão de Relações Públicas do Exército, *O seu exército* (N.p.: N.p., 1967), 23; and Joffre Gomes da Costa, *Marechal Henrique Lott* (Rio de Janeiro: N.p., 1960), 201.

9. Maj. Gen. Lauris Norstad, Director—Plans & Operations, to Chief of Staff, May 9, 1947, RG-319, P&O Decimal File, 1946–1948, Box 332, NA.

10. Ibid.

11. Norstad to Chief of Staff, May 9, 1947.

12. Ordway to Lott, October 7, 1947, RG-319, P&O Decimal File, 1946–1948, Box 332 (Sec. II) (Case 20 only) (Sub-Nos 1–), NA.

13. Ibid.

14. Saville to Chief of Staff, USAF, October 17, 1947, RG-319, P&O Decimal File, 1946–1948, Box 332 (Sec. II) (Case 20 only (Sub-Nos 1–), NA. October 17, 1947.

15. CNO to Senior Naval Member—JBUSMC, August 8, 1947, RG-319, P&O Decimal File, 1946–1948, Box 332 (Sec. II) (Case 20 only) (Sub-Nos 1), NA.

16. Ordway to Gen. A. C. Wedemeyer, December 2, 1947, RG-319, P&O Decimal File, 1946–1948, Box 32 (Sec. II) (Case 20 only) (Sub-Nos 1), NA.

17. Ordway to Wedemeyer, December 2, 1947; Wedemeyer to CNO, March 12, 1948, RG-319, P&O Decimal File, 1946–1948, Box 332 (Sec. II) (Case 20 only) (Sub-Nos 1), NA.

18. Lt. Col. H. G. Sparrow, Executive—Plans & Operations, to Operation Requirements Branch, General Officers Branch, and Overseas Assignment Branch, July 30, 1948, RG-319, P&O Decimal File, 1946–1948, Box 332, NA.

19. Sparrow to ORB, July 30, 1948; and CSG, P&O, to USAM, August 16, 1948, RG-319, P&O Decimal File, 1946–1948, Box 332, NA.

20. Quarterly Report of Activities, 1st Quarter 1949, United States Army Section, U.S. Military Mission to Brazil, March 31, 1949, RG-319, P&O Decimal File, 1949–February 1950, Box 534, 091 Brazil, (Sec. IB) (Book 1) (Cases 1–) (16 only) (Sub-Nos 1–), NA; and General Cordeiro de Farias et al., *Meio seculo*, 412–418.

21. Ibid.

22. Quarterly Report of Activities, 1st Quarter 1949, March 31, 1949, RG-319, P&O Decimal File, 1949–February 1950, NA.

23. Stepan, *Military in Politics*, 173–178.

24. Quarterly Report of Activities, September 30, 1949, RG-319, P&O Decimal File, 1949–February 1950, Box 534, 091 Brazil, NA.

25. Quarterly Report of Activities, March 31, 1949, RG-319, P&O Decimal File, 1949–February 1950, Box 534, NA; and Schneider, *Political System of Brazil*, 248.

26. The national security and development policies of the various post-1964 coup governments had their roots in early twentieth-century military thought. See Frank D. McCann, "The Formative Period of Twentieth-Century Brazilian Army Thought, 1900–1920," *Hispanic American Historical Review* 64:4 (November 1984): 765; and General Aúrelio de Lyra Tavares, *Segurança nacional, problemas atuais* (N.p.: José Alvaro Editor, S.A., n.d.), 258–259. McCann's article provides a detailed examination of the development of the early army thought that led to acceptance of the doctrine of national security. For an analysis of the military governments' application of doctrine taught at the ESG, see Stepan, *Military in Politics*, 183–187.

27. Stepan, *Military in Politics*, 183–187. For more on ESG ideology and the part the school played in the 1964 coup, see also General Carlos de Meira Mattos, "Doutrina política revolucinária Brasil—potência," *Revista do Clube Militar* 44:174 (April 1970): 16–18. "Extracto do discurso proferido pelo General do Exército Dwight D. Eisenhower na Escola de Estado Maior do Brasil, em 6 de Agosto de 1946," *A Defesa Nacional* 33:388 (September, 1946): 263; and Mike Burgess and Daniel Wolf, "The Concept of Power in the Brazilian Higher War College (ESG)" (Toronto: Latin American Research Unit, December 1979), 1–2. The doctrine of national security and development was being implemented at West Point at the same time.

28. Roger Hilsman, *The Politics of Policy Making in Defense and Foreign Affairs* (New York: Harper and Row, 1971), 76; Baily, *U.S. and Development of South America*, 146–147; and John Child, "Geopolitical Thinking in Latin America," *Latin American Research Review* 14:2 (1972): 92. For a summary of the ESG, see "Escola Superior de Guerra," *Dicionário Histórico-Biografico Brasileiro, 1930–1983*, vol. 2, ed. Israel Beloch and Alzira Alves de Abreu (Rio de Janeiro: Fundação Getúlio Vargas, Centro de Pesquisa e Documentação de História Contemporânea do Brasil, Forense-Universitária, 1984), 1181–1182.

29. Baily, *U.S. and Development of South America*, 146–147; and Fontaine, *Brazil and the U.S.*, 46. For examples of the anti-communist and anti-nationalist views of two of the ESG commandants, see Juarez Távora, "Escola Superior de Guerra," *A Defesa Nacional* 61:475 (February 1954): 111–120; and General Cordeiro de Farias address to the first graduating class in *O Estado de São Paulo* (São Paulo), December 23, 1950. Besides Cordeiro de Farias, the first staff members of the ESG included Cel. Sady Folch, Cel. Av. Ismar P. Brasil, Ten. Cel. Affonso Henrique de Miranda Correa, CF Celso A. de Macedo Soares Guimaraes, and Ten. Cel. Idálio Sardenberg. The first Americans included Col. William J. Verbeck, Col. Alvord Van Patten Anderson, Jr., and CMNG Lowe E. Bibby.

30. Arruda, *ESG*, 2–3; and Stepan, *Military in Politics*, 178–183. For more on the ESG, see Alexandre de Barros, "The Brazilian Military: Professional Socialization, Political Performance, and State Building" (Ph.D. diss., University of Chicago, 1978).

31. Ibid.

32. Burgess and Wolf, "Concept of Power," 1; and Carlos de Meira Mattos, *Brasil: Geopolítica e destino* (Rio de Janeiro: Biblioteca do Exército Editora with Livraria José Olympio Editora, 1975), 67. For a sketch of Mario Travassos as the commander of an FEB training depot, see Floriano de Lima Brayner, *Recordando os bravos: Eu convivi com eles—Campanha da Itália* (Rio de Janeiro: Editora Civilização Brasileira, 1977), 335–346.

33. Jan Knippers Black, *Sentinels of Empire: The United States and Latin American Militarism* (New York: Greenwood Press, 1986), 43; Schneider, *Political System of Brazil*, 120, 244, 250; and Stepan, *Military in Politics*, 180–181.

34. General Tristão de Alencar Araripe quoted in *A Defesa Nacional* 37:43 (June 1950): 5; General Aurélio de Lyra Tavares, *O Exército Brasileiro visto pelo seu ministro* (Recife: Universidade de Pernambuco—Imprensa Universitária, 1968), 51–52; "Exército—fator de integração nacional," *Revista do Clube Militar* 43:165 (June 1969): 10–11; "Segurança e desenvolvimento," *Revista do Clube Militar* 43:166 (July 1969): 8–10; and General Antônio Jorge Correa, "Escola Superior de Guerra—Laboratório de ideias," *A Defesa Nacional* 63:667 (May–June 1976): 9–11.

35. Comissão Diretoria de Relações Públicas do Exército, *O seu exército*, 22–23; and McCann, "The Military," 54.

36. Jeronymo Jorge Alves Silva, "Evolução histórica do militar brasileiro formou sua consciência democratica," *Revista do Clube Militar* 43:168 (October 1969): 43; Cel. Francisco Ruas Santos, ed., *Marechal Castello Branco: Seu pensamento militar (1946–1964)* (Rio de Janeiro: Imprensa do Exército, 1968), 252–253; and John W. F. Dulles, *Castello Branco: The Making of a Brazilian President* (College Station: Texas A&M University Press, 1978), 181–185.

37. Alves Silva, "Evolução histórica."

38. Ibid., 43; and Stanley E. Hilton, "The Brazilian Military: Changing Strategic Perceptions and the Quest for Mission," *Armed Forces and Society* 13:3 (Spring 1987): 331. For ECEME course content, see Frank D. McCann, "The Brazilian Army and the Problem of Mission, 1939–1964," *Journal of Latin American Studies* 12:1 (May, 1980): 123–125. For details on Mamede and his

link to the national security doctrine, see *Dicionário Histórico-Biografico*, 2056.

39. Hilton, "Brazilian Military," 331; Schneider, *Political System of Brazil*, 252; Alfred Stepan, "The New Professionalism of Internal Warfare and Military Role Expansion," in *Authoritarian Brazil: Origins, Policies, and Future*, ed. Alfred Stepan (New Haven: Yale University Press, 1973), 59; and Stepan, *Military in Politics*, 174–185.

40. Comissão de Relações Públicas do Exército, *O seu exército*, 22.

41. Fontaine, *Brazil and the United States*, 31.

42. General C. L. Mullins, Jr., to Colonel Paul L. Freeman, Jr., January 5, 1950, RG-319, P&O Decimal File, 1949–February 1950, Box 200, 334 JBUSMC TS (Sec. I) (Case 1–), NA; Lt. General Richard J. Seitz, Oral History, 1977, 13, USMHI; and Flynn, *Brazil*, 43, 321.

43. Michael L. Conniff, "The Tenentes in Power: A New Perspective on the Brazilian Revolution of 1930," *Journal of Latin American Studies* 10:1 (May 1978): 82; and McCann, "Formative Period of Twentieth-Century Brazilian Army Thought," 764.

44. Stephen G. Rabe, *Eisenhower and Latin America: The Foreign Policy of Anti-Communism* (Chapel Hill: University of North Carolina Press, 1988), 2, 26, 31–32, 34–35; Dwight D. Eisenhower, *Waging Peace, 1951–1961* (Garden City, N.Y.: Doubleday, 1965), 514–520; Weis, *Cold Warriors*, 89–90; and Joint Subsidiary Plans Division Memorandum for Director, Joint Staff, Subject: 10th Inter-American Conference, March 16, 1954, RG-218, Records of the JCS, CCS 4000.3295 (12-16-43) (Sec. 7), NA.

45. Herter to Embassy—Rio, March 12, 1959, RG-59, Records of the Department of State Relating to Internal Political and National Defense of Brazil, Decimal File, 1955–1959, 732, Micro. 1511, Roll 8, 732.5-MSB/1-2258-732.726/4-2356, NA.

46. The original size of three officers and three enlisted men had been reduced previously as an economy measure.

47. "Briefing Paper for Meetings with Brazilian Minister of War," March 27, 1959, RG-59, Records of the Department of State, Records of the Assistant Secretary of State for Inter-American Affairs (R. R. Rubottom), Box 11, 1959 Brazil, Lot 61D279; Department of the Army to CINCARIB, July 15, 1959, RG-218, JCS Central Decimal File, 1959, CCS 9/22/5440 Brazil, NA; Storrs, "Brazil's Independent Foreign Policy," 151–152; and José Honório Rodrigues, "The Foundations of Brazil's Foreign Policy," *International Affairs* 38:3 (July 1962): 324–338.

48. Woodruff Wellner to Secretary of State, May 26, 1959, RG-59, Records of the Department of State, 1955–1959, Micro. 1511, Roll 8, NA.

49. William T. Briggs to Woodruff Wellner, May 27, 1959, RG-59, Records of Assistant Secretary of State for Inter-American Affairs (R. R. Rubottom), Box 11, 1959 Brazil, Lot 61D279, NA.

50. Philip Rain, First Secretary of the Embassy, to Department of State, July 13, 1959, RG-59, Records of the Department of State, 1955–1959, Micro. 1511, Roll 8, NA.

51. Ibid. Lacerda was the leader of the Democratic National Union in Congress from 1957 to 1959. See John W. F. Dulles, *Carlos Lacerda, Brazilian Crusader,* vol. 1, *The Years 1914–1960* (Austin: University of Texas Press, 1991), 231–278.

52. Rain to Department of State, July 13, 1959, RG-59, Records of the Department of State, Micro. 1511, Roll 8, NA. Numerous works detail the chaotic state of Brazilian politics of the period. For the best example, see Skidmore, *Politics in Brazil.*

53. Chair, U.S. Delegation, JBUSMC, to CINCARIB, August 21, 1959, RG-218, JCS Central Decimal File, 1959, CCS 9/33/5440 Brazil, NA.

54. Dillon to Embassy—Rio, August 27, 1959, RG-59, Records of the Department of State, 1955–1959, Micro. 1511, Roll 8, NA.

55. U.S. Congress, Senate, Hearings Before the Subcommittee on Western Hemisphere Affairs of the Committee on Foreign Relations, *United States Policies and Programs in Brazil*, 92d Cong. 1st sess., May 4, 5, 11, 1971, 53; Dillon to Embassy—Rio, August 27, 1959; and Stepan, *Military in Politics*, 129.

.. 6 ..

The Korean War

With the dawning of the 1950s decade, Brazil–United States military relations settled into a mode reminiscent of the pre-war pattern. When objectives coincided, cooperation was relatively easy. When interests diverged, cooperation suffered. Absent were the common threats and shared goals that had brought the countries closer in the 1940s. Local debate in both republics over national and international policy affected diplomatic efforts on a number of military-political issues. The special relationship continued, but in a form shaped by post-war international politics and developments within Brazilian and U.S. society. Illustrative of the new contour of relations was the failed U.S. effort to secure Brazilian participation in the Korean conflict.

U.S. ECONOMIZING AND THE RELATIONSHIP

The changed nature of the relationship became clear as the cold war focused U.S. energy and resources on other areas in the world. Since the end of the war Brazilians had increasingly complained of U.S. inattention. Many in the Department of State considered the claim self-pity, which, they noted, was not shared by Spanish-speaking America. Nevertheless most U.S. military and political leaders defined Brazil as first among equals in Latin American relations.[1] The problem was that the Brazilians naturally considered their nation greater than any other in the region and deserving of assistance from its northern patron. By 1950, however, it was clear that the rewards of the magnitude expected from the wartime alliance would not appear.

The financial and diplomatic demands of cold war leadership led the United States to decisions inimical to the type of ties that existed during World War II. U.S. economizing efforts seemed to threaten the structures of military relations, and moves to embrace Argentina portended a different tone to the relationship. In response to the changes, Brazil returned to a more pragmatic approach to the Brazilian-American alliance. The process was gradual, beginning in the early post-war period when U.S. policies toward Latin America were confused.

For the U.S. military Brazil continued to occupy a dominant position in hemispheric considerations. In recognition of that fact U.S. strategists wanted the Brazilian military to assist in defense planning for the Caribbean-Panama-Galápagos sector under the Inter-American Defense Board's Military Plan.[2] However, in 1950 "economy" was the byword in Washington, and "equality of treatment" was the catchphrase at the Department of State. Efforts to reduce the size of the U.S. military presence in Brazil to save money fueled Brazilian fears because it seemed to indicate a general retrenchment in relations. Much like the squabbling that had occurred among U.S. service branches regarding the ESG Mission, proposed changes in the configuration of the JBUSMC were related more to U.S. frugality and military politics than retreat from commitment to close military relations.

Attempts to consolidate the various U.S. military activities in Brazil dated from the early post-war period. Recommendations from military leaders in Washington, responding to economizing pressures from Congress, prompted Ambassador William Pawley to raise discreetly the idea of changing the status of the JBUSMC and military missions into a single, smaller body. Pawley dropped the subject when the Brazilians emphatically informed him that they wanted no changes, especially one that included reductions.[3]

The issue lay dormant until early January 1950, when the chief of the U.S. delegation to the JBUSMC, Major General Charles Mullins, proposed including the U.S. Navy and ESG Missions under the JBUSMC umbrella as a means of streamlining military activities in

Brazil. Not only did the Brazilians resist the scheme, but also the U.S. Navy opposed consolidation. The army mission did little during World War II to build strong bridges to its Brazilian counterpart beyond the FEB. Naval relations had a long history and flourished as a result of joint sea and air operations in the Atlantic Ocean that predated the war and the personal activity of Admiral Jonas Ingram. The navy enjoyed a special place in Brazil–United States military relations and was antagonistic toward the plan. In 1948 similar army proposals led to a bitter fight with the navy that ended inconclusively. Nothing had occurred in the interim to change the navy position.[4]

U.S. Army officials understood the navy's motivation but could not comprehend Brazilian opposition to consolidation. Unlike the army, the navy required host governments to pay for services in dollars rather than in local currency. JBUSMC services cost Brazil nothing, so fusing the agencies had financial benefits. Nevertheless, an agreement for merging the various military activities required a change of the navy's attitude rather than that of the Brazilians, and there was little hope of such cooperation.[5]

Regardless of the outcome of any merging efforts, the maintenance of the JBUSMC as the primary military link was paramount. Army officials recognized that should economizing measures force cutbacks in militarily important Spanish-speaking countries, the existence of the commission, or at minimum its size, would be questioned. The prepared army defense for continuation of the JBUSMC, in the event one was needed, argued that it served the objectives of both countries.[6]

THE BRAZILIAN VIEW OF THE RELATIONSHIP

U.S. officers understood local military politics well but had little grasp of Brazil's desire for comprehensive ties. The Brazilians thought the alliance was slipping away and with it their international status and major source of aid. U.S. failure to acknowledge the Brazilians' motivations is puzzling because through a variety of channels they conveyed their feelings that the relationship had deteriorated. The Rio and Bogotá Treaties seemed to create a "leveling" that placed Brazil on the same plain as the smallest of its neighbors. The military expressed resentment openly, believing that the United States was treating it as a stepchild. Echoing the armed forces, diplomats pointed to the delay in the transfer of two navy cruisers the United States had agreed to sell and for which Brazil had already paid.[7]

Brazilian fears were real, even though Washington gave little heed to them. At a time when the United States was the only noncommunist country capable of providing assistance on a scale necessary for the modernization of Brazil's armed forces, any change in the existing structure of military relations could retard development. Economizing pressures ultimately forced a reduction in mission and JBUSMC personnel, but major changes did not materialize. Brazilian and U.S. Navy opposition was too strong; the basic forms of the relationship remained.

THE U.S. VIEW OF THE RELATIONSHIP

Particularly galling to the Brazilians was the U.S. attempt to bring Argentina back into the fold. With varying degrees of sensitivity, Department of State and army officials recognized that the move to embrace Argentina could cause Brazilian resentment. Some senior U.S. Army officers felt the United States had a moral obligation to maintain Brazilian pre-eminence, even though they supported rapprochement with Argentina.[8]

Department of State officials were less charitable. In late-1949 and early-1950 intradepartmental discussions of U.S.–Latin American policy, State officials accused Brazil of using Argentina as a "whipping boy" to obtain favors from the United States. Dean Acheson dismissed critics of the rapprochement policy, claiming "responsible Brazilians" understood and approved closer U.S.-Argentina ties.[9] Acheson's opinion reflected that of many in the U.S. government and military who ignored or lacked understanding of the Brazilian point of view. This fact became painfully apparent when hostilities erupted in Korea.

EVE OF THE KOREAN WAR

On the eve of the North Korean invasion of the South the main concern of U.S. officials was the effect on Brazilian-U.S. relations of a win by Getúlio Vargas in the October 1950 presidential election. The officials recognized that Vargas's nationalistic stance ran counter to U.S. international trade policies and that if elected, he would make aggressive claims for assistance. They believed, however, that the Brazilian military would prevent policies that deviated from those of the United States. Indeed, many in the United States, such as Dean Acheson, saw the army as a force for democracy that would prevent excesses by Vargas. Few expected Brazil to pursue a course in international affairs that differed from that of the United States.[10]

The reality of the situation was far different and indicated the degree to which U.S. officials failed to comprehend the nature of Brazilians military politics. Adherence to the U.S. line by the Brazilian military was not a forgone conclusion. Nationalism split opinion in the officer corps over numerous issues, including close ties with the United States. Two articles in the army publication *A Defesa Nacional* illustrate the point. The first decried South America's economic and political dependence but reiterated the traditional belief that Brazil could be the mediator between the United States and Spanish America. The second claimed that communism was winning the war for hearts and minds because unequal development in the post-war world made it easy for the USSR to convert people to its cause.[11] Few in the United States recognized the criticisms of U.S. policies or what they portended.

THE KOREAN WAR

Miscalculations over the nature of the Brazilian military's position and the U.S. ability to influence national decisions became evident after North Korea plunged south on June 25, 1950. As North Korean successes multiplied, the United States maneuvered the United Nations into condemning the invasion and called for military support for U.S. and South Korean forces. On the heels of its success at the United Nations the Truman administration sought OAS sanction of the U.S. request for condemnation of North Korea as an aggressor against the United States. Under the Rio Treaty such an action obligated the Latin American countries to join the conflict. The Truman administration feared that the Korean situation would lead to general conflagration and wanted ground forces from certain Latin American countries to become active in Asia, thereby freeing U.S. troops for rapid deployment to Europe should the need arise. The Department of Defense thought that under the scheme Brazil and Argentina could each immediately send an infantry division to Korea. Mexico could provide a regimental-sized combat team, while Chile, Peru, and Uruguay could each supply a battalion. The United States would assist in training, equipping, and supplying the units.[12]

The Joint Chiefs of Staff thought Latin America was the easiest place to obtain military contributions because of U.S. dominance in the region. The JCS was sure that because the United States viewed the conflict as a threat to the entire world, including the security of the Western Hemisphere, the Latin Americans would follow suit. At the March 1951 Consultative Meeting of Foreign Ministers in Washington President Truman requested token forces and increased production of strategic materials. The Latin Americans, however, refused to accept the proposition that the hemisphere was threatened and therefore saw no obligation under the Rio Treaty to supply troops. Economic matters were of greater concern. The Latin American nations promised to increase production of resources needed for the war but balanced their pledges by issuing a statement that addressed the region's need for economic development.[13] Implicit in the statement was the need for military assistance as well.

Although the United States promised to equip forces going to Korea, the Latin Americans were unhappy with the fact that under the Mutual Security Act of 1949 they could only purchase U.S. arms on a cash basis. And because the region had the lowest priority for availability of equipment, the countries with cash were unable to make purchases because of limited supply. What rankled the Latin Americans most was that while they kept their Lend-Lease financial obligations current, other countries received free military assistance.[14]

By October 1951 U.S. diplomacy had convinced only Colombia to provide an infantry battalion and a navy frigate. The Departments of Defense and State continued to push for Latin American participation, and Brazil became the focal point of U.S. efforts. Both agencies believed that if Brazil sent troops to Korea, the other Latin American countries would follow suit. With that aim in mind the U.S. military increased visits by Brazilian Army and Navy officers to the IADB in hopes of influencing them to support active participation in the conflict.[15]

There was ample reason to believe successful negotiations with Brazil would pull along even the most reluctant Latin American state. The Chilean ambassador and naval representatives indicated to General Charles L. Bolté and Brigadier General Edwin Sibert, the U.S. representatives on the IADB, that public opinion in their country would be swayed if Brazil took the first step. It would be difficult, reasoned the Department of State, for OAS member states to postpone decisions favorable to U.S. wishes if Brazilian leaders agreed to send troops to Korea. State Department officials believed that even Mexico, which had denied U.S. requests, would be hard-pressed to continue its refusal.[16]

CURRENTS IN BRAZIL

Political currents during the 1950 Brazilian presidential campaign made it difficult to determine if Brazil would join the fighting in Korea. In an interview aimed at U.S. leaders that was broadcast on Radio Continental shortly after the electoral victory, Vargas declared that "whoever wants our collaboration must aid us with our needs." He added that Brazil remained faithful to the Western bloc in the East-West split but expected help in resolving national problems. According to Vargas, Brazilian cooperation rested on the quality of reciprocity.[17]

The return of Vargas to the presidency coincided with a growing division in Brazilian society over development policy. Discussions on internal conditions could not be divorced from external relations, and that inevitably meant the close relationship with the United

States. Anti- and pro-American sides argued over U.S. involvement in the economy and the degree to which Brazil should be tied to the North American giant. The petroleum question sparked debates on the role of the United States in national affairs, and the issue of participation in Korea hardened the opposing sides.[18]

Brazilian editorial opinion reflected the division in political and military circles on the Korean question. The *Diário Carioca* (Rio de Janeiro) called for direct involvement in Korea while other newspapers were more cautious. The *Diário de Notícias* (Rio de Janeiro) argued that Brazil should participate but noted that the country should not "enter the conflagration already vanquished," as it had in World War II. The price of such precipitate action in the 1940s was continued underdevelopment. An editorial in the *Correio da Manha* (Rio de Janeiro) claimed the United States asked much for Brazilian participation, which meant little to the war's outcome. The Korean theater had little need for a few symbolic soldiers; moral support was all that was necessary given the regional nature of the conflict. If it turned into a general war, however, Brazil should then participate fully.[19]

More profound was the split in the Brazilian officer corps. The question of involvement in Korea did not create the division. Rather, it defined factions in the struggle for power within the military that had begun after the war and centered on petroleum policy.[20] At stake was not the singular question of Korea but the future direction of national and foreign policy.

Three factions vied for control of the military in post-war Brazil. The Sorbonne group, led by Castello Branco, consisted of many ex-*Febianos* who favored continued alliance with the United States despite a belief that Brazil's wartime contributions had been ignored. They did not oppose developmental nationalism but were pro–United States and anti-communist. Rivaling the Sorbonne group were the nationalists headed by Newton Estillac Leal and Nelson Werneck Sodré. The nationalists, whose members included many junior officers, wanted to de-emphasize the U.S. connection in favor of alliance with the underdeveloped countries in Latin America, Africa, and Asia. They stressed development through domestic, mainly governmental, means rather than reliance on foreign, and especially U.S., capital. The third group, the radical nationalists, was small in number, and its views were similar to those of the communists. Like the communists, they blamed the United States for the Korean conflict and argued against involvement in Korea and continuance of the U.S. connection.[21]

In the background the outlawed communists bitterly opposed Brazilian participation with the slogan "Not one soldier for Korea." Luís Carlos Prestes, the leader of the communists since the mid-1930s, urged the people to prepare for revolution. If the government did not deny the U.S. request, the people should change the government via the barrel of a gun.[22] Prestes and the communists lacked power but added to the growing division that threatened Brazilian society.

THE "CAPITÃO X" ARTICLE AND ITS AFTERMATH

The power struggle within the military centered on the nationalists and the pro-U.S. group, and the opening round came with the August issue of *A Revista do Clube Militar*, whose director held radical nationalists sentiments. An article entitled "Considerations About the War in Korea," anonymously signed under the nom de plume "Capitão X," accused the United States of aggression in Korea.[23] The article set off a firestorm of accusation and counteraccusation in the Brazilian officer corps.

Supporters of the idea of sending Brazilian troops to Korea responded immediately. Six hundred officers issued a manifesto denouncing the article's view as an imitation of the Soviet position. *A Defesa Nacional*, whose editorial board followed the high command's pro-U.S. stance, also carried rebuttals. Articles in the November 1950 and January 1951 issues blasted the Capitão X piece, arguing that Brazil should provide military support and could do so without surrendering its economic and political independence. Other articles in the journal claimed the nationalists were communists, especially the *moscovita* Capitão X, and demanded the purging of communists from the armed services. A similar editorial in the *Correio da Manha* accused Estillac Leal of communist tendencies and called on the minister of war, General Canrobert Pereira da Costa, to "decontaminate" the armed forces.[24]

Contributors to *A Defesa Nacional* and the *Correio da Manha* accepted the notion that the conflict in Korea represented a threat to the hemisphere and supported active participation. Nevertheless, they linked military cooperation with economic assistance. A thoughtful editorial in the *Correio da Manha* lamented the division in Brazilian society. Blaming the problem on a lack of conscience and spirituality that resulted from material impoverishment, the essay asserted that basic development was necessary to preserve the nation's institutions and to enable Brazil to fulfill its role in the United Nations. Brazil could "fight for democracy in the international sphere only if internal order was preserved," which required an economically developed society.[25]

After the initial harshness of the rebuttals in *A Defesa Nacional,* the journal showed that the high command had concerns about national development as well. An April 1951 editorial urged provision of troops for Korea but indicated reciprocity was vital. Brazil should avoid the mistakes made in World War II, when its transportation system was undeveloped, prices for its products were depreciated, and the dislocation of the labor force from the agricultural to the extractive sectors in exchange for industrial products did little for the economy.[26]

The more tempered articles and editorials in *A Defesa Nacional* may have been due to the silencing of the opposition organ. In December 1950 the Clube Militar Directorate suspended publication of *A Revista do Clube Militar,* citing a desire to maintain unity in the officer corps. The move was an attempt by Estillac Leal to disassociate the nationalists from the extremists.[27]

If Estillac Leal hoped to protect his supporters from retribution, he was unsuccessful. At the end of 1950 Canrobert Pereira da Costa transferred the most vocal members of the Clube Militar Directorate to barracks across the country. He sent the second vice president, Major Tactio Livio Reis de Freitas, to São Luiz in Maranhão, while Nelson Werneck Sodré, director of the cultural department, was ordered to Cruz Alta in Rio Grande do Sul. Estillac Leal remained in Rio de Janeiro and became the minister of war in the second Vargas government in January 1951. Despite the president's backing, Estillac Leal's opponents maneuvered his resignation in March of the following year.[28] Momentary victory by the pro-U.S. group did not end opposition or assure Brazilian troops would go to Korea.

NEGOTIATIONS FOR BRAZILIAN TROOPS

Negotiations for Brazilian participation stalled as a result of the presidential election but revived once the outcome was clear. On December 8, 1950, the pro–United States National Security Council met at Catete Palace to discuss the U.S. request but failed to reach a decision. The consensus was that at the time Brazil should concentrate on maintaining internal order and stockpiling primary goods and materials. In the meeting Góes Monteiro informed the group that Brazilian troops would be ineffective without lengthy preparation.[29]

Indications of the Brazilian mood also became evident when Vargas named Estillac Leal minister of war and refused to make any commitment beyond joining the other Latin American countries in agreeing to strengthen the collective defense of the hemisphere. U.S. diplomats and military leaders decided to wait until the March 1951 meeting of the Organization of American States to increase pressure on Brazil. At the meeting talks between Assistant Secretary of State for Inter-American Affairs Edward G. Miller and Minister of Foreign Affairs João Neves da Fontoura led the U.S. diplomat to believe that Brazil was seriously considering offering an army division to the U.N. Forces in Korea.[30]

Based on the talks Secretary of State Dean Acheson and General Charles Bolte met with Neves da Fontoura and his principal military adviser, General Paulo de Figueiredo, to delve into the matter. Neves da Fontoura and Figueiredo were noncommittal but left the impression that the Brazilian government and military were amenable to providing troops. Their stipulation was that the United States provide large-scale economic and military aid. At the foreign minister's suggestion Bolte and Figueiredo arranged further discussions to work out details. To emphasize the importance the United States placed on Brazilian involvement, President Truman sent a personal note to Vargas urging favorable consideration of the troop request.[31]

The foreign minister's hint of military support in return for widespread assistance was the second phase of a grand courtship that had begun shortly after the Brazilian presidential election. In an apparent bid to gain the backing of Vargas, the United States confidentially provided him with its topics for the March 1951 foreign ministers' meeting in Washington. The Brazilian president's response should have alerted Washington. Vargas claimed a desire to continue military cooperation, but without outlining the details. Much more specific were his proposals regarding government-to-government economic assistance and private investment needed by Brazil. Vargas told U.S. officials that he wanted a bilateral agreement with his country before the Washington conference.[32]

The Truman administration accepted a proposal by Vargas to initiate discussions and dispatched Edward G. Miller to Rio de Janeiro in February. But where Vargas was specific on economic collaboration and vague on military support, Miller emphasized political and military cooperation and was hazy on economic assistance.[33] The question seemed to be, Who would blink first? Brazil followed the United States into World War II under Vargas and supported the United States in international affairs in the post-war period. The talks with Vargas in February and between U.S. and Brazilian military personnel in April gave reason to believe the same would occur over Korea.

Neves da Fontoura further whetted U.S. appetites when he broached the idea of sending a Brazilian military mission to Korea to drum up public enthusiasm for a larger commitment. The Department of State saw additional evidence in Estillac Leal's visit to the United States in May 1951.[34] The fact that Estillac Leal was the nationalist president of the Clube Militar when the Capitão X article came out in the journal failed to evoke doubts.

The U.S. military and the Department of State received the idea of a mission enthusiastically. Brazil appeared to be taking action, a view supported in American eyes by talks in May between Neves da Fontoura and Ambassador Herschell Johnson in Rio de Janeiro on the prospects of the Korea mission. Mention of the mission ceased, however, after Neves da Fontoura made public statements that indicated a lack of support for sending troops to Korea, which caused

Washington to question his sincerity. Dean Acheson ordered Ambassador Johnson to inform the Brazilians that no mission should go to Asia unless it was a definite prelude to greater military participation.[35] It is unclear if the proposed mission was a trial balloon to test Brazilian public opinion, as Edward Miller believed, or if it represented a real desire to become involved in Korea. Either way, Brazil did not send a mission to Korea.

No mission went to Korea probably because Brazilian leaders did not want it construed as the first contingent of a larger involvement without first obtaining an agreement on economic assistance. Although there was a lack of consensus regarding the mission in the officer corps and Brazilian society as a whole, Vargas could have ordered a mission to Korea. But the main goal remained obtaining U.S. aid; without it the question of a mission or greater participation in Korea was a moot point. For the Brazilians economic assistance was linked to the provision of troops for the Korean conflict.[36]

GÓES MONTEIRO AND THE KOREA QUESTION

When the proposed military mission to Korea failed to materialize, some U.S. diplomats and military leaders believed the Brazilian government would never act. Others remained confident Brazil would send troops despite the setback. The Brazilians did nothing to dispel the latter belief. In June 1951 Góes Monteiro, chief of the General Staff, responded to a report in the leftist newspaper *Última Hora* (Rio de Janeiro) in a way that indicated troops might go overseas. The article claimed Brazilian soldiers would go first to Europe and then to Korea under Eisenhower's command. Góes Monteiro answered that there was no reason to send a contingent to Europe because Brazil had to prepare for the defense of the country and the continent. He noted, however, that defense might be accomplished best at a distance and that it was not "too much to think that the defense of the Western Hemisphere may begin in Berlin or more to the East."[37]

The following month Góes Monteiro traveled to Washington, saying that he would discuss how Brazil could best comply with the

U.N. call for additional troops. He added that his mission included talks on U.S. economic and military aid to make Brazilian military cooperation efficacious. To be effective, Brazil needed to obtain arms and equipment on the same basis as the NATO countries. Góes Monteiro added that economic development assistance was important because communist propagandizing of Brazil's underdevelopment influenced public opinion against a military contribution and therefore prevented his government from making a strong commitment.[38]

Miller believed the general was "the sacrificial offering in lieu of the late-lamented mission to Korea."[39] Rather than the sacrificial offering Miller believed, Góes Monteiro's trip was a last attempt to obtain assistance before Brazil decided on the U.S request. His instructions from Vargas reiterated what the Brazilian president's earlier letter to Truman had said and what Neves da Fontoura had repeated to Acheson and Miller. Brazil's priorities were international security and economic development. Participation in Korea would be conditioned on the amount and speed of U.S. economic and military aid. If the United States moved rapidly and generously, Brazil could act more quickly. At the time, Brazil was unprepared and would not determine the date it could fulfill U.N. obligations.[40] In short, Brazil wanted quid pro quo: Brazilian assistance in Korea for massive aid. The catch was that the Brazilians wanted a promise of assistance before an agreement to send troops. Vargas had made this mistake in 1942 and did not want to get fooled again. The United States wanted Brazilian commitment without prior agreement to provide aid.

U.S. COURTSHIP

Although Washington wanted a positive decision before providing aid, army officials hinted that assistance would follow a commitment pro forma. Latin America was last in U.S. military priorities, but if Brazil agreed to send a division, it would be lifted to Category I for military assistance. The United States would then supply the division completely and provide technical and training help. In addition, the United States would transport the Brazilian troops and provide for all their needs until they returned home. Although the

United States would carry the wounded and disabled home, arrangements for replacement personnel would be the responsibility of Brazil. Washington also intimated that equipment might be available to the police for internal security. Any military assistance provided, however, would be on a repayable basis rather than gratis because legislation still did not exist for such aid.[41] The discussions made clear both sides of the question.

Góes Monteiro also mentioned that any agreements had to be kept secret for at least six months because public opinion did not see Brazilian vital interests in the Korean situation. He told army officials that it would be easier to obtain favorable opinion for a war in Africa or Europe than in Korea. The Brazilian people, he said, saw Korea as a uniquely U.S. problem. Much as in World War II, public opinion had to be developed to ensure participation.[42]

Góes Monteiro made it clear that cooperation depended on the outcome of Minister of Finance Horacio Lafer's mission to the United States. Lafer came to Washington in September to negotiate financing of Joint Brazil–United States Economic Development Commission projects with the World Bank, the Export-Import Bank, and the U.S. government. Lafer succeeded in obtaining agreements increasing Brazil's loan limits, which led the United States to re-focus efforts to gain Brazilian participation in Korea.[43]

Military assistance questions remained, but U.S. officials thought the positive outcome of the Lafer mission and additional inducements would smooth any problems. Dean Acheson reiterated that Brazilian troops designated for Korea could receive U.S. training and equipment and even appealed to Brazil's desire for greatness by adding that enormous prestige would accompany involvement in the crusade against communism. In conversations with Neves da Fontoura five months earlier Acheson had said cash payment was unnecessary; the amount and method of payment could be worked out in the future after Brazil offered troops. Repayment was moot because Acheson was prepared to defer payment if that issue was all that stood in the way of an agreement.[44]

Willingness to defer reimbursement indicated how much the United States wanted Brazilian involvement. Deferment of aid payments was not a negotiating option open to other countries contributing forces; agreement with those countries had to be reached prior to provision of assistance. Moreover, because the Department of State, the army, and the air force believed Brazilian agreement would be the basis for negotiations for troops with the other Latin American republics, they argued that the lion's share of military grant aid appropriated under the newly passed Mutual Security Act of 1951 should go to Brazil.[45]

As in other instances, the navy disagreed. State, army, and air force officials wanted to provide Brazil with one-third of the $38,150,000 appropriated for Latin America, with the remaining two-thirds divided among Argentina, Chile, Colombia, Cuba, Ecuador, and Uruguay. The navy, however, preferred to spread the funds among as many countries as possible rather than concentrate on a few strategically important ones. Under the navy plan the seven countries favored by the other service branches and the Department of State would receive less so that cooperation could be purchased from more Latin American militaries.[46]

PRELIMINARY AGREEMENT

Proposed allocation of the majority of military grant aid to Brazil was an incentive for cooperation and a reward for perceived progress in negotiations with Góes Monteiro. The general insisted on discussing hemisphere defense concurrently with the Korea question, and in late September preliminary agreement seemed at hand. On September 27 General Charles Bolte sent Góes Monteiro a memorandum containing two draft agreements dealing with Brazilian assistance in Korea and defense of the hemisphere, the latter of which became the basis for the future military accord. Apparently to prevent any leaks, the Joint Chiefs of Staff kept the U.S. members of the JBUSMC ignorant of the progress of negotiations until dispatch of the drafts. Nor was advice requested of the delegation, even though it would be the agency responsible for implementing any agreement.[47]

The draft dealing with an infantry division for duty in Korea repeated the U.S. view outlined in earlier talks and included a number of provisions of future importance for the development of the

Brazilian military. Article 5 gave U.S. sanction to the development of an indigenous arms and munitions industry by granting Brazil appropriate export licenses and technical assistance. The United States also promised to make purchases from such an industry. Article 6 called for the development of local aircraft and naval construction and repair facilities, with U.S. technical aid, and the granting of export licenses. Projects contemplated under the two articles would be coordinated jointly through the JBUSMC.[48]

Góes Monteiro sent the draft agreements to Brazil but received no response before his return home. Nevertheless, on the eve of his departure both he and his American colleagues thought the difficult negotiations were coming to a fruitful end. Góes Monteiro told Dean Acheson that arrangements were near conclusion and that a meeting of the full JBUSMC had been set for the first two weeks in December to discuss joint plans for hemisphere defense and the dispatch of Brazilian troops to Korea. The Brazilian general hedged, however, warning that internal political problems, including the Clube Militar situation, could prevent ratification of the arrangement.[49]

If Miller and Acheson thought an arrangement was near, the Joint Chiefs of Staff was uncertain and planned accordingly. The JCS informed the chief of the U.S. delegation to the JBUSMC, General Charles Mullins, that the guiding principle in the December talks was to avoid emphasis on either hemisphere defense or Brazilian troops for Korea to such an extent that one prejudiced the success of the other. If it became evident that Brazil did not want to send a division to Korea, the subject was to be dropped. If Brazil agreed to send troops but could not simultaneously designate forces for hemisphere defense, Mullins was authorized to offer U.S. assistance in preparing Brazilian units for defense of the region, with the understanding that those forces could be used for internal security if necessary.[50]

ORIGINS OF THE 1952 ACCORD

Underlying Brazil-U.S. relations and the Korean issue was the question of assistance. Since the end of World War II the Truman administration and the military had placed their hopes on legislation that would allow military aid for the Latin Americans. The war in Korea and U.S. efforts to obtain Latin American troops underscored the importance of including the region in the military grant aid program. The Brazilians understood the problem and since 1948 had been trying to solve it by replacing the wartime military accord with a new one.[51] Brazilian troops might not go to Korea, but the 1951 draft agreement on hemisphere defense offered the chance to reach a new military agreement.

In 1948 a U.S. Air Force planning project asked its section of the JBUSMC about the possibility of rehabilitating the Belém and Natal air bases. Interpreting the request as an operational order, the air force officers mistakenly initiated discussions with the Brazilian air section of the commission. The Brazilians saw in the project an opportunity to revitalize the relationship so as to continue modernization plans and began work on the airfields. In conjunction with the work General Salvador Cesar Obino reassured the JBUSMC of Brazilian willingness to stand by the United States in case of world conflict. At the same time, he proposed a new military accord.[52]

Obino added that with a renewed alliance Brazil needed to increase the size, strength, and composition of the armed forces and to equip them with modern weapons. Of course, to do so while maintaining air and sea bases required U.S. assistance in training and matériel acquisition. For any military effort to be successful, he went on, Brazil had to have economic aid as well, especially with the means of production and transportation. According to Obino, this also meant Brazil would have to expend large amounts of money, and the best way to obtain public and legislative acquiescence for these expenditures was by establishing a new accord between the two governments.[53]

The U.S. response was noncommittal because of pending congressional action on the Inter-American Military Cooperation Act and plans for a multilateral defense scheme. In the meantime the air force section of the JBUSMC continued working with the Brazilians on rehabilitating the air bases. The Department of Defense admonished the officers to take care to avoid giving the Brazilians the impression that the work constituted tacit acceptance of the accord proposal. Similar admonitions went out from Omar Bradley to senior officers and civilians whom Minister of War Pereira da Costa planned to meet during a March 1949 visit to the United States. Bradley told the officials that, although Brazil should receive special consideration, they should sidestep the question of a new accord. He suggested that if the minister of war asked for a commitment, the officials should stick to a line that stressed pending legislation and urgent needs in other areas of the world.[54]

Concurrently, the JCS approved a recommendation from the army chief of staff to examine the peacetime legality of the 1942 agreement, because the agreement may have been invalidated with the war's end. After determining the legal basis of the old accord, the JCS would make recommendations concerning the desirability of extending it. In March 1949 the Joint Strategic Survey Committee (JSSC) concluded that the 1942 political-military arrangement was still in force and that the United States was committed under its terms. The JSSC pointed out, however, that those commitments ran counter to current U.S. strategic interests and that the national military establishment could not fulfill the obligations of providing arms until Congress provided a legal means to do so.[55]

The JSSC suggested that Brazil and the United States modify segments of the agreement to reflect the present state of affairs. One of the recommendations was to give de jure separate authorization for the functions of the JBUSMC and JBUSDC. Also recommended was an interim agreement that met U.S. strategic needs in Brazil regardless of congressional action and that was worded in a manner that would allow its registration with the United Nations. According to the JSSC, the temporary accord should be replaced with a new treaty once Congress passed legislation allowing hemisphere military assistance. The JSSC concluded that, although the JBUSMC and JBUSDC should be consulted in any negotiations for a new accord, they were not the proper agencies for discussing the larger collective defense scheme; the IADB was the organization created by the Rio Treaty for such talks. In that way a bilateral deal could be reached within a multilateral paradigm.[56]

The JBUSMC again overstepped its authority with the release of the JSSC report. Viewing the report's recommendations as a directive to undertake planning for the collective defense of Brazil, the commission submitted a study on air and coastal defenses. The JCS quickly ordered the U.S. delegation to cease strategic planning unless told otherwise.[57]

The consequences of the JBUSMC action were slight, for both militaries awaited the outcome of the 1949 Mutual Defense Assistance bill. The act passed, but its failure to offer the Latin Americans grant assistance prevented conclusion of a new defense pact. Economic and military aid continued to color any question of strengthening the relationship. Only after the outbreak of hostilities in Asia did conditions change to the point that a new military accord became possible. Nevertheless, Brazilian opposition, especially in the military, to participation in Korea threatened to split society and the officer corps. In addition, Brazil had no clear indications that it would receive benefits for providing troops if it had no commitment of assistance from the United States. As a result, Vargas did not approve the draft agreements negotiated by Góes Monteiro, and no Brazilian troops went to Korea.[58] Disagreement on cooperating with the United States in hemisphere defense also cropped up, but the advantages outweighed the drawbacks. Consequently, Brazil and the United States agreed to a new accord in 1952, using as its basis Bolte's draft agreement on hemisphere defense.

National interest had moved the Brazilians to form close military ties with the United States in the previous decade. The same motivation guided their cold war decisions. Many military and political officials influenced by the wartime experience viewed close relations with the United States in the post-war period as the best means of accomplishing institutional and national objectives, but cold war ideology and the perception that the relationship did little for development gave rise to opposition. Both proponents and opponents of the U.S. connection were nationalists who differed on the most efficacious manner of achieving national goals. The decisions not to send troops to Korea but to sign the 1952 accord must be seen as an effort by Brazilian military leaders to maintain institutional integrity while keeping the special relationship alive. At the same time, these decisions reflected the still strong but waning influence of the pro-American faction in intramilitary struggles.

NOTES

1. James E. Webb, Acting Secretary of State, Memorandum for President, October 6, 1950, White House Central Files—37, Folder 24, Box 37, HST Library; Memorandum by the Assistant Secretary of State for Inter-American Affairs (Miller) to Regional Planning Advisor (Halle), November 7, 1950, *FRUS 1950,* 626.

2. Memorandum of Conversation by Mr. Duncan A. D. Mackay of the Office of Regional American Affairs, Subject: Meeting with Representatives of the U.S. Delegation to the IADB to Consider Problems of Inter-American Military Collaboration, August 15, 1951, *FRUS 1951,* 1017.

3. Colonel Paul L. Freeman to Major General Charles L. Mullins, Jr., January 13, 1950, RG-319, P&O Decimal File, 1949–February 1950, 334 JBUSMC TC (Sec. I) (Case 1), NA.

4. Mullins to Freeman, January 5, 1950; Freeman to Mullins, January 13, 1950.

5. Freeman to Mullins, January 13, 1950.

6. Ibid.

7. James Webb, Memorandum for the President, October 6, 1950, White House Central Files—37; Dean Acheson, Memorandum of Conversation, October 9, 1950, Dean Acheson Papers, Box 65, HST Library.

8. Ridgeway to Bradley, July 28, 1949, Box 13, Official Papers Folder, Matthew B. Ridgeway Papers, USMHI.

9. Dean Acheson, "Effect in Brazil of Argentine Developments and Significance to Brazilian-American Relations of Possible Election of Vargas to Presidency," Memorandum for the President, May 1, 1950, White House Central Files—37, Folder 22, Box 37, HST Library; Memorandum Prepared in the Department of State, January 4, 1950, *FRUS 1950,* 597.

10. Dean Acheson, Memorandum for the President, May 10, 1950, White House Central Files—37, Folder 22, Box 37, HST Library. Concern over Vargas was long-standing. See Department of State, "An Estimate of the Political Potential of Getúlio Vargas," OIR Report No. 4324, May 9, 1947, Division of Research for the American Republics, NA.

11. Ten. Cel. Adelardo Filho, "Problemas do Brasil," Ten. Cel. J. H. García, "A outra guerra," *A Defesa Nacional* 37:430 (May 1950): 71–80, 95–96; Sodré, *História militar,* 304–355; and Skidmore, *Politics in Brazil,* 100–108.

12. Memorandum by Mr. Ivan B. White of the Office of Regional American Affairs to Assistant Secretary of State for Inter-American Affairs (Miller), February 14, 1951, *FRUS 1951,* 994–997; and Eric Goldman, *The Crucial Decade—and After, America 1945–1960* (New York: Vintage Books, 1960), 160.

13. Memorandum of Conversation, Secretary of State and Foreign Minister Manuel Tello, April 6, 1951, Dean Acheson Papers, Box 66, HST Library; Under Secretary of State (Webb) to Secretary of Defense (Lovett), October 10, 1951, *FRUS 1951,* 1022–1023; and Rabe, *Eisenhower and Latin America,* 23.

14. "United States Policy Regarding Hemisphere Defense, Provision of Armaments and Military Assistance to American Republics, and Participation by

American Republics in the Korean Conflict," February 13, 1951, *FRUS 1951*, 993.

15. Freeman to Mullins, January 13, 1950, RG-319, P&O Decimal File, 1949–February 1950, 334 JBUSMC TC (Sec. I) (Case 1), NA; Secretary of State to Embassy in Brazil, May 10, 1951, *FRUS 1951*, 1198; and "Inter-American Defense Board, 1948–1950," Willis D. Crittenberger Papers, USMHI.

16. Memorandum by Officer in Charge of General Assembly Affairs (Popper) to the Assistant Secretary of State for United Nations Affairs (Hickerson), Subject: Military Assistance for Korea, March 16, 1951, *FRUS 1951*, 1009; Memorandum of Conversation by Mr. Milton Barall of the Office of South American Affairs, Subject: Request for Assignment of Chilean Troops to Korea, April 7, 1951, *FRUS 1951*, 1275; and Under Secretary of State (Webb) to Secretary of Defense (Lovett), October 10, 1951, *FRUS 1951*, 1022–1023.

17. "Vargas fixa os rumos do futuro governo," *O Jornal*, November 5, 1950, 1–2; "Auto suficiência," *O Radical*, November 7, 1950, 2; and Embassy—Rio to Department of State, Embtel 622, November 9, 1950, RG-59, Records of the Department of State, Box 5860, NA.

18. For an analysis of the different views on economic development policy and political opposition, see Skidmore, *Politics in Brazil*, 81–112.

19. "A posição do Brasil," *Diário Carioca*, December 29, 1950, 4; "A Posição do Brasil," *Diário de Noticias*, December 7, 1950, 4; Tomas Collação, "Muito," *Correio da Manha*, March 29, 1951, 1; and Tomas Collação, "Tropas," *Correio da Manha*, October 18, 1952, 1.

20. Fontaine, *Brazil and the U.S.*, 55, 73; Edgard Carone, *A república liberal* (São Paulo: DIFEL, 1985), 50; and Wirth, *Politics of Brazilian Development*, 168. The military and Itamaraty are the two most important institutions in the shaping of foreign policy.

21. E. Bradford Burns, "Tradition and Variation in Brazilian Foreign Policy," *Journal of Inter-American Studies and World Affairs* 9:2 (April 1967): 206; Fontaine, *Brazil and the U.S.*, 73–74; and Skidmore, *Politics in Brazil*, 105–106.

22. Carone, *A República liberal*, 52–53. For the call to arms by Prestes, see the August issues of the *Imprensa Popular* and the *Voz Operária*.

23. Carone, *A república liberal*, 48–49; Fontaine, *Brazil and the U.S.*, 25; John W. F. Dulles, *Vargas of Brazil: A Political Biography* (Austin: University of Texas Press, 1967), 334; and Skidmore, *Politics in Brazil*, 105. Some years later Department of State officials claimed Capitão X was Lt. Colonel Humberto de Andrade, who had just been promoted by Marshal Lott to a position in the General Headquarters in the Ministry of War. See "1959 Brazil," n.d., RG-59, Records of the Department of State, Box 11, NA.

24. Ten. Cel. Riograndino da Costa e Silva, "O communismo e as forças armadas," *A Defesa Nacional* 38:437 (December 1950): 115–117; Editorial, *A Defesa Nacional* 38:438 (January 1951): 4; Solon Lopes de Oliveira, "Uma opinião," *A Defesa Nacional* 38:444 (July 1951), 128; "A política externa e as forças armadas," *Correio da Manha*, December 7, 1950, sec. 2, 1; and Skidmore, *Politics in Brazil*, 105.

25. "Exame de consciência," *Correio da Manha*, December 1, 1950, sec. 2, 1.

26. Editorial, *A Defesa Nacional* 38:441 (April 1951), 3–4.

27. Skidmore, *Politics in Brazil*, 105–106.

28. Ibid.; and Carone, *A república liberal*, 55–56.

29. "O Brasil e a situação internacional," *Correio da Manha*, December 9, 1950, sec. 2, 1; and Dulles, *Vargas of Brazil*, 309. Members of the council included General Newton Cavalcanti—secretary general; General Alvaro Fuiza de Castro—chief of staff of the army; Raúl Fernandes—foreign minister; Ovidio de Abreu—president of the Bank of Brazil; General Salvador Cesar Obino—chief of staff of the armed services; and Manoel Guilherme de Silveira—finance minister.

30. Memorandum by the Officer in Charge of General Assembly Affairs to the Assistant Secretary of State for United Nations Affairs, "Military Assistance for Korea," March 16, 1951, *FRUS 1951*, 1009; Carone, *A república liberal*, 44; Lieuwen, *U.S. Policy in Latin America*, 87; and Storrs, *Brazil's Independent Foreign Policy*, 136–137.

31. "Economic and Military Cooperation Between Brazil and the United States," April 5, 1951, Dean Acheson Papers, Box 66, HST Library; Truman to Vargas, April 9, 1951, White House Central Files—38, Folder 36, Box 38, HST Library; and Acheson, *Present at the Creation*, 497–498.

32. Ambassador in Brazil (Johnson) to Secretary of State, January 15, 1951, *FRUS 1951*, 1184–1187.

33. Memorandum by Economic and Financial Advisor of the Bureau of Inter-American Affairs (White), February 6, 1951, *FRUS 1951*, 1191–1194.

34. Assistant Secretary of State for Inter-American Affairs (Miller) to Commander-in-Chief, United Nations Command (Ridgeway), August 10, 1951, *FRUS 1951*, 1211–1212.

35. Secretary of State to Embassy in Brazil, May 10, 1951, *FRUS 1951*, 1198; and Assistant Secretary of State for Inter-American Affairs to Commander-in-Chief, United Nations Command, August 10, 1951, *FRUS 1951*, 1211–1212.

36. For a good analysis of Brazil during the period, see Skidmore, *Politics in Brazil*, 81–142. For Brazilian military politics, see Sodré, *História militar*, 304–355. For Brazilian foreign policy during the negotiations for participation in Korea, see Amado Luiz Cervo and Clodoaldo Bueno, *História da política exterior do Brasil* (São Paulo: Editora Atica S.A., 1992), 252–253.

37. *Última Hora*, June 19, 1951, 1; and "Em Berlim ou mais para leste," *A Noite*, June 20, 1951, 1, 9. The article in *Última Hora* came out of a proposal by Oswaldo Aranha to send an army division to Germany. Aranha opposed participation in Korea but thought Brazil should cooperate with the United States in the Atlantic. See Luíz Alberto Moniz Bandeira, *A presença dos Estados Unidos no Brasil* (Rio de Janeiro: Editora Civilização Brasileira, 1973), 329–330.

38. Memorandum of Conversation, "Korean and Uniting for Peace Aid from Brazil," August 3, 1951, Dean Acheson Papers, Box 66, HST Library; Miller to Ridgeway, August 10, 1951, *FRUS 1951*, 1211–1212; Miller to Johnson, October 23, 1951, *FRUS 1951*, 1229; Bandeira, *Presença*, 331; and Hilton, "United States, Brazil, and the Cold War," 611.

39. Assistant Secretary of State for Inter-American Affairs to Ambassador in Brazil, October 23, 1951, *FRUS 1951*, 1229.

40. Memorandum of Conversation by Officer in Charge of Brazilian Affairs (Kidder), Subject: Discussions with General Góes Monteiro on His Mission to U.S., August 17, 1951, *FRUS 1951*, 1213–1214; and Secretary of State to Embassy in Brazil, August 21, 1951, *FRUS 1951*, 1216–1217. Some scholars argue that Góes Monteiro's trip was a classic case of "para Ingles ver" (for the English to see) and that he was Miller's sacrificial lamb.

41. Ibid.

42. Memorandum of Conversation (Kidder), August 17, 1951; Secretary of State to Embassy in Brazil, August 21, 1951, *FRUS 1951*, 1213–1217; William O. Briggs to the Department of State, October 23, 1952, RG-59, Records of the Department of State, 1950–1954, Box 5860, NA; and Bandeira, *Presença*, 333.

43. Miller to Bunker, September 10, 1951, *FRUS 1951*, 1106–1108; Miller to Johnson, September 14, 1951, *FRUS 1951*, 1222–1224; and Weis, *Cold Warriors*, 45–46.

44. Memorandum of Conversation, "Korean and Uniting for Peace Aid from Brazil," August 3, 1951; "Economic and Military Cooperation Between Brazil and the United States," April 5, 1951, Dean Acheson Papers, Box 66, HST Library; and Under Secretary of State to Secretary of Defense, October 10, 1951, *FRUS 1951*, 1022–1024. Góes Monteiro spoke of the friendliness of his brothers in arms during the meetings but castigated civilian government officials as untrustworthy and indifferent to the fate of Brazil. See Bandeira, *Presença*, 332–333.

45. "Mutual Security Program, FY 1952—Latin America," October 29, 1951, *FRUS 1951*, 1024–1027; and Under Secretary of State to Secretary of State, October 10, 1951, *FRUS 1951*, 1022–1024.

46. Ibid.

47. Deputy Chief for Plans, Department of the Army (Bolte), to Chief of the Joint Staff, Brazilian Armed Forces (Góes Monteiro), September 27, 1951, *FRUS 1951*, 1224–1228; Assistant Secretary of State for Inter-American Affairs to Ambassador in Brazil, October 23, 1951, *FRUS 1951*, 1234; and Memorandum for Major General C. L. Mullins, Jr., Military Commission, Subject: Relationship Between the Requirements for a Brazilian Division in Korea and Requirements for Brazilian Forces to Assist the U.S. in the Defense of the Western Hemisphere, n.d., RG-218, JCS Geographic Decimal File, 1951–1953, Box 10, CCS 092.2 Brazil (1-11-49) Sec. 1, NA.

48. Bolte to Góes Monteiro, September 27, 1951.

49. Memorandum of Conversation, "Farewell Visit by General Góes Monteiro—Brazil-U.S. Military Cooperation," October 15, 1951, Dean Acheson Papers, Box 66, HST Library; Miller to Johnson, October 23, 1951, *FRUS 1951*, 1229–1230; and Acting Secretary of State (James Webb) to Secretary of Defense, November 9, 1951, *FRUS 1951*, 1028.

50. Memorandum, JCS to Major General C. L. Mullins, Jr., n.d., RG-218, JCS Geographic File, 1951–1953, Box 10, CCS 092.2 Brazil (1-11-49), Sec. 1, NA.

51. "Current Status of the Military Aspects of Brazilian-U.S. Relations," March 28, 1949, RG-319, P&O Decimal File, 1949–February 1950, Box 534, 091 Brazil, NA.

52. Chief, Brazilian General Staff (Obino), to Senior General, U.S. Delegation JBUSMC, n.d.; Chief of Staff, USAF, to JCS, "Proposal by Brazilian Government for an Accord," January 11, 1949; and "Current Status of the Military Aspects of Brazilian-U.S. Relations," March 28, 1949, RG-319, P&O Decimal File, 1949–February 1950, Box 534, 091 Brazil, NA. Bandeira claims the impetus for an accord came from the Americans in 1951. See Bandeira, *Presença*, 334. Obino's proposal points to the opposite being the case.

53. Ibid.

54. Major General S. E. Anderson, USAF, Director, Plans & Operations, to Commanding General, U.S. Air Force Section JBUSMC, December 30, 1948; and Memorandum for Secretary of Defense, Secretary of the Army, Secretary of the Navy, Secretary of the Air Force, General Eisenhower, Admiral Denfield, General Vandenberg, Military Aides to President, Chairman of the Munitions Board, Executive Secretary—NSRB, and Director of the Joint Staff from Omar Bradley, March 28, 1949, RG-319, P&O Decimal File, 1949–February 1950, Box 534, 091 Brazil, NA.

55. A Report by the Joint Strategic Survey Committee, "Proposal by Brazilian Government for an Accord," March 21, 1949; and JSSC to JCS, "Secret Political-Military Agreement of 1942 Between the United States and Brazil," February 19, 1950, RG-319, P&O Decimal File, 1949–February 1950, Box 534, 091 Brazil, NA.

56. Ibid.

57. JBUSDC to Secretary, Joint Chiefs of Staff, June 4, 1949, RG-319, P&O Decimal File, 1949–February 1950, Box 524, 091 Brazil, NA.

58. Dulles, *Vargas of Brazil*, 298, 309. The only Latin American country to send troops to Korea was Colombia, which provided a one-thousand-man infantry battalion. Many scholars believe Colombian president Laureano Gomez sanctioned participation to rid himself of a group of liberal army officers during *la violencia*. See Robert H. Dix, *Colombia: The Political Dimensions of Change* (New Haven: Yale University Press, 1967); and Ernesto Hernandez, *Colombia en Correa* (Bogotá: Imprenta de las Fuerzas Armadas, 1953).

.. 7 ..

The Military Accord
and Post-Korea Relations

The Korean War was still raging when Dwight D. Eisenhower won the 1952 presidential election. Despite the promise of a "new look" in foreign policy, the Eisenhower administration continued to define the Soviet Union as the major threat to peace. The cold war conflict, however, shifted the bipolar rivalry to the underdeveloped world. In the Western Hemisphere U.S. political objectives encompassed the aims of broad support for U.S. policies, access to strategic raw materials, the fostering of anti-communism and reduction of anti-Americanism (or nationalism), and capitalist development. Standardization of military organization, training, doctrine, and armament endured as the staple of hemisphere defense policy, even though efforts to obtain Latin American participation in Korea failed.[1]

Brazil remained central to U.S. defense plans, and in 1952 the two countries signed a new military accord. Nevertheless, the question of assistance persisted as the main point of contention in military relations. Negotiations regarding Brazil's role in hemisphere defense, U.S. requests for communications and radar sites in the Northeast and for a missile-tracking station on Fernando de Noronha Island, and Brazilian desires to change the composition of the JBUSMC and JBUSDC all centered on the aid issue. Influencing those negotiations, and straining ties, was the rise of Brazilian nationalism.[2]

THE 1951 MUTUAL SECURITY ACT

Efforts during the Truman presidency to organize, train, and indoctrinate the Latin American armed forces along U.S. lines were relatively successful. Arms standardization fared less well because of the lack of legal mechanisms for arms assistance. The Surplus Property Act provided diminishing amounts of weapons from 1946 to 1948, when the act expired, but after that there were no legal means to supply the Latin Americans. Increasing tension with the Soviet Union, however, moved Congress to make provisions for military aid through the Mutual Defense Assistance Program (MDAP) in 1949. Although Secretary of State George Marshall wanted military alliances embracing all the countries of the hemisphere, the program did little to achieve that goal. MDAP guidelines excluded the region from receiving grant aid and worked against military unification; Latin American militaries could only purchase U.S. arms.[3]

Truman supported the Inter-American Military Act in 1946 and again in 1947 as a means of supplying the region's armed forces, but Department of State and congressional opposition killed the legislation. Another effort to expand military assistance came in April 1950 when National Security Council Report 68 called for quick action because of the danger of a new world war. The administration's backers again placed a proposal before Congress to widen the military aid and sales program, but the Korean War erupted before a vote could be taken. Subsequent failure of the Washington Conference in March and April 1951 to elicit Latin American military participation in the war spurred Congress to pass the Mutual Security Act later that year. Under the act any nation that opposed communism could receive military grant assistance or purchase weapons if U.S. officials viewed such actions as buttressing U.S. security.[4]

The act also sought a hemispherewide defense under the "General Military Plan for the Defense of the American Continent," which had been approved by the Inter-American Defense Board in November 1951. Although the IADB concocted the plan, the United States eschewed the multilateral agency in Mutual Security Program negotiations with the Latin Americans. Military assistance under the program was available only if the Latin American republics signed bilateral agreements.[5] Such arrangements allowed the United States to provide assistance to countries considered important rather than spread it regionwide. This narrow approach favored Brazil.[6]

Mutual security legislation, however, offered unattractive financial terms to participating countries. The bill provided only $38 million for fiscal year (FY) 1951 and $52 million for FY 1952 for the entire hemisphere and required recipient countries to cut commercial ties with communist nations. By limiting the Mutual Security Program to two or three years and forbidding the use of funds for internal security, Congress made the program unappealing to the Latin American militaries.[7]

The U.S. military did not regard grant aid quid pro quo for the committing of forces to Korea, even though it hoped that extension of such assistance would have that effect. Grant aid offered the extra advantage of furthering standardization and gaining influence with recipient governments and their militaries. In short, the primary objective of the Military Assistance Program was to keep the Latin American militaries on the side of the United States in the cold war. General Charles Bolte argued that earlier failure to obtain Latin American military participation in Korea was in part the fault of the United States because of the way requests were made. If the United States was to succeed in obtaining troops for Korea, it would have to make supply of matériel easier, and grant aid was the best method.[8]

Despite the 1951 act's drawbacks, it allowed the Brazilian military the means to pursue its modernization plans and to maintain special ties with the United States. When Góes Monteiro returned to Brazil with a draft agreement on Korea, he also carried a draft of a new accord that offered Brazil long-term benefits. Even though Brazilian participation in Korea was a dead issue, U.S. officials hoped a new bilateral arrangement would keep the special relationship alive. It would also enhance Brazil's ability to obtain assistance denied under the multilateral approach. Thus, in March 1952 Brazil and the United States signed a new bilateral military accord.[9]

At the same time, Brazil was sinking into a political crisis that quickly focused negative attention on the accord. Vargas's Brazilian Labor Party saw it as a U.S. ruse to force Brazil into the Korean conflict and to steal the country's natural resources. According to the PTB, the agreement would subordinate Brazil to U.S. whims. The National Democratic Union party, despite its pro-U.S. stance under the leadership of Eduardo Gomes, also opposed the accord. The UDN worried little about U.S. domination but feared the agreement would increase Vargas's prestige.[10]

Opposition to the accord highlighted the split in the officer corps over the Vargas presidency. Although most officers supported the treaty, the nationalists fought its ratification. Minister of War Estillac Leal, who was under attack for his nationalist stance, resigned in protest shortly after the agreement was signed; it had been negotiated without his advice or approval. The debate carried into the 1952 elections for the leadership of the Clube Militar, which pitted Estillac Leal and Horta Barbosa against the more internationalist generals Alcides Etchegoyen and Nelson de Melo. The latter pair won the election with the support of the Democratic Crusade, a right-wing, pro-U.S., and anti-Vargas pressure group whose honorary president was Eduardo Gomes.[11]

The victory by Etchegoyen and Nelson de Melo ensured official military backing of the treaty. It did not, however, end the intraservice battle for control of the army or for congressional approval of the accord. Estillac Leal's forced resignation and Góes Monteiro's removal as army chief of staff bore graphic proof that the struggle for supremacy in the military left casualties. Opposition was so great that Góes Monteiro suggested that Vargas withdraw the treaty from the ratification process.[12]

Debates in the Brazilian Congress over the treaty mirrored those in the military and delayed ratification for over a year. The issue was politically awkward for Vargas. Although he spoke in favor of the treaty, he did not support the pro-accord members of Congress with the full weight of his office. Not until Vargas named Eduardo Gomes head of the Brazilian delegation of the JBUSMC in early 1953 did the UDN give its support, thereby ensuring ratification. But there were conditions. The Chamber of Deputies voted favorably but issued a declaration against the use of Brazilian troops in Korea. The Senate followed suit with little debate.[13]

The Mutual Security Program and the accord were too late and offered too little to draw Brazil into Korea or to guarantee that arms would be obtained exclusively from the United States. Pro-U.S. officers controlled the Brazilian military and used their influence to see the bilateral accord ratified but refused to wreak further havoc on their institution over the Korea issue. Their support for the treaty was as pragmatic as it was ideological, for it meant continued access to military hardware. In early 1950 the United States was still the best source of armament, even though European arms manufacturers again were entering the Latin American market. The brotherhood of arms did not prevent Brazil from obtaining equipment under the best terms. Reflective of this was a 1952 deal with Great Britain whereby Brazil exchanged cotton for jet aircraft without prior notification to the United States.[14]

ATTEMPTED CHANGES IN FORMAL STRUCTURES

Despite current events, the Brazilian military maintained a desire for special military relations with the United States and sought to reconfigure the agencies charged with planning and implementing joint projects as a means of doing so. In 1951 during a trip to the United States Góes Monteiro suggested upgrading the JBUSMC and the JBUSDC to restore their functions to wartime levels. Revitalization would be accompanied by the creation of an umbrella management organization comprising representatives of the JBUSDC, the JBUSMC, the U.S. Department of State, and the Brazilian Foreign Office. Since the war, the JBUSMC had operated on a reduced scale commensurate with the nature of post-war necessities; JBUSDC activities were moribund. Creation of a joint defense board staffed by military and diplomatic representatives, however, would elevate relations to a level reminiscent of the war years.[15]

The idea of a new defense board derived from similar Canadian-U.S. and Mexican-U.S. military agencies. The board would meet quarterly and alternate between Washington and Rio de Janeiro. The U.S. military found merit in the suggestion and began discussing the formulation of such an agency. At first, military officials agreed that diplomatic representatives should sit on the board, as well as on the JBUSDC and JBUSMC. They later modified their positions and tried to exclude civilian diplomats.[16]

Negotiations to work out the configuration of a new defense structure began in Rio de Janeiro in September 1952, and verbal agreement was reached quickly. The name selected for the agency was the Permanent Combined Board on Defense, Brazil–United States. According to the agreement, the Brazilian Armed Forces General Staff and the U.S. Joint Chiefs of Staff would have a secret arrangement under which they would define the "objectives, functions and procedures for the two commissions and the new board." The board would meet annually, alternating between the two nations' capitals.[17]

Before formal notes could be exchanged, bickering erupted between Department of State officials and the Defense Department over the name of and participation on the new defense board. The Department of State balked at naming the new organization the Permanent Combined Board on Defense, Brazil–United States because it bore a close resemblance to the Permanent Joint Board on Defense, United States–Canada. The U.S. ambassador to Canada and State Department officials argued that use of the name would "arouse Canadian anxieties, hurt Canadian sensibilities, and otherwise needlessly injure our relationship with Canada." The diplomats exhibited less concern with offending Brazilian "sensibilities." As the Brazilians cared less about the name than they did about the establishment of such a board, the Joint Chiefs of Staff accepted the Department of State recommendation to call the new agency the Combined Board on Defense, Brazil–United States. The Brazilians agreed without protest.[18]

Although willing to compromise on the name, the Joint Chiefs of Staff refused to budge on the question of civilian participation on the board. The U.S. delegation of the JBUSMC, the embassy in Rio de Janeiro, and the Brazilian government favored civilian membership because of the political role of Brazil's officer corps. The deputy secretary of defense agreed verbally that representatives of the

Department of State and the Itamaraty should be permanent members of the proposed board. The JCS rejected the idea in December 1952, May 1953, and April 1954, arguing that civilian presence would make the board a government-to-government body dealing with political and economic matters, as well as military ones, on the order of the Canada-U.S. board. The JCS wanted the new defense board to be strictly military.[19]

The Department of State quarreled with JCS assumptions on the grounds that when dealing with the military in Latin America, one also dealt with a powerful entity comprising individuals with potential impact on the nation's politics. Because many of the problems facing a new board would have political ramifications, Itamaraty and Department of State membership would be invaluable in reaching solutions. Current negotiations for extensive facilities and base rights were examples. Besides, argued State Department officials, acrimony over military issues had reached the point of threatening political relations with Brazil. The JCS position was therefore dangerous.[20]

RENEWED ASSISTANCE REQUESTS

One of the issues that concerned the Department of State was a $50 million equipment program for the Brazilian armed forces. On January 13, 1954, the JBUSMC submitted a plan to equip additional Brazilian forces that included matériel for one airborne regimental combat team, two infantry regimental combat teams, and a battalion of medium tanks. The commission further recommended that the navy receive sixteen destroyer escorts, five destroyers, and four fleet-type submarines and that the air force get one squadron (twelve airplanes) of C-32 Fairchilds, one squadron of PB4Y Privateers, and ten H19 helicopters. Although the program would expand the Brazilian military, the JBUSMC claimed it was necessary for Brazil to execute its mission in defense of the hemisphere.[21]

The size of the project shocked the U.S. Joint Chiefs of Staff. They were hesitant to support the plan because it entailed assistance "of a much greater magnitude than has heretofore been considered feasible."[22] With the negative response, Brazil modified the JBUSMC recommendation by requesting a small aircraft carrier, two submarines, and four destroyer escorts. Rear Admiral Richard F. Whitehead, chief of U.S. Navy activities in Brazil, and Vice Admiral Ernesto de Araújo, inspector general of the Brazilian Navy, came to Washington to press for favorable action but were confronted by JCS delaying tactics. Navy officials informally told Araújo that the U.S. reserve fleet was too small to justify approval of the request. They intimated, however, that perhaps the Department of State could come up with a political reason to justify obtaining special congressional approval for transfer of the vessels.[23]

The Brazilians were unhappy with the JCS refusal to transfer the ships and with the delay in establishing the combined defense board. Ambassador João Carlos Muniz pressed the Department of State on several occasions to find the political justification supposedly wanted by the JCS. The Brazilian military took a more direct approach. Encouraged by the JBUSMC to expect few problems in obtaining the vessels, Admiral Renato de Almeida Guilhobel threatened to decrease the number of U.S. Navy Mission personnel, to reduce the privileges of the radio facility operated by the U.S. Navy in Recife, and to delay improvements of Brazilian Navy bases important to hemisphere defense. The JCS position was especially odious because Brazil paid $16 million between 1952 and 1954 to satisfy wartime Lend-Lease obligations.[24]

The Communications and Missile-Tracking Stations

Mystifying the Department of State was the obstinacy of the JCS and navy in light of the Pentagon plan to request facility and basing rights in Brazil. U.S. military leaders wanted to expand U.S. presence on a relatively large scale. The army wished to obtain 1,150 acres of land in Maceió to build a worldwide radio communications station to be operated by about 500 officers and enlisted men. Moreover, the navy wanted to continue operation of the Recife naval radio station. Reflecting modern warfare technology, air force desires were more comprehensive and proved to be the focus of contentious negotiations. The air force wanted to establish a missile-tracking station on Fernando de Noronha Island, build three new air bases, and obtain users rights at airports in Rio de Janeiro, Belém, and Natal. The air force also wanted to place 840 military personnel on those bases.[25]

The Department of State was doubtful any of the military's objectives could be fulfilled unless the combined board included civilian membership and unless the Pentagon provided the Brazilians with at least part of the matériel recommended by the JBUSMC. State officials were partially correct: JCS opposition prevented the creation of the new defense organization; on September 28, 1955, the two governments exchanged notes reaffirming the JBUSDC as the principal agency in Washington and the JBUSMC as the primary agency in Rio de Janeiro for military collaboration.[26] State officials were wrong about negotiations for facilities: the United States reached agreement with Brazil only after promising to examine the arms request.

Negotiations for facilities and rights proceeded despite the failure to create the combined board. The consequence of that failure, however, was that the Brazilian stance became harder than expected. In December 1955 the Department of Defense decided the missile-tracking station had the highest priority. U.S. officials accepted higher than normal construction costs for reaching an agreement for the station and concentrated efforts toward that goal.[27] Discussions for the radio station and Coast Guard LORAN radar sites waited on the outcome of Fernando de Noronha talks.

U.S. Army and Air Force desires for a missile-tracking station on Fernando de Noronha Island and a communication center in Maceió dated from late 1952. The issue was not explored at that time because the Brazilian Congress and press were attacking the government for concluding the 1952 Military Defense Assistance Agreement. In November 1953, after the accord's ratification, Brazil allowed the U.S. Air Force to survey possible sites for the missile-tracking station. Nevertheless, the project languished until late 1955 when the U.S. delegation of the JBUSMC broached the subject. The Brazilian political situation delayed matters further until General Lott's preventive coup ensured that Juscelino Kubitschek de Oliveira (1956–1961) occupied the presidency.[28]

In January 1956 the United States informally suggested station locations, but a number of months passed before discussions began in Rio de Janeiro. Interestingly, the talks showed the validity of the Department of State's argument for civilian membership on the proposed combined board. Participants in the negotiations included U.S. Embassy and Itamaraty officials, along with military attachés and the JBUSMC.[29]

RECOMMENDATION NO. 18

Brazilian dissatisfaction boiled up during the talks. A number of points irritated the Brazilians, one of which was the issue of assistance. In January 1954 the JBUSMC issued Recommendation No. 18, which called for an increase in force levels for Brazil with a corresponding increase in Military Assistance Program assistance in the amount of $50 million. The JCS delayed approval of the recommendation until January 1956 but increased the amount to include one airborne battalion combat team and one aircraft transport squadron. The extras were not without strings: provision of the airplanes was contingent on Brazilian agreement to purchase U.S. aircraft and one year's supply of spare parts.[30]

The Brazilian military considered the quantity of assistance and the delivery time of matériel inadequate to perform its hemisphere defense mission. Equally rankling was the perception that the United States failed to acknowledge and treat Brazil as more important than its Spanish-speaking neighbors. Ambassador Ellis O. Briggs agreed and argued for a policy of treating Brazil as the "first friend and ally" of the United States in Latin America. Briggs explained that the dollar cost of assistance was not as important as how it was done. As an example he cited the decision to offer the Brazilian Navy two destroyers, two submarines, and one minesweeper. Although the offer seemed generous, it was not well received because the Brazilians compared it with a simultaneous offer to Chile of two destroyers and two submarines. Briggs contended the United States should recognize Brazil as the dominant power in Latin America even if doing so created initial difficulties with the other countries in the region, including Argentina.[31]

The Department of State agreed that the amount of assistance offered under Recommendation No. 18 was insufficient to secure

Brazilian agreement for the Fernando de Noronha station. The charge that the United States placed Brazil in the same category as the Spanish-speaking countries in the region was another matter. Ernest Siracusa of the Office of East Coast Affairs told Briggs that, although Brazil's special place was not openly acknowledged, the United States in effect had a separate policy for that country. Brazil received more aid proportionately than the other Latin American countries. The Brazilian military rejected Siracusa's argument and took the position that the missile-tracking station meant increased responsibilities, hence the need for expanded aid. The key issue in negotiations was assistance. Permission to build and man the station hung on arranging an acceptable aid package. The Brazilians wanted quid pro quo, the station for assistance.[32]

The United States eschewed the quid pro quo stance, claiming the facility was a scientific station. Dissatisfaction over assistance should not be linked to the Fernando de Noronha talks, U.S. negotiators argued, but discussed at a later date. In reality the Pentagon was responsible for site selection and pursued negotiations under the 1952 MAP Treaty. The station was clearly military because its primary mission was tracking intercontinental ballistic missiles (ICBMs). The protracted negotiations not only slowed agreement but also delayed scheduled testing of ICBMs. In Brazil failure to reach quick agreement gave nationalists time to mount an attack. Decrying the country's dependency, congressional opponents claimed the station would make Brazil a target for a Soviet nuclear attack and would mean U.S. military occupation of the island.[33]

KUBITSCHEK AND THE MISSILE-TRACKING STATION

The matter stalled until Kubitschek and Minister of War Lott leaked to the press a proposal for massive quid pro quo aid. The tactic prompted President Eisenhower to send Kubitschek a personal note appealing for cooperation. Eisenhower admitted that, although the Brazilians would have maximum participation in non-classified areas of the project, they would be denied access to classified equipment. He also promised that the United States would give serious consideration to Brazilian assistance requests.[34]

Ironically, the happenstance of a missile veering off course from Florida and crashing in the Amazon jungle provided a boost to negotiations. An astute Kubitschek promptly declared that the tracking station would prevent future mishaps. More important was pressure from the Brazilian Navy and Air Force for an agreement. The two services wanted the equipment that would accompany construction of the station and argued that the army's desires could be satisfied by further negotiations.[35]

Opponents of the arrangement relented after Kubitschek published his government's conditions for an agreement. They appeared to give Brazil control of the station because only the Brazilian flag would be flown on the island; the installation would be under Brazilian command; U.S. technicians would train, be assisted by, and eventually replaced by Brazilians; and ownership of the station would pass to Brazil in five years. The Brazilian president's personal intervention eased nationalist fears, and a deal was consummated under the auspices of the 1952 bilateral accord.[36] The degree to which pressure from the military spurred Kubitschek's efforts is unclear. In all probability he was acting to appease the politically important segment in the military that considered close ties with the United States synonymous with modernization, of which the missile-tracking station was an important element.

The Agreement and Assistance

Anxious to conclude a deal, the Brazilian government accepted the Eisenhower proposal and entered into the arrangement without first determining the amount of U.S. aid. Under Article 6 of the agreement, the United States promised to examine the issue of new responsibilities for the Brazilians and a concomitant increase in military assistance.[37] A last-minute hitch threatened to derail the process when military and press opponents who were unhappy with Article 6 forced the government to seek specific U.S. recognition that the Fernando de Noronha station implied greater economic and military responsibilities for Brazil. They also wanted the United States to say it would review immediately with the Brazilian government technical and material aid.[38]

The abrupt demands took U.S. negotiators by surprise. It appeared that the agreement was about to slip away, which led Ambassador Ellis Briggs to comment "that few things in Brazil seem to be in the bag until the neck thereof is padlocked and sealed." Brazil relented only after receiving reassurances that aid would be reviewed. On January 21, 1957, Ambassador Briggs and Minister of Foreign Affairs José Carlos Macedo Soares exchanged notes approving U.S. construction of the missile-tracking station.[39]

Immediately thereafter the JBUSMC began unauthorized discussions on aid. Claiming that Brazilian officials possessed strongly negative views of the military relationship as a result of the Fernando de Noronha deal, the U.S. delegation urged the JCS to expedite delivery of equipment and assign Brazil a higher priority. The National Security Council continued to give Latin America the lowest place for MAP aid but placed Brazil at the top of the regional list. To assuage the Brazilians, and to provide incentive for negotiations on the Maceió communications center and the Coast Guard LORAN sites, the JCS offered two extra destroyers for anti-submarine warfare duties. The Department of Defense wished to forge ahead with discussions on new base requirements and hoped the gesture would avoid a replay of the Article 6 problem. The Department of Defense did not, however, want it to appear to be a quid pro quo payment for cooperation in developing the sites.[40]

ASSISTANCE AND BASE RIGHTS

Bargaining over Article 6 of the Fernando de Noronha agreement and negotiating over the Maceió and LORAN sites were to occur simultaneously but on separate tracks. The JBUSDC gained a short-lived renewed importance as Article 6 was negotiated at the military level between the JBUSMC and the JBUSDC. In the meantime Brazilian and U.S. military and diplomatic representatives conducted the radio and radar station discussions on a broader plane.[41] On the surface it appeared the relationship was returning to a more intense level reminiscent of earlier times. Closer examination reveals, however, that the new negotiations occurred only when they were in

U.S. interest. Rarely, if ever, did the United States respond with alacrity to Brazilians initiatives.

Prior to the beginning of discussion two incidents occurred that delayed and set the tone for the talks. The first occurred when the February 20 issue of *O Jornal* (Rio de Janeiro) reported that Foreign Minister Macedo Soares had leaked to the *Diários Associados* (Rio de Janeiro) news of the U.S. desire for the Maceió and LORAN sites and for expansion of Military Air Transport System (MATS) air base facilities. Angered by the leak, the Department of State called in the Brazilian ambassador to make clear its disapproval of the tactic and express displeasure because it meant negotiating under publicity.[42]

The second incident affected the Brazilian military directly. In a December 1956 letter to Kubitschek, Eisenhower indicated that Brazilians would have limited access to the Fernando de Noronha station. It is unclear if Kubitschek communicated the president's message to the military leadership or if the agreement convinced it that previous constraints no longer applied. According to Article 4 of the agreement, the station was to be operated under U.S. command assisted by Brazilian technicians and military personnel. Article 5 implied joint operation by stating that U.S. technicians would be replaced gradually by Brazilians. Regardless of the language, the issue of access caused heated arguments.[43]

In April 1957 Major Clifford A. Wiggers, a liaison officer from the U.S. Air Force Missile Test Center, angered the chief of staff of the Brazilian Army. Wiggers rather arrogantly informed the G-2 of the Army General Staff that no Brazilian would participate in the operation of telemetry and data gathering or missile-impact locating equipment. He said that Brazilians could take part as weather observers, exterior security guards, housekeepers, and control tower operators only. Wiggers' announcement infuriated the Brazilians. Their main interest was in the training that joint operations would provide, allowing them to operate the station in the future, and the NIKE missiles they hoped would be placed in the Northeast.[44] The Brazilians angrily claimed that denial of access was contrary to Articles 4 and 5 of the agreement. Wiggers' statement irritated the Department of State as well. State officials accused the air force of failing to provide adequate guidance to the major regarding the delicateness of the issue. The JCS answered that Wiggers had spoken the truth and then sought Department of State help in finding language with which to tell the Brazilians they were to be denied access to buildings and equipment on their own territory.[45]

Softer language did not smooth ruffled Brazilian feelings, but the whole issue soon became moot. In June 1957 a U.S. military review determined that Fernando de Noronha was no longer needed. Although U.S. technicians continued manning underwater sound and communications equipment, on June 9 a reduction of force began. A phased withdrawal of all U.S. personnel began, and control of the station was passed to the Brazilians, with the United States retaining the right of access should it be needed.[46]

The news leak and the flap over access to classified material occurred in the context of a relationship adjusting to a rapidly changing world. With worldwide responsibilities, the United States hoped to get more for less. Brazilian motivations changed little. If Brazil was to play a role in the international arena, its national interest required that the maximum be obtained from basing and aid agreements with the United States. For both countries that meant the assumptions on which each side based its negotiating stance for Article 6 and the Maceió and LORAN sites had to be defined before talks could begin in earnest.

The Brazilian ambassador in Washington, Ernani do Amaral Peixoto, informed U.S. officials early on that Brazil viewed discussion on these issues as a crossroads in the relationship. The Brazilians wanted an equal partnership. Negotiations on Article 6 and on the radio and radar stations were not separate matters but should "be viewed as a single and indivisible program." In return, Amaral Peixoto said, Brazil would not insist on a quid pro quo linking of economic aid to military assistance.[47]

The level of U.S. assistance continued to be an important issue. The Brazilian military agreed to the missile-tracking station because of recognition that the United States and Brazil were allies. Though Article 6 was fuzzy, it gave the military a claim on additional hardware. The military was unwilling, however, to agree to U.S. requests for the Maceió and LORAN sites unless Brazil received assistance over and above that provided in the current MAP program. Articles 66 and 87 of the Brazilian Constitution forbade foreign troops on national soil without congressional approval, and nationalist congressmen and officers could prevent ratification of an agreement unless large-scale aid was forthcoming. The United States could get the Maceió and LORAN sites only if it was willing to pay the price.[48]

THE MACEIÓ AND LORAN STATIONS

Brazilian efforts to gain maximum advantage in the negotiations began with the location of the discussions. U.S. negotiators wanted to hold the talks in Rio de Janeiro, but Ambassador Amaral Peixoto and Foreign Minister Macedo Soares proposed that discussions take place in Washington. According to the ambassador and foreign minister, negotiations should take place away from the Brazilian public's scrutiny so both men could present any agreement on Article 6 and the radio and radar sites as mutual defense arrangements initiated by Brazil. If presented as a Brazilian initiative under the 1952 accord, congressional ratification could be avoided, and each side would obtain what it wanted in a "package." The Maceió radio station and the LORAN sites would be included among the list of defense projects, which would parry criticism of U.S. endangerment of Brazilian sovereignty.[49]

U.S. diplomatic and military officials refused to accept the ploy, arguing that the JBUSMC in Rio was in charge of Article 6 negotiations. The Maceió and LORAN stations were separate issues. Although the latter were important, they were not indispensable. The United States did not quash negotiations, emphasized the value of the LORAN stations to Brazilian aerial and surface navigation, and tentatively offered to establish a school for the Brazilian Signal Corps in conjunction with the Maceió installation.[50]

The Brazilians gave in yet another time. In early May 1957 the Brazilian Embassy indicated a willingness to negotiate Article 6 and the Maceió and LORAN stations separately but concurrently.[51] Brazilian capitulation probably was motivated less by U.S. arguments than by a recognition of the facts. Having agreed to the Fernando de Noronha deal without specifying the amount of aid, Brazil was in a weak bargaining position. Better to obtain the maximum in negotiations along with a signal school, and in the future the radio and radar stations, than sink the deal at the outset, especially given that technological advances in communications and navigation were making the stations unnecessary.

Additional motivation may have come from knowledge of JCS plans to change force levels for Brazil, with an accompanying reduction in FY 1959 MAP aid. The JCS did not plan to inform the Brazilians until after an agreement on the Maceió and LORAN sites had been reached. Regardless of the reason, negotiations on the radio and radar stations began on May 9, 1957, in Washington, D.C. Talks on Article 6 were scheduled for a later date.[52]

U.S. officials expected the Brazilians to contend that the communication and LORAN centers increased their defense responsibilities, which therefore required greater assistance. To counter that position, the United States considered giving the LORAN stations to Brazil as grant aid at a later date or, in a reversal of its earlier position, using them as quid pro quo. The effect of the Fernando de Noronha missile-tracking station arrangement on subsequent negotiations, however, was not expected.[53] Political turmoil resulting from the outcome of the January agreement created barriers that influenced these discussions. Similar to the problems Vargas faced regarding the 1952 accord, the agitation showed that Brazilian politics and Brazil-U.S. relations could not be separated.

The Kubitschek administration's use of the 1952 accord to outmaneuver opposition on the missile-tracking station angered many deputies in Congress. Shortly after the agreement had been signed, UDN deputy Sexias Doria sponsored a committee to investigate Kubitschek's conduct of foreign affairs. The committee, which received strong support from Vice President João Goulart's PTB and Kubitschek's own PSD, claimed the agreement was offensive, rather than defensive, in nature because guided missiles could be launched from the site. In reality, argued the opposition, the station was a U.S. ploy to draw a first strike on Brazil. The committee also declared that the real purpose of the Maceió and LORAN stations was to gain control of Brazil's petroleum.[54]

Department of State officials doubted the committee could force Kubitschek to renounce the missile-tracking station agreement but worried that such opposition could make the Maceió and LORAN talks difficult. It soon became clear their fears were justified. Nationalist opposition in Congress and the military forced the Itamaraty to deny a U.S. request to conduct a technical survey of the communications site. Strong political opposition required Kubitschek to submit any agreement to Congress for ratification instead of relying on the 1952 accords, as had occurred with the Fernando de Noronha deal. Complicating matters was the Brazilian Constitution's limitation on stationing foreign troops on national territory. U.S. officials understood that under the circumstances arranging a status of forces agreement would be politically impossible. Any U.S. military personnel stationed at new facilities would be subject to Brazilian civil and criminal jurisdiction whether on or off duty.[55]

The elements against reaching a successful arrangement were too great. By August 1957 the Departments of Defense and State had come to the conclusion that the obstacles to establishing the Maceió and LORAN stations were too formidable, especially given that alternative sites were available. Another four months passed, however, before a Department of Defense review led to a decision to withdraw the request for the LORAN sites and to locate the communications center in Puerto Rico. Technological advances that obviated the need for base rights in Brazil helped make the decision easier, but political reasons were equally important. The Department of State feared that acrimonious negotiations could destroy the military relationship and thus political relations. As a result, on January 10, 1958, the Department of State informed the Brazilian ambassador of the decision to drop the requests.[56]

ARTICLE 6

The whole episode reflected a disillusionment on both sides that had been brewing since the Korea affair. Admiral Arthur Radford, chairman of the Joint Chiefs of Staff, was angry over Brazilian demands and wanted "to condemn them [the Brazilians] to Stone

Age existence." The Brazilians were unhappy as well. Although Kubitschek assured Eisenhower that Brazil would stand by the United States in case of war, growing nationalist sentiment in the armed forces and demands for a more independent foreign policy created conditions for a changed military relationship. Warnings of Brazilian disillusionment had been evident in military and civilian circles for some time. The military suspected the United States was stalling on Article 6 aid and was behind a Costa Rican proposal to cut military expenditures in Latin America in favor of economic development assistance. Even the pro-American publisher of *O Estado de São Paulo* (São Paulo), Dr. Júlio de Mesquita, was pessimistic. Mesquita told the U.S. consul he believed Brazil-U.S. relations had been damaged irretrievably.[57]

Brazilian suspicions were near the mark. For over a year the United States had delayed addressing the specifics of military aid under Article 6 because of the political situation in Brazil. Close to the scene, Ambassador Briggs urged immediate action on the aid issue because debate in Brazil centered on expansion of diplomatic and economic ties to the USSR and Eastern bloc countries. According to Briggs, the chiefs of the Brazilian armed forces opposed renewal of ties with the United States, so it was the "psychological moment" to show goodwill toward the military. Giving substance to the talks in Washington would also ease military nervousness over limited Brazilian participation at the Fernando de Noronha station regardless of U.S. force reduction plans.[58]

After much posturing by both sides, formal discussions on Article 6 began on June 28, 1957. Little occurred until the following month when the first of a series of compromises set the stage for agreement. The first compromise involved U.S. acceptance of Brazilian desires to conduct negotiations in Washington and Brazil's agreement to hold talks at the military level under JBUSDC aegis. Nothing changed in each side's negotiating position. The Brazilians continued to argue that construction of the missile-tracking station increased defense responsibilities. They kept the quid pro quo stance and presented a $600 million list of equipment deemed adequate for "new" defense requirements. U.S. representatives also refused to budge, claiming the station did not increase Brazilian defense responsibilities—especially to the amount of $600 million.[59]

Negotiations remained deadlocked until two small concessions, one by Brazil and one by the United States, gave momentum to the talks. An earlier Vargas request for an aircraft carrier had been lost in the political chaos after his death, but the Kubitschek government revived the issue at the start of the Fernando de Noronha negotiations. The JCS turned down the request on the grounds that a carrier was beyond Brazil's needs and that Argentina would want one too. Besides, U.S. assistance to the navy already was greater than that given to the army or air force.[60]

With the rebuff, Brazil immediately purchased a carrier from Great Britain (renamed the *Minas Gerais*) and requested U.S. electronic equipment for the ship under MAP. Although this time the Department of Defense supported the request, the Department of State did not, which angered the Pentagon. Using the none-to-subtle art of blackmail, navy officials informed the Department of State that they and the JCS would fight to the end to supply the desired equipment. Such a fight, they added, could protract other negotiations. Wishing to avoid such a situation, State Department officials agreed to provide the equipment in April 1958 but on a reimbursable basis rather than as grant aid. In return the United States promised to train Brazilians for carrier duty under 1959 MAP funding.[61]

Brazil made the second concession that moved Article 6 negotiations off center. At the same time U.S. military officials requested the missile-tracking, radio, and radar stations, they made known their desire for broader use and expansion of MATS air bases in Belém and Natal. Despite the lack of agreement on Article 6, Brazil agreed to expand the facilities, increase MATS traffic, and allow a small increase in U.S. personnel at the bases.[62]

The concession cost Brazil little and gained a great deal. Domestic political opposition was negligible because the military benefited from the physical expansion of the airfields. More important, the concession moved the JCS to finally review the Brazilian list of desired equipment and arrive at a figure. In May 1958 the JCS offered a three-year aid program valued at $87.1 million. The Brazilians accepted the offer, although they were unhappy with the amount. They noted that, although the sum was sufficient for the FAB and the navy, it did not fulfill army needs. The chief of staff of the Brazilian armed forces, General Edgar do Amaral, told the head of the U.S. delegation of the JBUSMC that "in reality it is recognized that the materiel now offered has little significance in relation to Brazil's needs." As a result, Brazil sought to continue discussions regarding matériel not included in the Article 6 agreement.[63]

The road to agreement on Article 6 was long and often difficult; the process and results of negotiations satisfied neither side completely. Nevertheless, the compromises both countries made indicated that the military relationship was strong enough to withstand the problems. The JBUSDC returned to a secondary role after the talks, and the JBUSMC again became pre-eminent. With the difficult bargaining over, military relations settled into a cooperative rhythm, as the two sides worked at the day-to-day tasks of fulfilling the new agreement. The negotiations indicated, however, that Brazil's political and military development was maturing to a point where more assertive stances could be adopted in military relations. Nevertheless, military ties remained close as each side adapted to rapidly changing local and international situations.

NOTES

1. Rabe, *Eisenhower and Latin America*, 2.

2. Ibid., 2, 26, 31–32, 34–35; Eisenhower, *Waging Peace*, 514–520; and Joint Subsidiary Plans Division Memorandum for Director, Joint Staff, Subject: 10th Inter-American Conference, March 16, 1954, RG-218, Records of the JCS, CCS 4000.3295 (12-16-43) (Sec. 7), NA.

3. Rabe, *Eisenhower and Latin America*, 15; and Weis, *Cold Warriors*, 20–21. Brazil received permission to buy two light cruisers under MDAP but only after Argentina was allowed to purchase two as well. See *FRUS 1950*, 767–768, 774–775.

4. "United States Objectives and Programs for National Security," April 7, 1950, *FRUS 1950*, 235–292; and Weis, *Cold Warriors*.

5. Memorandum of Conversation by Mr. Duncan A. D. Mackey of the Office of Regional American Affairs, Subject: Meeting with Representatives of the U.S. Delegation of the IADB to Consider Problems of Inter-American Military Collaboration, August 15, 1951, *FRUS 1951*, 1016–1018.

6. For the key country approach, see *FRUS 1951*, 1024–1029.

7. U.S. Congress, Senate, Committee on Foreign Relations, *Hearings: Mutual Security Act of 1952*, 82d Cong, 2d sess., 1952, 730; and Weis, "Roots of Estrangement," 190. The Department of Defense recommended $100 million

in grant aid for the region's armed services for FY 1952, but Congress refused to provide that amount. See Secretary of Defense (Marshall) to Secretary of State, January 10, 1951, *FRUS 1951*, 990–991.

8.   "Discussions by General Bolte of Grant Aid to Latin American Countries," Minutes of the Third Meeting of the International Security Affairs Committee, Held in the Department of State, February 13, 1951, *FRUS 1951*, 991–994.

9.   Weis, *Cold Warriors*, 47–48.

10. Memorandum by Under Secretary of State to Executive Secretary of the National Security Council, "First Progress Report on NSC 144/1, United States Objectives and Courses of Action with Respect to Latin America," July 23, 1953, *FRUS 1952–1954*, 20; and Weis, *Cold Warriors*, 48–50.

11. Sodré, *História militar*, 323; and Flynn, *Brazil*, 165.

12. Lourival Coutinho, *O General Góes depoe* (Rio de Janeiro: Livraria Editora Coelho Branco, 1956), 517; Sodré, *História militar*, 323; and Skidmore, *Politics in Brazil*, 106.

13. Luíz Alberto Moniz Bandeira, *Brasil–Estados Unidos: A rivalidade emergente (1950–1988)* (Rio de Janeiro: Civilização Brasileira, 1989), 25–48; and Weis, *Cold Warriors*, 50.

14. Minutes of the Meeting Between the Department of Defense—State Department Latin American Coordinating Committee, November 25, 1952, *FRUS 1952–1954*, 135–136.

15. Dean Acheson to Embassy in Brazil, August 21, 1951; and Edward G. Miller, Jr., to Ambassador in Brazil, October 23, 1951, *FRUS 1951*, 1216, 1229–1231.

16. Memorandum on Substance of Discussions at a Department of State–Joint Chiefs of Staff Meeting, Held in the Pentagon, April 1, 1954, *FRUS 1952–1954*, 648.

17. Enclosure "B" in Report of the Chair, JBUSDC, August 30, 1954, RG-218, JCS Geographic Decimal File, 1954–1956, Box 11, Folder CCS 092.2 Brazil (1-11-49) Sec. 4, NA; Edward G. Miller, Jr., to the Ambassador in Brazil, October 23, 1951, *FRUS 1951*, 1229–1231; Under Secretary of State to Executive Secretary, NSC, July 23, 1953, *FRUS 1952–1954*, 23; and Third Progress Report on NSC 144/1, "United States Objectives and Courses of Action with Respect to Latin America," *FRUS 1952–1954*, 61.

18. Acting Deputy Under Secretary of State to the Secretary of Defense, October 12, 1953, *FRUS 1952–1954*, 631–633; and Henry Holland to Deputy Under Secretary of State, August 2, 1954, RG-59, Records of the Department of State, Records of the Assistant Secretary of State for Inter-American Affairs (Henry F. Holland), 1953–1956 Country File (Brazil-Chile), Box 2, Lot 57D295, NA.

19. Ridgeway to Admiral Arthur W. Radford, Chief of Staff, Subject: Proposed Defense Organization, Brazil-U.S., April 29, 1954, RG-218, JCS Chairman's File, 1953–1957, 091 Brazil, Box 5, NA; Memorandum for Secretary of Defense—Proposed Defense Organization Between the United States and Brazil, RG-218, JCS Geographic Decimal File, 1954–1956, Box 11, Folder CCS 092.2 Brazil (1-11-49), Sec. 4, NA; Holland to Deputy Under Secretary, August 2, 1954, RG-59, Records of the Assistant Secretary of State for Inter-American Affairs, 1953–1956, Country File (Brazil-Chile), Box 2, Lot

57D295, NA; and Holland to Acting Secretary of State, May 18, 1954, *FRUS 1952–1954*, 651.

20. Memorandum on Substance of Discussion at a Department of State–Joint Chiefs of Staff Meeting, Held in the Pentagon, April 9, 1954, *FRUS 1952–1954*, 648–649; and Memorandum by Assistant Secretary of State for Inter-American Affairs to Deputy Under Secretary of State, July 12, 1954, *FRUS 1952–1954*, 653–655.

21. Memorandum for President, Joint Brazil–United States Military Commission, n.d., RG-218, JCS Geographic Decimal File, 1954–1956, Box 11, NA; and Memorandum by the Assistant Secretary of State for Inter-American Affairs to Deputy Under Secretary of State, July 12, 1954, *FRUS 1952–1954*, 653–657.

22. Report of the Chair—JBUSDC, August 30, 1954, RG-218, JCS Geographic Decimal File, 1954–1956, NA.

23. Memorandum by Assistant Secretary of State for Inter-American Affairs to Deputy Under Secretary of State, July 12, 1954, 656.

24. Ibid.; and Editorial Note, *FRUS 1952–1954*, 652.

25. Memorandum by Assistant Secretary of State for Inter-American Affairs to Deputy Under Secretary of State, July 12, 1954, 656–657.

26. Report by Chairman, U.S. Delegation, Joint Brazil–United States Defense Commission, to Joint Chiefs of Staff on Proposed Combined Meeting of JBUSDC and JBUSMC, September 18, 1956, RG-218, JCS Geographic Decimal File, 1954–1956, Box 11, CCS 092.2 Brazil (1-11-49), Sec. 6, NA; Shoultz, *Human Rights and U.S. Policy*, 239; and Barber and Ronning, *Internal Security and Military Power*, 285–287.

27. Statement by the Bureau of Inter-American Affairs of the Department of State for the Foreign Relations Committee, May 14, 1959, RG-59, Records of the Department of State, Office of East Coast Affairs (Brazil), 1956–1957, 3322.b.3 Folder 4, Box 3, Lot 62D308, NA; and Ronald M. Schneider, *Brazil: Foreign Policy of a Future World Power* (Boulder, Colo.: Westview Press, 1976), 46.

28. Lott and other senior officers supporting the constitutionally elected Juscelino Kubitschek's and his vice president, João Goulart's, right to take possession of their offices acted to prevent right-wing officers and politicians from launching a coup to deprive the two of their seats. See Maria Victoria de Mesquita Benevides, *O Governo Kubitschek: Desenvolvimento econômico e estabilidade política* (Rio de Janeiro: Paz e Terra, 1979), 179–183; John W. F. Dulles, *Unrest in Brazil: Political-Military Crisis, 1955–1964* (Austin: University of Texas Press, 1970), 3–61; Nelson Werneck Sodré, *Memórias de um soldado* (Rio de Janeiro: Civilização Brasileira, 1967), 485; Stepan, *Military in Politics*, 92, 106–107, 184; Skidmore, *Politics in Brazil*, 143–158; and Sodré, *História militar*, 364–366.

29. Statement by the Bureau of Inter-American Affairs, May 14, 1959; Memorandum by Under Secretary of State to Executive Secretary of the National Security Council, "Second Progress Report on NSC 144/1, United States Objectives and Course of Action with Respect to Latin America," November 20, 1953, *FRUS 1952–1954*, 39; and Memorandum from Deputy Assistant Secretary of State for Inter-American Affairs to Deputy Under Secretary of State, July 20, 1956, *FRUS 1955–1957*, 715.

30. Under Secretary of State to Deputy Secretary of Defense, June 9, 1955; Deputy Assistant Secretary of Defense for International Affairs to Secretary of State, April 20, 1955; and Deputy Under Secretary of State to Assistant Secretary of Defense for International Affairs, May 8, 1957, *FRUS 1955–1957*, 222, 229, 288.

31. Briggs to Department of State, December 18, 1956, *FRUS 1955–1957*, 731–732; and James Wilson to Dillon, "Increased Military Assistance to Brazil," April 23, 1958, RG-59, Records of the Department of State, 1955–1959, Micro. 1511, Roll 8, NA.

32. Under Secretary of State to Deputy Secretary of Defense, June 9, 1955; Deputy Under Secretary of State to Assistant Secretary of Defense for International Security Affairs, January 24, 1957, *FRUS 1955–1957*, 229, 749–750; Siracusa to Briggs, May 2, 1958, RG-59, Office of East Coast Affairs (Brazil), 321.1 Folder 1, Box 3, Lot 62D308, NA; Briggs to Secretary of State, January 22, 1958; and Wilson to Dillon, "Increased Military Assistance to Brazil," n.d., RG-59, Records of the Department of State, Micro. 1511, Roll 8, NA.

33. Wilson to Dillon, April 23, 1958, RG-59, Records of the Department of State, Micro. 1511, Roll 8, NA; and Weis, *Cold Warriors*, 100–102.

34. Briggs to Secretary of State, January 22, 1958; Wilson to Dillon, April 23, 1958, RG-59 Records of the Department of State, Micro. 1511, Roll 8, NA; and Weis, *Cold Warriors*.

35. Briggs to Secretary of State, November 20, 1958, RG-59, Office of East Coast Affairs (Brazil), 1956–1957, 332.b.3 Box 3, Folder 4, Lot 62D308, NA; and Weis, *Cold Warriors*, 100–102.

36. Briggs to Secretary of State, November 20, 1958.

37. See *Current History* 32:188 (April 1957): 239, for the text of the full agreement.

38. Briggs to Department of State, January 19, 1957, *FRUS 1955–1957*, 747; and Deputy Under Secretary of State to Assistant Secretary of Defense for International Security Affairs, January 24, 1957, *FRUS 1955–1957*, 749–750.

39. Briggs to Department of State, January 19, 1957.

40. Briggs to Secretary of State, January 19, 1957, *FRUS 1955–1957*, 747; Deputy Under Secretary of State to Assistant Secretary of Defense for International Security Affairs, January 24, 1957, *FRUS 1955–1957*, 749–750; and Memorandum for the Secretary of Defense, March 12, 1957, RG-218, JCS Geographic Decimal File, 1954–1956, CCS 092.2 Brazil (1-11-49), Sec. 7, NA. The latter memo was found in the JCS 1954–1956 file. Apparently archivists incorrectly placed the file under an incorrect heading.

41. Memorandum of Conversation, February 25, 1957, RG-59, Office of East Coast Affairs (Brazil), 1956–1957, Box 3, Folder 5, Lot 62D308, NA.

42. Memorandum of Conversation, February 25, 1957; and Barreto Leite Filho, "Nova fase nas negociações Brasil-EE.UU. para defesa do continente americano," *O Jornal*, February 20, 1957, 1.

43. Chair, USDEL JBUSMC, to JCS, April 9, 1957, RG-59, Office of East Coast Affairs (Brazil), 1956–1957, Box 3, Folder 5, Lot 62D308, NA.

44. Briggs to Secretary of State, April 2, 1957, RG-59, General Records of the Department of State, 1955–1959, Micro. 1511, Roll 8; and Chair, USDEL JBUSMC, to JCS, April 9, 1957.

45. Sayre to Siracusa, April 18, 1957; JCS to USDEL, JBUSMC, May 15, 1957; and Memorandum for William Briggs, Brazilian Affairs Desk, June 21, 1957, RG-59, Office of East Coast Affairs (Brazil), 1956–1957, Box 3, Folder 5, Lot 62D308, NA.

46. William F. Sandusky, Major, USAF, AFMTC Liaison Officer, to General Honorato Pradel, President, COPANE, and Commander, 4th Army, "Statement Concerning Reduction of Station," June 17, 1957, RG-59, Office of East Coast Affairs (Brazil), 1956–1957, Box 3, Folder 5, Lot 62D308, NA.

47. Memorandum of Conversation, February 25, 1957; and Transcript of Meeting, "Meeting of Brazilian and United States Representatives in Regard to Agreements for an Army Communications Facility at Maceió and Three Coast Guard LORAN Stations," May 9, 1959, RG-59, Office of East Coast Affairs (Brazil), 1956–1957, Box 3, Folder 5, Lot 62D308, NA.

48. Acting Assistant Secretary of State for Inter-American Affairs to Chairman of the JCS, April 10, 1957; Briggs to Department of State, July 18, 1957, *FRUS 1955–1957*, 284–285, 757–759.

49. Memorandum of Conversation, February 25, 1957, RG-59, Office of East Coast Affairs (Brazil), 1956–1957, Box 3, Folder 5, Lot 62D308, NA; and Briggs to Department of State, July 18, 1957, *FRUS 1955–1957*, 757–759.

50. Memorandum for the Secretary of Defense, February 19, 1957, RG-218 JCS Geographic Decimal File, 1954–1956, Folder CCS 092.2 Brazil (1-11-49), Sec. 7; and Memorandum of Conversation, February 25, 1957, RG-59, Office of East Coast Affairs (Brazil), 1956–1957, NA.

51. Memorandum of Conversation, May 6, 1957; Department of State to Inter-American Affairs Subcommittee of the Senate Foreign Relations Committee, May 14, 1959, RG-59 Office of East Coast Affairs (Brazil), 1956–1957, Box 3, Folder 5, Lot 62D308; and Memorandum for the Secretary of Defense, May 7, 1957, RG-218, JCS Geographic Decimal File, 1954–1956, Box 11, Folder CCS 092.2 Brazil (1-11-49), Sec. 8, NA.

52. Ibid.

53. Siracusa to Sayre, March 21, 1957, RG-59, Office of East Coast Affairs (Brazil), 1956–1957, Box 3, Folder 1, NA.

54. Siracusa to Rubottom, April 3, 1957, RG-59, Office of East Coast Affairs (Brazil), 1956–1957, Box 3, Folder 1, NA.

55. Ibid.; Siracusa to Rubottom, July 23, 1957; and Memorandum for the Chief Signal Officer, "Status of Negotiations for Base Rights for ACAN TROPACON Station in Brazil," n.d., RG-59, Office of East Coast Affairs (Brazil), 1956–1957, Box 3, Folder 1, NA.

56. Siracusa to Wallner, August 1, 1957; Siracusa to Briggs, December 4, 1957, RG-59, Office of East Coast Affairs (Brazil), 1956–1957, Box 3, Folder 1, NA; and Department of State to Inter-American Affairs Subcommittee of the Senate Foreign Relations Committee, May 14, 1959, RG-59, Office of East Coast Affairs (Brazil), 1956–1957, Box 3, Folder 4, NA.

57. Wallner to Siracusa, July 25, 1957, RG-59, Office of East Coast Affairs (Brazil), 1956–1957, Box 3, Folder 1; Briggs to Secretary of State, April 23, 1958, May 5, 1958, RG-59, General Records of the Department of State, 1955–1959, Micro. 1511, Roll 8, NA; Memorandum of Conversation, September

16, 1957, RG-59, General Records of the Department of State, Central Decimal File, 1955–1959, Box 5225, Folder 932.00, NA; and Memorandum of Conversation, President Eisenhower and Ambassador Peixoto, March 12, 1957, *FRUS 1955–1957*, 754–755.

58. Briggs to Department of State, December 27, 1957, *FRUS 1955–1957*, 770; and Briggs to Secretary of State, February 1, 1958, RG-59, General Records of the Department of State, 1955–1959, Micro. 1511, Roll 8, NA.

59. Wilson to Dillon, April 23, 1958, RG-59, General Records of the Department of State, 1955–1959, Micro. 1511, Roll 8, NA; Statement by the Bureau of Inter-American Affairs of the Department of State for the Senate Foreign Relations Committee, May 14, 1959, RG-59, Office of East Coast Affairs (Brazil), 1956–1957, 332.b.3 Box 3, Folder 4, Lot 62D308, NA; and Weis, "Roots of Estrangement," 204.

60. "Negotiations for Defense Sites Agreement with Brazil," June 29, 1956, RG-59, Office of East Coast Affairs (Brazil), 1956–1957, Box 4 Folder 5, Lot 62D308, NA; and Weis, "Roots of Estrangement," 201–202.

61. Memorandum of Conversation, "Military Aid for Brazil—Electronic Equipment for Aircraft Carrier," March 20, 1958, RG-59, General Records of the Department of State, 1955–1959, Micro. 1511, Roll 8, NA.

62. Briggs to Secretary of State, April 10, 1958, RG-59, General Records of the Department of State, 1955–1959, Micro 1511, Roll 8, NA.

63. General of the Army Edgar do Amaral to President of the JBUSMC, October 21, 1958; and Ambassador Ernani do Amaral Peixoto to John Foster Dulles, November 6, 1958, RG-59, General Records of the Department of State, 1955–1959, Micro. 1511, Roll 8, NA. The equipment transferred to Brazil under the arrangement included fifty aging jet aircraft, two World War II–era submarines, four destroyers, two minesweepers, and over a dozen helicopters. See Kaplan, "U.S. Arms Transfers," 414.

.. 8 ..

Civic Action, Counterinsurgency, and the 1964 Coup

The military alliance withstood the adjustments of the 1950s and remained firmly rooted as the new decade began. Pro-U.S. officers remained in control of the Brazilian military and valued close ties despite ruffled feelings over the Fernando de Noronha, radio, LORAN, and Article 6 negotiations. The United States also desired maintenance of intimate relations. At the beginning of the 1960s U.S. political and military officials recognized the importance of the Brazilian military in national life and considered it a model for the Third World.

The relationship was not without its critics, for a new generation of voices in Brazil and the United States heralded changes that meant military relations would continue adapting to a different set of internal and external dynamics. The refocusing of U.S. military assistance to counter internal threats and Brazil's military and political evolution resulted in further adjustments in the relationship. Particularly important was Brazil's move toward greater independence from its northern patron in international affairs.

JUSTIFYING MILITARY ASSISTANCE

Criticism of U.S. military assistance increased in the latter half of the 1950s. Members of the U.S. Congress and the Latin American "Democratic Left" questioned the Eisenhower government's support of repressive regimes in the name of anti-communism. Reviving old arguments, critics claimed that provision of U.S. weaponry to the region's militaries helped dictators oppress their own populations because no external threat existed. Aid dollars earmarked for military equipment would best be spent on economic development, they argued. Reservations about military aid also existed in the Brazilian and U.S. militaries but remained hidden behind institutional doors.[1] In Brazil radical nationalist and leftist sentiment in the officer corps that questioned the connection during the 1950s was still present, but pro-Americans controlled the military and quashed dissent.

In response to the detractors, President Eisenhower and the U.S. Congress initiated separate studies that re-examined U.S. assistance policy on a worldwide basis. In 1956 the President's Citizen Advisors on the Mutual Security Program, headed by U.S. Steel Corporation president Benjamin Fairless; a House study; and a Senate study under the charge of the former ambassador to Argentina, Undersecretary of State David K. E. Bruce, reached the same conclusions. Conforming to cold war ideology, the three studies praised the Mutual Security Program as a means of preventing the spread of communism and called for an expansion of military assistance. Bruce's report went further, recommending a broader role for the Inter-American Defense Board.[2]

Supported by the studies, the Eisenhower administration asked Congress for an increase in MAP funding that nearly doubled that previously apportioned. Congress accepted the premises of the various studies and complied with presidential wishes. Eisenhower had less success with an effort to join the IADB to an OAS/NATO alliance with joint maneuvers and planning. The idea was to form a strategic "Atlantic Triangle" that would act as a barrier to any communist threat. Brazil and Peru supported the concept, but Latin American opponents deflected the move by arguing such action would militarize the OAS. Increased MAP funding in 1957–1958 seemed to reduce the need for such an action, and regional opposition blunted any new adventures.[3]

Two events shook the United States into a reappraisal of the focus of military aid. Vice President Richard M. Nixon's disastrous goodwill tour of South America in 1958 and Fidel Castro's victory over Cuban dictator Fulgencio Batista in 1959 stimulated new administration and congressional examinations of U.S. policy in the region. This time the executive and legislative bodies reached different conclusions. Soon after the Nixon debacle the Senate Foreign Relations Committee began a wide-ranging review of U.S. Latin American policy. Democratic presidential hopefuls Hubert H. Humphrey and John F. Kennedy and the administration's most vociferous congressional critics, Wayne Morse and J. William Fulbright, accepted the overall policy of anti-communism and U.S. hegemony in the region but attacked Eisenhower's emphasis on military, rather than economic, aid to achieve objectives. Morse, in his criticism, singled out Brazil as a recipient of excessive military aid, which elicited an angry Brazilian response.[4]

To deflect congressional criticism, Eisenhower quickly formed a new group to study the situation. Under the leadership of former army undersecretary Major General William Draper the President's Committee to Study the United States Military Assistance Program aimed to reappraise military assistance and make recommendations regarding U.S. aid. Members of the Draper Committee, as it came to be called, included many individuals who left their imprint on U.S. post-war anti-communist policy. Among the military members of the committee were Admiral Arthur Radford (Ret.), former chairman of the Joint Chiefs of Staff; General Alfred M. Gruenther (Ret.), former NATO head; and General Charles Bolte, who had been the chief of the army's Latin American division. Civilians included future ambassador to Brazil Lincoln Gordon and Paul Nitze and James Webb of the Department of State.[5]

To gauge the efficacy of policy in Brazil, the committee dispatched James Webb to Rio de Janeiro with a series of questions for the U.S. delegation of the JBUSMC that were designed to determine the effects of reduced FY 1960 MAP. The JBUSMC delegates predictably declared that reduction would retard Brazil's ability to maintain equipment and an appropriate level of munitions. Mainly, they claimed, reduction in MAP would alienate elements of the politically important officer corps, "with resultant negative attitudes towards U.S. objectives."[6]

Although there were some new elements in the Draper Committee's report, its conclusions differed little from the 1956 presidentially inspired study. According to the findings, the Mutual Security Program was a militarily and economically sound concept in the anti-communist crusade. As with earlier studies, the final report called for permanence of the program and increased MAP funding. Departing from previous views, the committee urged that greater emphasis be given to the underdeveloped world and greater involvement by the Department of State in military assistance planning and coordination.[7] Interestingly, the committee's recommendation for better cooperation between the Departments of Defense and State endorsed an idea rejected earlier by the military during efforts to establish a new joint Brazil-U.S. defense board.

Two of the committee's recommendations, which reflected U.S. dominance in the region, gained increased acceptance in the early 1960s. Both changed the U.S. military's conception of the mission of the Latin American militaries and had a profound effect on local societies. Viewing the region's armed forces as the only institutions capable of unifying their countries, the committee suggested the Latin American militaries redirect their energies toward nation building. Much of their equipment and training could be utilized in a civic role to help national development, just as the U.S. military had played in the growth of the United States in the nineteenth century. The committee believed that the Brazilian military was an image of its northern tutor and held it up as the twentieth-century model for underdeveloped countries. Logic dictated that Brazil be the testing ground for civic action. U.S. assistance in the form of training would, of course, be invaluable and should be expanded.[8] The committee's recommendation regarding the Latin Americans' defense missions indicated the degree to which assistance could be used to influence national decisions in pursuit of U.S. interests. It also reflected the doctrinal thinking that had been evolving in the U.S. and Brazilian service schools.

Along with suggesting a civic role for the militaries, the Draper report urged a change from an externally oriented defense role to an internal orientation to match new battlefield tactics. Communist-inspired wars of national liberation in Cuba and Southeast Asia eschewed set battles between large armies in favor of small, highly mobile forces using unconventional tactics. To meet the threat, the committee recommended increased training in anti-guerrilla warfare by U.S. instructors.[9]

The Eisenhower administration used the conclusions of the Draper Committee to justify continuance of MAP. The rationale changed, however, from anti-submarine warfare and defense against invasion from external foes to civic action and counterinsurgency. The enemy came from within and had to be defeated by internal action. Although unrealistic, arms standardization remained an important goal and reflected a holdover from the past focus of defense policy.

The Senate Foreign Relations Committee study came to much different conclusions. The Senate report, which came out in 1960, validated congressional cuts in 1959 and 1960 overall military assistance funding and stressed the importance of economic aid. The report represented a new vision and methodology for defeating perceived enemies. Despite the promotion of a new approach, military aid programs to Latin America experienced growth during the Eisenhower administration.[10]

BRAZIL'S INDEPENDENT FOREIGN POLICY

The dawning of a new decade coincided with a break from old ideas. The Senate committee's conclusions reflected the emergence of different attitudes as a new generation of leaders who wished to avoid the mistakes of the past began to assert themselves. The cold war mentality that stressed a bipolar world with military might as a deterrent to aggression was in the process of change. Although prewar beliefs and ways of conducting international affairs did not disappear, world recovery from the chaos and destruction of the 1940s and early 1950s provided the conditions necessary for new approaches to old problems. A dominant theme was that old alliances hindered development. National interests could best be served by the creation of new relationships.[11]

New actors questioned U.S. leadership in the new multipolar world. Although the process of change began well before John F. Kennedy in the United States and Jânio Quadros in Brazil achieved prominence, they reflected the energy that promised new directions in Brazil-U.S. relations. Quadros's approach to international affairs was especially telling. His attempt to steer a course independent from that of the United States shaped Brazil's adaption to the changing world scene and threatened to alter the old military alliance.[12]

Alexandre de S. C. Barros dates the change in Brazilian diplomatic outlook from the inauguration of Juscelino Kubitschek. Evidence of a willingness to diverge from the United States, however, existed well before that event. As early as 1948 the CIA noted that, even though Brazilian policy usually paralleled that of the United States, there was a tendency to adopt independent approaches on some matters. Nevertheless, little substantive difference was evident until Jânio Quadros (January–August 1961) and his foreign ministers guided Brazil toward a foreign policy that did not intertwine Brazilian interests with those of the United States. In a 1961 article in *Foreign Affairs* Quadros outlined Brazil's desire to have closer ties with underdeveloped countries in Africa and Asia because they shared common views on anti-colonialism and on development. Similarly, Quadros explained, relations with communist bloc countries were necessary for development because those states represented new markets for Brazilian products.[13]

Quadros attempted to steer a middle course in the East-West struggle, especially over Cuba. Prior to the Bay of Pigs invasion President Kennedy sent Adolf Berle to Brazil to inform Quadros of U.S. plans. Quadros tried to head off the attack by instructing his ambassador to Cuba, Vasco Leitão da Cunha, to present Fidel Castro an unsigned letter drafted by Foreign Minister Afonso Arinos de Melo Franco that praised the Cuban leader's anti-imperialism but urged an abandonment of Sovietization. In the letter Quadros argued that communism was alien to Latin America and urged Castro to take an international position similar to Finland's. Cuba could then be neutral toward the United States and open to the USSR without forging a formal alliance with the Soviets.[14]

Some Brazilian officers favored an independent foreign policy, a tendency noticeable since the beginning of the cold war. Opposition by the Estillac Leal and Horta Barbosa factions to participation in Korea showed the strength of that proclivity. Nationalist and leftist officers lost control of the armed forces in 1952, but at the end of the decade the struggle intensified as senior World War II veterans began retiring and more independent-minded younger officers began to rise. Even some ex-FEB officers, such as General Luíz Cunha Mello, adopted political philosophies that contained anti-U.S. strains.[15]

Quadros's *Foreign Affairs* article echoed the philosophy that General Antônio de Souza Junior had elucidated in his 1959 work entitled *O Brasil e a Terceira Guerra Mundial*. In the book Souza Junior argued that Brazil could assume a prominent international position by following a path between the United States and the USSR. By attaching the country to "Afro-Asiatic interests through the Luso-Brazilian Community and to Latin American interests" through shared economic problems, Brazil would be a "Third Force" while serving its own national interests. In so doing, Brazil would contribute to world peace.[16]

Souza Junior's book publicized a trend already in motion. In May 1958 military representatives from Argentina, Brazil, Paraguay, and Uruguay met in Buenos Aires to lay the groundwork for a purely Latin American regional defense organization. The goal was to set up a coordinating structure for the protection of maritime traffic, the standardization of arms and equipment, and the exchange of military intelligence, as well as creating agencies for joint planning. Although little resulted, the meeting pointed to a willingness to undertake independent projects without U.S. guidance.[17]

Quadros's move away from U.S. foreign policy dominance was not a new idea, nor was it driven by a particular anti-American ideology. Rather, it reflected the same pragmatic effort to achieve great nation status as that which drove Brazilian leaders to form an alliance with the United States in 1942. The independent foreign policy earned Quadros political support from nationalists, the Left, industrialists, businessmen, and diplomats who recognized the utility of non-alignment in a fiercely competitive world market. The developing Brazilian economy needed new markets even if they were in communist countries. Adherence to Washington's cold war ideology was a costly hinderance. Re-establishment of ties with the Soviet Union and disagreement with the United States over Cuba, however, were related to Brazil's development goals rather than major ideological shifts.[18]

CIVIC ACTION AND COUNTERINSURGENCY

Regardless of foreign policy independence moves, the military leadership remained firmly anti-communist and pro–United States. Conservative officers Odílio Denys, Silvio Heck, and Gabriel Grün Moss were ministers of the army, navy, and air force, which guaranteed limits to the new foreign policy. Despite Quadros's proclivities, the Kennedy administration believed Brazil could act as a bulwark against Cuba in Latin America and sought closer links; the United States did not alter military assistance. Washington gave Latin America a high priority for the first time since World War II, but policy continued to be forged by the anti-communist cold war logic after John F. Kennedy took office. What changed was the way aid was applied. During the 1960 presidential campaign Kennedy castigated the incumbent administration's inability to prevent the establishment of a "communist satellite" in Cuba and promised a different approach in foreign affairs. When Soviet premier Nikita Khrushchev endorsed wars of national liberation in the Third World, the Kennedy government searched for new ways to defeat communism.[19]

At first JFK's foreign policy rejected the rigid cold war ideology that stressed military deterrence for one that emphasized development. To reduce the poverty that enhanced the allure of communism in the underdeveloped world, and to gain supporters of U.S. policy, Kennedy adopted the idea of nation building. According to the concept, lack of development prevented countries from building modern democratic states. Therefore, U.S. assistance should focus on economic programs while stressing the need for political reform. To those ends the Kennedy administration initiated the Alliance for Progress, a multibillion dollar aid program to improve the economies of Latin American countries and the lives of their citizens. Success depended to a large degree on Brazil's willingness to cooperate.

The program resembled major components of Kubitschek's 1958 proposal Operação Pan America, which had been rejected by the United States.[20]

Kennedy was also a pragmatist. Although the Alliance for Progress aimed to raise standards of living to remove the attraction of communism, stability was necessary for development, and communist-inspired guerrilla movements fomented instability. After the failed Bay of Pigs invasion Kennedy came to lean more and more on the military, the institution most resistant to change, and adopted some of the recommendations of the Draper Committee. U.S. military aid shifted its primary emphasis from external defense to internal security. On December 18, 1961, Kennedy issued a directive to incorporate civic action into the Military Assistance Program. One month later a national security memorandum called for the development of counterinsurgency methods to suppress "subversive insurgency." The United States would provide equipment and training through MAP, which would be administered by the United States Military Group in each country. In Brazil that meant the JBUSMC.[21]

General George S. Beatty, former chair of the Rio commission, testified before the U.S. Senate that the U.S. military gave no advice to the Brazilians regarding internal security. He admitted, however, that some training provided by the United States supported such a mission. Beatty did not mention the June 19, 1962, National Security Action Memorandum No. 119, which directed U.S. personnel to prepare internal security plans for selected countries and to train local police, paramilitary, and military forces. The memorandum especially targeted middle-grade and senior officers for training at the Jungle Warfare School at Fort Gulick in the Canal Zone and at the Special Forces School at Fort Bragg, North Carolina.[22]

The Brazilian Army needed no prodding to adopt civic action or counterinsurgency. The concepts had been discussed at the ESG and the ECEME well before Kennedy's December directive. The difference in 1961 was that U.S. aid allowed theory to be put into action. The Kennedy administration thought the internal security programs would have a salubrious effect on Brazil–United States relations and would increase U.S. prestige elsewhere. One optimistic report suggested that the trained Brazilians could pass their know-how on to neutralist African countries that wished to avoid the appearance of intimate relations with the United States.[23]

The refocusing of assistance served U.S. anti-communism goals and helped maintain close ties with conservative officers. Such aid failed, however, to prevent Brazil's continued move toward an independent foreign policy. That fact became evident following Jânio Quadros's dramatic resignation. Whether civic action aid won the people to the U.S. cause is questionable, for one of the consequences of the program was the 1964 coup. The effect on the military was clear. It gave the Brazilian military added confidence in its ability to manage and develop the country. After 1964 the military applied its new skills to suppress armed and unarmed opposition to the new regime.[24]

CRISIS IN BRAZIL

Political tensions in Brazil increased during Quadros's few months in office. The enigmatic president created animosity between his detractors and supporters in the UDN, PTB, and PSD with his domestic and foreign policies and his attempts to isolate Vice President João Goulart. Congressional support waned because of neglect, and the armed forces abandoned him because of his "leftist" foreign policies. Especially galling to the conservative officers was Quadros's decoration of Ernesto "Che" Guevara with the Cruzeiro do Sul, Brazil's highest award, in August 1961.[25]

Despite the unstable situation, there was no powerful demand from the major political players to oust Quadros. Instead, the president initiated his own crisis by resigning on August 25, 1961. Apparently his plan was to provoke military and political leaders into refusing the resignation and giving him greater powers rather than accept Goulart as president. The tactic failed. No political party called for his return, and the masses did not take to the streets in his support. More important, the majority of the senior military officers no longer trusted Quadros. Influential political groups, including the military, accepted his departure without hesitation.[26]

Quadros's actions precipitated a succession crisis that ultimately led to military government in Brazil. The question of allowing Goulart to accede to the presidency, as called for in the Constitution, divided society. The UDN and prominent conservatives opposed Goulart, while the PTB and most of the unionists supported constitutionalism. The issue also split the final arbiter of Brazilian politics, the military officer corps. The three military ministers, Odílio Denys, Gabriel Grün Moss, and Silvio Heck, and their supporters favored intervention to prevent Goulart (who was abroad at the time) from occupying the presidential palace. The formidable Marshal Henrique Texeira Lott and his followers supported the constitutional process. Unfortunately for the constitutionalists, in 1961 conservative officers controlled the armed forces more effectively than they had in 1950s. In an effort to prevent a replay of the1955 countercoup, the conservative officers imprisoned Lott and other legalist officers.[27]

While in confinement Lott made an impassioned appeal for the military to honor the Constitution. Congress, including the UDN deputies, responded to Lott's arrest and appeal by calling for legality with protests and declarations of solidarity. Tension filled the air, and the split between legalist officers and interventionists seemed to portend civil war. To forestall such an outcome, Congress reached a compromise in which the Constitution was modified to create a parliamentary system whereby the president had limited powers.[28]

The tactic allowed João Goulart (1961–1964) to occupy the presidency and temporarily assuaged the anti-Goulart officers. The U.S. response was wary, even after Goulart went to Washington to assure the Americans that he opposed totalitarian regimes such as the one in Cuba. U.S. Embassy officials revealed their reservations about Goulart by justifying the actions of interventionist officers during the succession crisis. They argued that the United States should not overlook the "fact" that the motivation of the interventionist officers stemmed from a genuine desire to preserve democratic values even though the officers contravened the Constitution. Goulart's trip to the United States and the U.S. response changed nothing regarding Brazil's independent foreign policy, which had been evolving irregularly since Getúlio Vargas's second presidency.[29]

Indications of Goulart's intention to stay the independent course came in January 1962 at a meeting of inter-American foreign ministers at Punta del Este. Francisco San Tiago Dantas, the minister of foreign affairs, made clear Brazil's opposition to U.S. dominance and to Washington's demand for Cuba's ouster from the Organization of American States.[30] His position had support from a broad spectrum of Brazilian society, but U.S. officials regarded any stance unsupportive of U.S. views as sympathetic to Marxist ideals.[31]

A Brazilian diplomat during the period provided one of the best explanations of the framework in which Brazilian foreign policy was developing. José M. Villar de Queiroz eschewed communism but reasoned an independent foreign policy was necessary to pursue national interests and development. According to Villar de Queiroz, four principles guided Brazilian national interests: preservation of peace and peaceful solutions to controversy, self-determination, observance of international obligations, and inter-American solidarity. Stemming from these were four corollaries: the struggle against underdevelopment, peaceful coexistence, non-intervention, and anti-colonialism. These principles and their corollaries determined Brazilian policy toward the nations of the world, even if that meant adopting positions opposite those of the United States.[32]

If Villar de Queiroz's article caused unease, a CIA report and a circular from the Itamaraty must have convinced U.S. leaders that Brazil could become the next Cuba. An August 1963 CIA report said that the Soviets had offered economic aid to the Goulart government in return for the establishment of a military mission in Brazil. A November 1963 Itamaraty circular stated that Brazil no longer believed the world was bipolar. Tensions within the Western nations and within the communist bloc, and between developed and undeveloped countries, substantiated the existence of a multipolar world. As a result, Brazil belonged to no particular military bloc but to Western civilization, and there was no correlation between civilization and military alliances. Hence, the circular proclaimed, Brazil did not consider itself militarily allied to any nation.[33]

An earlier CIA intelligence memorandum that claimed communist penetration of the police and armed forces at the highest levels had caused alarm in Washington. The memo said that a pro-communist, Colonel Carlos Cairoli, had been appointed chief of police in

Brasília and that General Oromar Osório, the highest ranking fellow traveler in the armed forces, was slated to become the commander of the strategically important Vila Militar in Rio de Janeiro. The appointments could pose a serious threat to U.S. interests, asserted the CIA, because of the influence the two men could exert in key institutions. Even though the number of communists in the Brazilian Army was slight, it was larger than in any of the other Latin American militaries.[34] Although unsubstantiated, the information seemed to validate the proposition that Goulart intended to turn Brazil into a Soviet vassal. Fears were so great that in 1962 the United States provided funds to Goulart opponents to counter the Brazilian president's influence.[35]

THE 1964 COUP

Brazil's troubled economic situation and Goulart's mid-1963 turn to the radical nationalist view that the roots of this problem were external set the stage for another test of Brazil-U.S. military relations. The story of the development of opposition among conservative politicians and businessmen, and their link with military officers through the Instituto de Pesquisas e Estudos Sociais (IPES, or Institute of Social Studies and Research) has been amply treated elsewhere. The polarization within the Brazilian military also has been scrutinized. In short, the events leading to the April 1964 overthrow of the Goulart government and establishment of military rule are discussed in detail elsewhere and are beyond the scope of this work.[36]

Similarly, U.S. preparedness to aid the coup with small arms and ammunition, fuel oils, and communications support through the secret "Brother Sam" plan has been examined in detail.[37] Less clear is the role played by U.S. military representatives in Brazil. As early as March 1963 CIA representatives described their meetings with General Olympio Mourão Filho, Admiral Silvio Heck, General Amaury Kruel, Marshal Odílio Denys, and General Nelson de Melo to discuss plans for a coup against Goulart. As the conspirators were short on funds and arms, they solicited support from the CIA, U.S. military attaché Vernon Walters, and Ambassador Lincoln Gordon.

Considering that such meetings occurred and that the local aspects of "Brother Sam" had to be coordinated, the JBUSMC could not have been uninvolved. Some weight is given to that proposition by José Stacchini's claim that an officer attached to the U.S. Embassy met, at the American's request, a ranking Brazilian officer to offer matériel assistance for the coup. Although the Brazilian answered that the conspirators needed only fuel, any logistics in moving such aid would have been within the expertise of commission members.[38]

Vernon Walters was key. During World War II Walters had been the U.S. liaison officer with the FEB in Italy, where he established a close friendship with then Lieutenant Colonel Humberto Castello Branco and other Brazilian officers. So strong were Walters's ties to the officer corps that when he arrived in Brazil prior to the coup to take up the duties of the U.S. military attaché, thirteen generals were on hand to greet him. In his memoirs Walters claims that once coup plotting commenced, he quit visiting Castello Branco and other officers to avoid the perception of U.S. involvement. Although he may have ceased direct contact with Castello Branco, Walters kept in constant touch with General Floriano de Lima Brayner, one of the main conspirators, who provided him with details of the progress of coup planning.[39]

Radical nationalists claim that the coup began in Washington, and to a certain extent they are correct. After the death of John F. Kennedy and the replacement of his appointees, U.S. anti-communist policy became more hard-line. President Lyndon B. Johnson appointed Thomas C. Mann, a fervent anti-communist, to the post of assistant secretary of state for inter-American affairs. Mann returned to a policy of containing Latin American radical elements, which he identified with communism. He made clear that the United States would not oppose coups it believed were aimed at preventing or overthrowing communism.[40] Thirteen days after Mann articulated the Johnson administration's policy of selectively recognizing regimes established by coup, the Goulart government fell.[41]

Harder to determine is the degree of influence exerted by U.S. military representatives. The communication link between the conspirators and Walters does not by itself indicate overwhelming influence, although his charge was to stay informed of coup plotting and to influence Brazilian armed forces' actions. Nor did JBUSMC contacts with civilian agencies such as the Ministry of Finance, Chief of Police, Director of Traffic, Inspector of Customs, Vehicle Registration Bureau, and Ministry of Foreign Affairs ensure automatic acceptance of U.S. views. More important was the fact that of the line generals on active duty at the time of the coup, about one-third had received training at U.S. service schools or from U.S. personnel in Brazil.[42]

U.S. military personnel probably lobbied their colleagues in military and civilian circles while providing the conspirators with mutual support through the communication linkages. Willard Barber and C. Neale Ronning mention unconfirmed reports that U.S. officers throughout the region exerted influence by word or deed on the action of local militaries in times of political crisis during the 1960s. Jan Black goes further, claiming U.S. military representatives coordinated coup plotting. Whether U.S. military personnel actively worked with coup plotters is uncertain, though logistics of the Brother Sam operation would indicate some prior planning. It is clear, however, that U.S. instructors and their Brazilian colleagues hammered the anti-communist theme in courses at the ESG and the ECEME. And the U.S. government and many Brazilian officers associated Goulart with communism.[43]

To gauge the degree, if any, of influence the U.S. delegation of the JBUSMC had on the Brazilian section is difficult. In testimony to the U.S. Senate JBUSMC chairman General George S. Beatty claimed that U.S. officers on the commission did not get involved in Brazilian political affairs. A cursory glance at a list of Brazilian heads of the JBUSMC, however, indicates that many were among the 1964 coup conspirators (See Appendix A). There is little doubt that the U.S. members supported the ideology of the conspirators.[44]

Perhaps most revealing of the ideology shared by the U.S. military and the Brazilian conspirators was a remark made by a high-ranking U.S. general intimately involved in U.S.-Brazil relations. General Paul Freeman, a former JBUSMC delegate, attempted to justify the coup by claiming that democracy had never worked in Brazil. Therefore, it was better to have dictators with U.S. weapons and advisers than a variety of foreign missions and arms because the former gave the United States control over the dictators' actions. Post-coup repression in Brazil invalidates Freeman's assertions.[45]

Brazilian military officers needed no tutoring, especially those who were already pro–United States or who held anti-communist views. Those individuals played vital roles in propagandizing the anti-communist theme with U.S. help. Two closely linked conservative organizations, the Brazilian Institute of Democratic Action and the Institute of Research and Social Studies Research, employed retired officers to pressure their active-duty brothers in arms and to produce for widespread distribution literature that heralded the evils of communism in Brazil. Both organizations received funds from the United States to promote "democracy." Headed by the pro-U.S. geopolitician General Golbery do Couto e Silva, and including former members of the FEB, the political bent of the latter group was clear.[46]

The Johnson administration showed its joy over the success of the coup by recognizing the new Brazilian government in less than twenty-four hours after the military took control. U.S. dollars also evinced Washington's happiness over the ouster of Goulart. Shortly after the installation of the military government the United States provided $453 million in loans and agreed to a repayment schedule for Brazil's creditors. The following year the International Monetary Fund and the International Bank for Reconstruction and Development supplied Brazil with loans and credits worth $204.5 million.[47]

The U.S. military gave its sanction to the post-coup government as well, particularly in preparing Brazilians for internal security roles that came to be associated with torture. Testifying before a House of Representatives hearing on foreign assistance, Lieutenant General George M. Seignious III of the Pentagon said that MAP funds were used to train security police, criminal investigators, and personnel in disaster control at U.S. service schools.[48] Protestations that the U.S. military had nothing to do with oppression in Brazil appear weak at best. Although extralegal methods of obtaining information or confessions were well known by personnel in those agencies before U.S. assistance, such training is suggestive of an acceptance of immoral activities.[49]

U.S. support for the coup and the installation of Castello Branco (1964–1967) in power realigned Brazil closely with U.S. foreign policy in the short term. Participation in the Dominican Republic intervention signaled such a course. Realignment failed, however, to arrest Brazil's independence of the United States in world affairs or the continued development of independent thought in the military. If cooperation in the Dominican Republic represented the swan song of intimate military ties between Brazil and the United States, Brazilian refusal to participate in Vietnam and abrogation of the military accord gave clear evidence of the enormous changes the relationship had undergone since the end of World War II.

NOTES

1. Francis, *Attitudes of U.S. Government*, 222; and Weis, "Roots of Estrangement," 205–206.

2. U.S. Congress, House, Committee on Armed Services, *Military Assistance Advisory Groups* (Porter Hardy Report), 84th Cong., 2d sess., 1956; U.S. Congress, Senate, Special Committee to Study the Foreign Aid Program, *Report on United States Foreign Assistance Program: South America (Peru, Chile, Argentina, Uruguay, and Brazil)*, by David K. E. Bruce, 85th Cong., 1st sess., 1957; and Weis, *Cold Warriors*, 103.

3. Child, *Unequal Alliance*, 125–127; Harold Hovey, *United States Military Assistance: A Study of Policies and Practices* (New York: Praeger, 1965), 140–143; Michael J. Francis, "Military Aid to Latin America in the U.S. Congress," *Journal of Inter-American Studies* 87:1 (February 1982): 396–397.

4. Wallner to Secretary of State, June 1, 1959, RG-59, General Records of the Department of State, 1955–1959, Micro. 1511, Roll 8, NA; Rabe, *Eisenhower and Latin America*, 97–98; and Weis, *Cold Warriors*, 114–115.

5. Weis, *Cold Warriors*; and Weis, "Roots of Estrangement," n. 56.

6. Wallner to Department, February 26, 1959; enclosure No. 2, "Statement for Webb Sub-Committee," in Wallner to Department of State, February 26, 1959, RG-59, General Records of the Department of State, 1955–1959, Micro. 1511, Roll 8, NA.

7. President's Committee to Study the United States Military Assistance Program, *Interim Report*, March 17, 1959, Library of Congress [hereafter cited as LC]; and Weis, *Cold Warriors*, 130–132.

8. Weis, *Cold Warriors*.

9. Rabe, *Eisenhower and Latin America*, 147–148.

10. U.S. Congress, Senate, Committee on Foreign Relations, *The Mutual Security Act of 1960*, Report 1286, 86th Cong., 2d sess., 1960, 6–9; U.S. Congress, Senate, Appropriations Committee, *Hearings: Mutual Security Appropriations*

for 1960, 86th Cong., 2d sess., 1960, 742–744; U.S. Congress, House, Foreign Affairs Committee, Report 354, 86th Cong., 1st sess., 1960, 6–8; and
Rabe, *Eisenhower and Latin America*, 107–108.

11. Walter LaFeber believes that there were two cold wars. The first occurred
from 1945 to 1955 and reflected the bipolar power competition between the
United States and the USSR. Beginning in 1956 the post-war power structure
underwent change because of economic recovery in Europe and Japan, rising
nationalism, Soviet advances as a military and scientific nation, and the slow
decline of the U.S. ability to influence events. According to LaFeber, a "new
cold war" that adapted to a multipolar world developed in the years from
1956 to 1962. See LaFeber, *Inevitable Revolutions*, 138.

12. The key person in formulating Brazil's independent foreign policy was Fran-
cisco Clementino de San Tiago Dantas, Quadros's foreign minister. See Peter
D. Bell, "Brazilian-American Relations," in *Brazil in the Sixties*, ed. Riordan
Roelt (Nashville, Tenn.: Vanderbilt University Press, 1972), 77–102; Francisco
Clementino de San Tiago Dantas, *Política externa independente* (Rio de Ja-
neiro: Editora Civilização Brasileira, 1962); Marcilio Marques Moreira, *De
Maquiavel a San Tiago: Ensaios sobre política, educação, e econômia* (Bra-
silia: Editora Universidade de Brasília, 1981); and Fontaine, *Brazil and the
United States*. This movement was strong enough to give birth to a short-lived
journal, *Política Externa Independente* (Rio de Janeiro: Editora Civilização
Brasileira), that published issues beginning in May 1965 (vol. 1), to August
1965 (vol. 2), and then to January 1966 (vol. 3) before it was closed down.

13. CIA, *Brazil*, November 30, 1948, S-17, President's Secretary's File, Central
Intelligence Reports—Situation Reports, Box 260, HST Library; Alexandre de
S. C. Barros, "The Formulation and Implementation of Brazilian Foreign Policy: Itamaraty and New Actors," in *Latin American Nations in World Politics*,
ed. Heraldo Muñoz and Joseph S. Tulchin (Boulder, Colo.: Westview Press,
1984), 32; Jânio Quadros, "Brazil's New Foreign Policy," *Foreign Affairs* 40:1
(October 1961): 19–27; Flynn, *Brazil*, 211–216; and Adolf A. Berle, *Latin
America—Diplomacy and Reality* (New York: Harper and Row, 1962), 79–
82.

14. H. Jon Rosenbaum, "Brazil's Foreign Policy and Cuba," *Inter-American Economic Affairs* 23:3 (Winter 1969): 27–29.

15. Gordon to Mann, March 4, 1964, U.S. Department of State, DDRS-1975,
84-E, LC; Barber and Ronning, *International Security and Military Power*, 43;
and Walters, *Silent Missions*, 381. Cunha Mello later became a member of
João Goulart's *dispositivo* and supported a new alignment of Brazil's foreign
relations.

16. General Antônio de Souza, Junior, *O Brasil e a Terceira Guerra Mundial* (Rio
de Janeiro: Biblioteca do Exército Editora, 1959), 285.

17. Foreign Policy Research Institute, *A Study of U.S. Military Assistance Programs in Underdeveloped Areas* (Philadelphia: University of Pennsylvania,
April 8, 1959), 84–85.

18. Flynn, *Brazil*, 213, 215–216.

19. Thomas G. Paterson, "Bearing the Burden: A Critical Look at JFK's Foreign
Policy," *Virginia Quarterly Review* 54:2 (Spring 1978): 193–212; Lieuwen,
U.S. Policy in Latin America, 113; Baily, *U.S. and Development of South
America*, 94; Rosenda A. Gomez, "The Marxist Approach to Latin America:

Marx, Lenin, Stalin, and Mao," in *The Political-Military Defense of Latin America*, ed. Bruce B. Mason (Tempe: Bureau of Governmental Research, Arizona State University, 1963), 5; and Leacock, *Requiem for Revolution*, 19.

20. Jerome Levinson and Juan de Onis, *The Alliance That Lost Its Way: A Critical Report on the Alliance for Progress* (Chicago: Quadrangle Books, 1970), 48–50; and Weis, *Cold Warriors*, 141. For an articulation of the concept that development blunted communist expansion, see Walt. W. Rostow, *The Stages of Economic Growth: A Non-Communist Manifesto*, 2d ed. (Cambridge: Cambridge University Press, 1960).

21. John M. Baines, "U.S. Military Assistance to Latin America: An Assessment," *Journal of Inter-American Studies and World Affairs* 14:4 (November 1972): 473–474; Joyce Carol Townsend, *Bureaucratic Politics in American Decision Making: Impact on Brazil* (Washington, D.C.: University Press of America, 1982), 5, 49; Baily, *U.S. and Development of South America*, 84, 91, 94; John Duncan Powell, "Military Assistance and Militarism in Latin America," *Western Political Quarterly* 28:2, pt. 1. (June 1965): 382; Francis, *Attitudes of U.S. Government*, 272; and Leacock, *Requiem for Revolution*, 47, 73–78.

22. Joint Chiefs of Staff, National Security Action Memorandum 119—"Civic Action," *Counterinsurgency Bluebook Fiscal Year 1966*, November 15, 1966, DDRS 242-D, 1–3, 41–42, LC; U.S. Congress, Senate, *United States Policies and Programs in Brazil*, 92d Cong., 1st sess., May 4, 5, 11, 1971, 86–88; "President's Talking Paper," President Kennedy Papers, NSF Countries—Brazil, 3/16/62–3/31/62, Box 11-13, John Fitzgerald Kennedy Library [hereafter cited as JFK Library]; Lester D. Langley, "Military Commitments in Latin America: 1960–1968," *Current History* 56:334 (June 1969): 351; and Lieuwen, *U.S. Policy in Latin America*, 101–103.

23. "Brazil as an Instrument of Western Influence in Africa," n.d., President Kennedy Papers, NSF Countries—Brazil, 6/61–7/61, Box 11-13, JFK Library; and Frederick M. Nunn, "Military Professionalism and Professional Militarism in Brazil, 1870–1970: Historical Perspectives and Political Implications," *Journal of Latin American Studies* 4, pt. 1 (May 1972): 53– 54.

24. Baines, "U.S. Military Assistance to Latin America," 477; and Stepan, *Military in Politics*, 126–127, 210–211. The military had nothing to do with Quadros's resignation and had not been plotting his overthrow. See Leacock, *Requiem for Revolution*, 36.

25. Skidmore, *Politics in Brazil*, 200–204; and Vladimir Reisky de Dubnic, *Political Trends in Brazil* (Washington, D.C.: Public Affairs Press, 1968), 54–56.

26. Amir LaBak, *1961: A crise de renuncia e a solução parlamentarista* (São Paulo: Editora Brasiliense, 1986), 15–52; Skidmore, *Politics in Brazil*, 200–204; and Flynn, *Brazil*, 219–220.

27. Skidmore, *Politics in Brazil*, 206–211; and Mario Victor, *Cinco anos que abalaram o Brasil (de Jânio Quadros ao Marechal Castelo Branco)* (Rio de Janeiro: Civilização Brasileira, 1965), 320–322.

28. Skidmore, *Politics in Brazil*, 209–215; and Victor, *Cinco anos*, 334–335. A reproduction of Lott's manifesto can be found in Sodré, *História militar*, 474.

29. Bond to Secretary of State, September 7, 1961, President Kennedy Papers, NSF Countries—Brazil, 8/61–9/61, Box 11-13, JFK Library.

30. For Brazil's independent foreign policy during the period, see San Tiago Dantas, *Política externa independente*, 15–25.

31. Flynn, *Brazil*, 235–236; and F. Parkinson, *Latin America, the Cold War, and the World Powers, 1953–1973* (Beverly Hill, Calif.: Sage, 1974), 165. According to Vernon Walters, Goulart at first agreed to support U.S. initiatives in the U.N. and OAS regarding the Cuban situation. Walters claims Goulart later failed to do so despite the advice of his military chiefs to follow the U.S. lead, especially during the missile crisis. See Walters, *Silent Missions*, 376.

32. J. M. Villar de Queiroz, "Bloco ocidental: Problemas, políticos, econômicos, e militares," *Revista Brasileira de Política Internacional* 6:2 (September 1963): 450–451.

33. CIA, Information Report, "Establishment of Soviet Military Mission Tied to Soviet Offer of Aid to Brazil," August 8, 1963, DDRS 13-F, LC; and J. O. de Meira Penna, *Política externa, segurança, e desenvolvimento* (Rio de Janeiro: Livraria AGIR Editora, 1967), 36–37, 112.

34. CIA, Office of Current Intelligence, Current Intelligence Memorandum, Subject: Communist Inroads in the Brazilian Government, September 27, 1961, JFK Library.

35. Lincoln Gordon Interview, *Veja*, March 9, 1977, 4; and Flynn, *Brazil*, 278.

36. A number of works examine the events leading to the 1964 coup. See, for example, Luíz Alberto Moniz Bandeira, *O Governo João Goulart: As lutas sociais no Brasil, 1961–1964* (Rio de Janeiro: Editora Civilização Brasileira, 1978); Renee A. Dreifuss, *1964: A conquista do estado; ação política, poder, e golpe de classe* (Petrópolis: Editora Vozes, 1981); Flynn, *Brazil*; Hélio Silva, *1964: Golpe ou contragolpe?* (Rio de Janeiro: Editora Civilização Brasileira, 1975); Schneider, *Political System of Brazil*; Skidmore, *Politics in Brazil*; Thomas E. Skidmore, *The Politics of Military Rule in Brazil, 1964–1985* (New York: Oxford University Press, 1988); Heloisa Maria Murgel Starling, *Os senhores das Gerais: Os novos inconfidentes e o golpe de militar de 1964* (Petrópolis: Editora Vozes, 1986); Dulles, *Unrest in Brazil*; Phyllis R. Parker, *Brazil and the Quiet Intervention, 1964* (Austin: University of Texas Press, 1979); and Leacock, *Requiem for Revolution*.

37. See Parker, *Brazil and the Quiet Intervention*, 72–83; and Stepan, *Military in Politics*, 124–133. For an interpretation that places U.S. support of the coup in the broader context of U.S. involvement in Brazilian society, see Jan Knippers Black, *United States Penetration of Brazil* (Philadelphia: University of Pennsylvania Press, 1977).

38. CIA, Information Report, "Plans of Military Coup Directed by General Amaury Kruel, Minister of War, Marshall Odylio Denys, General Nelson de Mello, and Others to Discuss Plans for an Anti-Government Coup," March 13, 1963, DDRS 11-E, LC; CIA, Information Report, "Plan Within Brazilian Second and Third Armies for Coup Against Goulart Administration," April 10, 1963, DDRS 12-B, LC; "Acordo Militar Brasil-EUA ainda dura um ano," *Jornal do Brasil*, March 12, 1977, 20; Robert G. Wesson, *The United States and Brazil: Limits of Influence* (New York: Praeger, 1981), 374; and José Stacchini, *Março 64: Mobilização de audacia* (São Paulo: Companhia Editora Nacional, 1965), 89–90.

39. Walters, *Silent Missions*, 374, 376, 381–382; and Parker, *Brazil and the Quiet Intervention*, 77, 236 n.

40. Townsend, *Bureaucratic Politics*, 57. For a radical nationalist view of U.S. complicity in the 1964 coup, see Edmar Morel, *O golpe começou em Washington* (Rio de Janeiro: Editora Brasiliense, 1965).

41. Schneider, *Political System of Brazil*, 121–124; Skidmore, *Politics in Brazil*, 124–133, 322–330; and Ruth Leacock, "Promoting Democracy: The United States and Brazil, 1964–1968," *Prologue* 13:2 (Summer 1981): 79.

42. Gordon to Mann, March 4, 1964, DDRS 84-E, LC; CIA, Information Report, "Plans of General Olimpio Mourão Filho to Overthrow the Brazilian Government," April 30, 1963, DDRS 12-D, LC; Black, *U.S. Penetration of Brazil*, 162–178, 220–221; Winkelman and Merrill, "United States and Brazilian Military Relations," 64; and Leacock, *Requiem for Revolution*, 128.

43. Barber and Ronning, *International Security and Military Power*, 219; Black, *Sentinels of Empire*, 43; and Leacock, *Requiem for Revolution*, 113.

44. Testimony of General George S. Beatty, in U.S. Senate, *United States Policies and Programs in Brazil*, 56. For an example of U.S. JBUSMC members' philosophical support of the coup, see General George R. Mather, Oral History, January 19, 1972, 4, USMHI.

45. General Paul L. Freeman, Oral History, November 30, 1973, 89, USMHI. For post-coup repression, see Maria Helena Moreira Alves, *State and Opposition in Military Brazil* (Austin: University of Texas Press, 1988); and Skidmore, *Politics of Military Rule*.

46. Eloy Dutra, *IBAD, sigla da corrupção* (Rio de Janeiro: Editora Civilização Brasileira, 1963), 5, 13; Stepan, *Military in Politics*, 154; Philip Agee, *Inside the Company: CIA Diary* (Harmondsworth, England: Penguin, 1975), 321; and Black, *U.S. Penetration of Brazil*, 72–77. For a detailed examination of the IPES role in the 1964 coup, see Dreifuss, *1964*.

47. Skidmore, *Politics of Military Rule*, 36; and Flynn, *Brazil*, 315–316, 329–330.

48. U.S. Congress, House, *Hearings on Foreign Assistance and Related Agencies Appropriations—1973*, 92d Cong., 2d sess., April 12, 1973, part 1.

49. For the use of torture, see Ralph Della Cava, "Torture in Brazil," *Commonweal* 6:112 (April 24, 1970): 135–141; and Archdiocese of São Paulo, *Brasil: Nunca mais*, with a preface by Dom Paulo Evarito Arns (Petrópolis: Editora Vozes, 1985). Martha K. Huggins, "U.S.-Supported State Terror: A History of Police Training in Latin America," in *Vigilantism and the State in Modern Latin America: Essays on Extralegal Violence*, ed. Martha K. Huggins (New York: Praeger 1991), 219–242, provides an analysis of U.S. training of security police.

.. 9 ..

The Dominican Republic, Vietnam, Abrogation of the Accord, and Post-1977 Relations

The success of coup plotters and the installation of Castello Branco in the presidency pulled Brazilian foreign policy back into the cold war framework. Castello Branco shelved the non-alignment stance of the Quadros and Goulart governments, abandoned praise of Cuba, and dropped efforts to extend ties to China and the Soviet bloc. The idea of creating a third force between the capitalist and communist worlds evaporated as Brazil returned to the U.S. fold. The new regime strengthened ties with the United States and renewed Brazil's importance to the inter-American defense system.[1]

Cooperation with the United States in the 1965 Dominican Republic intervention illustrated the return to the cold war ethos but also provided Brazil with the opportunity to extend its influence in the hemisphere. However, the joint venture in Caribbean politics was a watershed. Anti-communism and close military ties remained central in Brazil-U.S. relations, but after 1967 Brazil again chartered its own foreign policy course. The move toward greater independence in foreign affairs begun by Vargas in the 1950s and nurtured by Kubitschek, Quadros, and Goulart came to fruition under the military elites that did so much to oppose the constitutional presidents. The development of a local arms industry and pragmatism in world politics led to a contradiction between Brazil's increasing drive to become a world power and its deferential pro-U.S. policies, which often worked against attainment of *grandeza*.[2]

The Brazilians gradually gained the confidence to break away from U.S. dominance without destroying the special relationship between the military establishments of the two countries. Participation in the Dominican Republic occupation helped build that confidence. The decision not to send troops to Vietnam and the abrogation of the accord in 1977 confirmed the maturity of Brazil-U.S. military relations. The relationship warmed under the Reagan administration's courtship, and the Brazil-U.S. brotherhood of arms again became cordial but lacked the strength of past ties.

THE DOMINICAN REPUBLIC

Brazilian-U.S. cooperation in the Caribbean grew out of civil war in the Dominican Republic. On April 24, 1965, supporters of Dominican president Juan Bosch, who had been deposed in a military coup in 1963, took up arms. Their primary aim was to restore Bosch to office. U.S. Embassy and military officials, however, accepted the Dominican military's assertion that Bosch's return meant a victory for communism and pressed Washington for intervention. Fearing another Cuba, President Lyndon Johnson ordered units of the Eighty-second Airborne Division into the Dominican Republic. The action was unilateral; the OAS was "advised" of the deployment of U.S. troops after the fact.[3]

President Johnson faced great domestic opposition to the intervention. To blunt criticism, and to give a multilateral look to the action, the administration went to the OAS for sanction. Dispatch of the Eighty-second Airborne angered many of the OAS member states because such unilateral action portended a return to gunboat diplomacy. In 1961 a U.S. proposal for a permanent inter-American military force had met OAS refusal because of fear the United States would misuse it. The U.S. intervention in the Dominican Republic seemed to justify that earlier criticism. Now the U.S. ambassador to the OAS, Ellsworth Bunker, turned the argument around by claiming that unilateral action resulted from the lack of a hemisphere military police force. The United States had been forced to go it alone. On May 1 Bunker proposed that member states provide military contingents for duty in the strife-torn country.[4]

During discussions of Bunker's proposal the United States sent experienced diplomat Avril Harriman to Brazil as part of a regional lobbying effort for support. Harriman's work bore fruit largely because of Vernon Walters's friendship with Brazilian president Castello Branco. Walters informed Castello Branco of the purpose of the trip before Harriman arrived in Brazil and presumably added a recommendation of the troop request.[5]

On May 8 the Council of the OAS authorized the military force, designating it the Inter-American Armed Force. For propaganda purposes the council later changed the name to the Inter-American Peace Force (IAPF). The IAPF's charge was to restore peace in the embattled Caribbean country. The U.S. proposal for the joint military force came less from a belief in multilateral action than from a desire to avoid criticism. A U.S. general provided the best explanation of U.S. motives by remarking that the United States devised the IAPF concept "for the purpose of giving an international cover to American military involvement in the Dominican Republic."[6]

With the council's approval of a military force, the main question of who was to command the operation arose in light of the fact that U.S. troops already were in the Dominican Republic. As the United States would have the largest force under the scheme, U.S. officials wanted command of the IAPF under a U.S. general. General Bruce Palmer, commander of the U.S. forces already in the Dominican Republic, argued for overall U.S. command with only one brigade of U.S. troops under the jurisdiction of a Latin American officer.[7]

Brazilian Command of the IAPF

Latin American members of the OAS Council objected to a U.S. commander and demanded the subordination of all U.S. troops under the operational control of a Latin American IAPF commander. Otherwise, they said, the proposal would not be acceptable to their countries. Palmer, the JCS, and the CIA continued to oppose the idea until agreement was reached to name a Brazilian chief of the operation. The IAPF was to consist of two forces, one United States and the other Latin American. The Latin American Brigade was composed of a Brazilian infantry battalion and a "fraternity" battalion made up of a Brazilian Marine company and units from other Latin American countries, with a Brazilian in command of the latter. This composition and command structure made the Dominican intervention a U.S. and a Brazilian affair.[8]

Clash Between General Alvim and General Palmer

On May 24 the first contingent of the Brazilian Inter-American Peace Force (FAIBRAS) left Galeão Airport under its commander, Colonel Carlos de Meira Mattos. Command of the IAPF fell to General Hugo Panasco Alvim. On arriving in the Dominican Republic, Alvim immediately clashed with Palmer by making it clear that he was the chief of forces in fact as well as in name. Over Palmer's objections Alvim assumed direct command of the Eighty-second Airborne and named a Latin American officer chief of staff. Palmer still influenced the shape of operations, however, by arranging to have Alvim's headquarters staffed mainly by U.S. enlisted men. As a result, all orders to U.S. forces passed through his headquarters for modification before being forwarded to field commanders. Palmer also exerted control by having one of his staff officers detail the U.S. general's wishes to a U.S. officer on the combined staff to develop them as if they came from IAPF personnel.[9]

Palmer did not care much for Alvim or the Brazilians. He later accused the Brazilians of racism toward the Dominicans and criticized their abilities in civic action and counterinsurgency.[10] Palmer expressed his distaste of Alvim and the Brazilians so openly that Washington eventually recalled him.

Alvim provoked another controversy with Palmer during negotiations between the Dominican military and the opposing constitutionalist forces. When an agreement between the conflicting factions seemed imminent, the United States decided to remove some of its troops to deflect charges of U.S. imperialism. Alvim, however, halted the withdrawal for fear that the warring parties would discontinue talks if U.S. troops left. The incident caused an angry Palmer to remark that the United States should never have allowed a non-American full command. The Johnson administration accepted Alvim's argument only after the U.S. choice for provisional president of the Dominican Republic, Hector García-Godoy, pleaded not to be left at the mercy of his own military.[11] The decision to postpone troop withdrawal until a later date avoided conflict between allies, but the episode foreshadowed a clash that led to the replacement of both Alvim and Palmer.

When García-Godoy assumed the office of provisional president on September 3, 1965, conditions were still dangerous. A Trujillo-era army remained rebellious, and the well-armed constitutionalists were bitter, while the provisional president attempted unsuccessfully to balance the two sides. In January 1966 the Dominican Army seized the radio and television stations and threatened to bring down the shaky government. García-Godoy followed previously established procedures and formally requested that the OAS Ad Hoc Committee order IAPF forces to remove the rebellious military from the stations and set up guard patrols around the national palace. The Ad Hoc Committee, to whom Alvim was responsible, sent a letter of request rather than a direct order to the IAPF commander. Alvim, who had grown closer to the Dominican military chiefs since summer 1965, when he was prevented from launching a final offensive against the constitutionalists, refused to honor the request. Although the IAPF had earlier undertaken police functions, Alvim distrusted García-Godoy and claimed that such a move was too dangerous and that therefore a political solution would have to be found.[12]

With the support of the OAS Council, Ellsworth Bunker, de facto head of the Ad Hoc Committee, demanded that Alvim take action. Alvim reluctantly complied, but the incident had already sown the seeds of his dismissal. Following the incident Bunker made a secret visit to Brazil to seek the Brazilian general's removal. Castello Branco agreed to remove the IAPF commander only after Bunker accepted the simultaneous replacement of Palmer. To save face, Alvim and Palmer relinquished command under the guise of rotation of duty. In January 1966 Brigadier General Robert Linville replaced Palmer, and the intensely pro-U.S., ex-*Febiano* Major General Alvaro Alves da Silva Braga took command of the IAPF. Castello Branco probably agreed to Bunker's demands to preserve U.S. support for his government.[13]

The replacement of Alvim and Palmer reduced friction between the Brazilians and Americans and coincided with the winding down of operations. At the end of September 1966, after five hundred days in the Dominican Republic, the FAIBRAS returned home. Its role in the intervention had been varied and included providing security in Santo Domingo and patrolling the interior. During the five hundred days more than three thousand Brazilian Army, Marine, Navy, and Air Force personnel participated in the operation in three contingents at six-month intervals. Four Brazilian soldiers died and eight were wounded during the period.[14]

WHY BRAZIL PARTICIPATED IN THE INTERVENTION

The question of why Brazil joined in the intervention remains to be answered. Castello Branco's statement that the OAS only acted in a crisis and the "crisis or emergency is characterized almost always by the direct or indirect interest of the United States" suggests that ordinarily Brazil would not have participated in such an affair. He told Avril Harriman that Brazil would not participate without OAS sanction.[15] In public Castello Branco portrayed Brazil's participation as fulfilling its obligations under the 1947 Rio Treaty and in the fight against international communism. In a May 28, 1965, speech in Teresina, Piauí, he said Brazil entered the fray to protect the continent from communism and to ensure democracy in the Dominican Republic. By intervening in the Caribbean, Brazil would be protected because "each front of subversion is a threat to our back and puts in jeopardy the liberty of all people. Today it opens in the Caribbean and no one doubted that if it succeeds in fixing itself there, it won't delay in selecting and attacking a new victim."[16] General Silva Braga probably echoed the feelings of many officers in remarking that he hoped Brazilian participation would prove Brazil was the special friend of the United States and therefore deserved treatment different from the other Latin American countries. Brazil had proven it in World War II and now again in the Dominican Republic.[17]

Luís Viana Filho provides another view as to why Brazil participated in the IAPF. Viana Filho claims that Castello Branco did not want unilateral action by anyone, especially the United States, regarding the security of the continent. Therefore, he was willing to take a risk and engage in collective action in the Dominican Republic.[18] However, with the Americans and Brazilians providing the vast majority of the troops, this was clearly a bilateral, rather than an inter-American, operation.

Latin American critics of the Dominican intervention accused Brazil of acting as an "American viceroy" in Latin America. The United States denied the accusation. According to Lincoln Gordon, the U.S. ambassador to Brazil, the closest approach to that idea was exploration of the concept of "ideological frontiers" to protect capitalist democracy. Many Brazilian officers supported the creation of a permanent inter-American defense force for such a purpose. When the United States discarded the scheme as unviable, it quickly disappeared.[19] The idea of ideological frontiers may have originally come from the Brazilians. In conversations with President Kennedy in 1961 Kubitschek commented that lines on a map did not make the borders of countries. Rather, they were "frontiers where common principles and ideas were to be defended."[20]

More likely, Brazil participated in the IAPF because the political and military risks were low and the possible gains high. The 1964 coup and the OAS sanction minimized domestic opposition, and the Dominican affair gave an active outlet for many of the violently anticommunist officers. In addition, the operation provided valuable experience for the army, air force, and navy personnel who participated in the intervention.[21] Despite the conflict between Alvim and Palmer, Brazil gained moral capital with the United States and further cemented ties between the two militaries. The intervention also allowed the Brazilian officer corps a rare opportunity to work at its trade and must have increased the military men's confidence in their ability to manage state affairs. Perhaps more important, participation offered Brazil the chance to act with and as a great power in the region, another step on the road to *grandeza*.

THE VIETNAM WAR

The Brazilian response to the Vietnam situation was much different. Involvement was too risky because the potential for higher casualties, domestic opposition, and financial cost was greater. Moreover, no international sanction to U.S. intervention had been given by the United Nations. Little could be added to Brazil's international prestige. As a consequence, Brazil refused U.S. requests to join the battle against communism in Southeast Asia. In 1966 and 1967 President Lyndon Johnson asked for Brazilian Army, Air Force, and Navy units, along with medical doctors, for duty in Vietnam. The Brazilian government privately and publicly supported U.S. actions, including the bombing of the North, and indicated the country would go to war if the fighting escalated to a worldwide scale. But because the war was localized Brazil gave only token assistance. By January 1967 Brazilian support consisted of a small quantity of medical supplies and one thousand bags of coffee.[22]

Although the level of material support was low, many Brazilian officers favored greater involvement in Vietnam. A Department of State background paper claimed that on December 31, 1966, Pio Correa, secretary general of the Foreign Ministry, offered a formula to Ambassador Lincoln Gordon that would give the Brazilian military a presence in Southeast Asia. Reportedly speaking with the explicit approval of the navy and implicit approval of Castello Branco, Correa requested that Brazil receive two long-desired "B" class destroyers rather than older "C" class ships scheduled for delivery. Brazilian Navy personnel would take possession of the ships in Honolulu and embark on a "shakedown" cruise that took them into Vietnamese waters. The cruise would include joint exercises, which might involve the Brazilians in combat.[23]

Correa's plan offered a vehicle for gradual expansion of participation, smoothing the way for entry into Vietnam while meeting Brazilian desires for naval modernization. U.S. officials were skeptical, fearing the formula was another quid pro quo assistance deal. They believed a Brazilian contribution of naval forces in Vietnam would be followed by a request for additional vessels. That, U.S. officials feared, would lead to Brazilian demands for a return to pre-1966 levels of military assistance and for further concrete signs of the special relationship. The Department of State rejected the plan, and Brazilian forces did not go to Vietnam. The only Brazilian military who went were the FAB pilots who delivered the coffee and medical supplies.[24]

The cost of Brazilian involvement in Vietnam would have been too much for both countries. With Vietnam gobbling up valuable resources, the United States reduced MAP aid to a number of countries, including Brazil. Resources for counterinsurgency had priority over capital military goods. For example, in 1966 Brazil had the largest number of Counterinsurgency Mobile Training teams in the Canal Zone school, and the Agency for International Development (AID) in Brazil provided police training to certain military personnel. The U.S. desire to avoid quid pro quo negotiations of the type encountered in the Fernando de Noronha, Maceió, LORAN, and Article 6 negotiations also influenced the U.S. decision.[25] Besides, token forces from Brazil would have little practical value in Vietnam operations.

BRAZIL'S RETURN TO AN INDEPENDENT FOREIGN POLICY

The price for Brazilian participation in Vietnam was too great. Token participation would not garner additional military assistance, and greater attention had to be directed toward internal threats. Equally important was a return to a more independent foreign policy as Brazil became fully integrated into the world economy during the presidency of Artur da Costa e Silva (1967–1969). Costa e Silva had not been a member of the FEB or the ESG group and had no special attachments to the United States. In public and private statements he expressed his desire to move away from close identification with U.S. foreign policy. He was particularly angry over the U.S. refusal to furnish Brazil with F-5 jet fighters. Reacting to the decision, his government promptly bought French Mirage jets and continued to disengage from dependence on U.S. weaponry. Between 1968 and 1972 Brazil spent nearly $500 million on European military equipment.[26]

OPERATION TOPSY

An increase in nationalism within the military and criticism of the ubiquitous presence of U.S. officials throughout Brazil coincided with the official distancing. Of the approximately one thousand U.S. government employees in Brazil in 1967, twenty-two percent were military personnel. To blunt criticism and streamline operations, Ambassador John Tuthill initiated "Operation Topsy" to reduce personnel. Tuthill argued that it was more cost effective for technical advisory roles to be carried out by experts on temporary duty rather than to maintain a large number of people in the country. The main point of contact, he said, was the JCS, not the JBUSMC. The Johnson administration agreed, despite Department of Defense and JBUSMC objections to the reduction. From June 1966 to January 1972 U.S. military personnel, excluding attachés and embassy guards, was reduced forty-seven percent.[27]

Reduction of personnel through Operation Topsy was part of a larger scale-down of operations in Latin America. With Vietnam taking more and more resources, U.S. policy in the region favored self-sufficient military establishments. The plan called for the gradual phasing out of grant assistance while sales of military equipment increased. Grants of matériel to deal with emergency situations would be handled on an ad hoc basis. After 1968 Brazil received no new grant matériel aid from the United States, but grant training programs and military missions remained in place as a means of continuing the U.S. presence. In addition, U.S. advisers and their Brazilian trainees kept in touch through visits and personal communications.[28]

Termination of grant aid had a major impact on the Brazilian military. Reductions in matériel from the United States forced Brazil to turn to France, Great Britain, and West Germany for weaponry. More important, U.S. actions spurred a national program for arms manufacture that made Brazil the world's tenth largest arms exporter and major provider of arms to Third World nations.[29]

Brazil had long sought self-sufficiency in arms production. Early in the cold war Brazilian officers spoke of the ability to produce their own weaponry as the only guarantee of the defense of the country. A 1948 article in the *Revista do Clube Militar* claimed that arms standardization and development could be achieved by the manufacture of equipment under U.S. patent in Brazilian factories. General Carlos de Meira Mattos argued that Brazil had to be able to protect its own maritime and air routes in the South Atlantic by the end of the century. A national arms industry would remove dependence on foreigners and give Brazil the capability to carry out that mission. To those ends Brazil founded the *Empresa Brasileira de Aeronáutica,* a national aircraft industry, in 1969 and the *Indústria do Material Bélico do Brasil,* a state-owned agency charged with coordinating Brazil's seven most important factories producing military equipment, in 1975.[30]

By 1976 Brazil was producing most types of ammunition, wheeled vehicles, and some tracked vehicles. The program was so successful that Brazil has become a major exporter of military hardware. Brazilian vehicles showed up in the 1973 Arab-Israeli conflict and in the Iran-Iraq War. Brazil also sold Libya Cascavel tracked vehicles over U.S. protests in 1974. The vehicles proved their worth in the Libyan-Egyptian conflict in 1977. From 1980 through 1988 Iraq was Brazil's largest arms customer. President João Baptista de Oliveira Figuereido's response to the critics of Brazilian arms sales was that "they can object, we sell to whoever wants to buy." Sales to Middle Eastern and North African countries supported national industries and brought in hard currency and oil.[31]

Development of an indigenous arms industry allowed the Brazilian military to operate independently of the United States. Relations remained cordial, but with a handshake rather than an embrace. The JBUSMC still functioned even though there was no joint planning for operations; all efforts focused on training. According to a former president of the JBUSMC, General Idálio Sardenberg, after 1969 the military accord lapsed practically, if not officially. The JBUSMC continued operation at a reduced level, and the JBUSDC did little. Other agencies, such as the Brazilian Military Purchasing Commission, the military attaché office in Washington, and the IADB handled most of the old duties of the JBUSDC.[32]

Nuclear Technology

Relations continued on the back burner until the 1973–1974 Arab oil embargo put Brazil and the United States on a collision course. The problem was nuclear technology. Brazil's interest in nuclear energy dated from 1946, when it rejected the Baruch plan for international control of atomic energy. Brazilian leaders believed that their country held vast quantities of uranium deposits and that international control would limit Brazil's development of a nuclear capability. The Brazilian representative on the United Nations Commission on Atomic Energy, Admiral Alvaro Alberto, argued that Brazil could accept the Baruch plan only if the United States and Great Britain guaranteed Brazil a supply of oil and coal in lieu of nuclear energy.[33] Brazilian development required an energy source, and the country had as yet little known fossil fuel deposits. Beyond that, the major powers had nuclear capabilities, and the military believed that atomic energy was one of the means by which Brazil would achieve greatness.[34]

Four years later Brazil tried unsuccessfully to obtain nuclear technology by offering an exchange of uranium ore for technical know-how. Then in 1951 Brazil secretly tried to purchase gas centrifuge equipment from Germany to enrich uranium. U.S. pressure prevented the deal but only temporarily checked Brazilian desires to enter the nuclear field. Brazil finally obtained nuclear technology under a 1955 Atoms for Peace agreement, although it was in the confines of the U.S. development program, which was built on the use of enriched uranium reactor fuels. Until the USSR entered the market in 1971, the United States was the only international supplier of enriched uranium reactor fuels, and that made Brazil dependent on the United States. In the move toward greater independence in 1961 Brazil broke away by converting to natural uranium reactors.[35]

Brazil's change to natural uranium reactors was part of the larger drive to lessen U.S. dominance. After the 1964 coup and realignment with the United States the military government re-committed to enriched uranium reactors and technology. That decision put Brazil further behind its Argentine neighbor in developing nuclear capabilities and later influenced relations with the United

States. Brazil soon contracted with U.S. companies to build power reactors and signed an agreement with Washington for the supply of enriched fuel. By 1973 Brazil had received five enriched uranium reactors under the 1955 Atoms for Peace agreement. In 1974 an event far from Brazil reversed the situation and led to strained relations with the United States.[36]

The 1974 explosion of a nuclear device by India frightened the United States into announcing it would let no new contracts for enriched fuel. Of more consequence for Brazil, in July 1974 the Atomic Energy Commission informed the Brazilian government that it would not provide enriched fuel for which Brazil had contracted and paid. As Brazil had refused to sign the 1967 Nuclear Non-Proliferation Treaty, the United States feared it too would develop atomic weapons. Additionally, with the 1973–1974 Arab oil embargo the United States wanted to preserve enriched fuel for its own energy needs. The action meant Brazil had no reliable source of fuel, which rendered its energy program vulnerable.[37]

The Brazilian military was unhappy with the Atomic Energy Commission decision. Since 1971 the ESG had stressed three themes: the East-West ideological conflict, economic and technical differences between developed and non-developed countries, and the gap between nuclear and non-nuclear states. Brazil needed reliable energy and atomic weapons capability if it was to reach its potential.[38] Brazil-U.S. relations had reached a low point with the actions of the United States.

The Nixon administration tried to repair diplomatic and military ties in 1973 by transferring several World War II destroyers under the Mutual Aid Agreement and facilitating the sale of forty-two F-5E supersonic jet fighter aircraft on credit. The effort did little to compensate for the lack of a well-developed nuclear program of the scale the Brazilians wanted, especially once Argentina's Atucha reactor came on line in 1974. Brazil turned to West Germany when the United States failed to fulfill Brazilian nuclear aspirations. In 1975 Brazil signed a deal with the Kraftwerk Union in West Germany for the construction of enriched uranium reactors and for assistance in building full fabrication and processing facilities, including an enrichment plant. The U.S. Congress opposed the agreement, but the caretaker administration of Gerald Ford played down the deal. Ford's successor, Jimmy Carter, had different ideas.[39]

Inaugurated in January 1977, Carter stressed respect for human rights and the non-proliferation of nuclear technology, themes that caused Brazilians to bristle. In his first year in office Carter tried to pressure Brazil into halting its nuclear program and repudiating the West German deal. When that failed, he dispatched Vice President Walter Mondale to Europe in an attempt to force West Germany to abrogate the agreement. Carter failed to obtain German cooperation but succeeded in raising Brazilian ire. Even the pro-U.S. General Carlos de Meira Mattos attacked the effort as an "unjustified limitation" because nuclear energy production was needed not only for development but also for ends required by Brazil's "scale of power," meaning *grandeza*.[40]

NIXON AND BRAZIL

The Carter administration attacked Brazil's human rights record at the same time that it tried to prevent the nuclear reactor agreement. U.S. criticism of the military government's human rights violations dated from the end of 1968, when the Costa e Silva government turned more authoritarian. Reports of torture in the early 1970s finally led congressional critics to threaten suspension of aid, especially military assistance. The Nixon administration, relying on the South American militaries to protect U.S. interests, refused to back such calls. While cutting back economic aid to the region, the Nixon government provided as much military assistance as possible. The provision of jet fighters and navy vessels reflected Nixon's attempt to mend the bruised Brazilian relationship.[41]

Nixon's actions patched up relations with the Brazilians, but it was evident the United States needed to take a different approach to the relationship. During a December 1971 visit to the United States President Emílio Garrastazú Médici (1969–1974) reaffirmed Brazil's friendship with the United States but noted that close cooperation in the future required a new relationship. The two countries' positions could not and should not be expected to be the same with every international problem. Médici said efforts should be made "to make our policies converge without requiring that they coincide in every case."[42]

An example of a convergence of interests came in 1971 when Brazil entertained thoughts of invading Uruguay. In the late 1960s and early 1970s Uruguay suffered from internal upheaval as Tupamaro revolutionaries carried out violent acts in the hope of establishing a leftist regime. The situation caused great concern in Brasília. With elections in Uruguay scheduled for November 1971, Brazil's military government feared that the Frente Amplio, a collection of left-leaning factions, would be victorious. In that case an antagonistic government capable of supporting subversive schemes of exiled Brazilians could be dangerous. To meet that threat, the army developed "Operation Thirty Hours," a plan to prevent the leftists' assumption of power should they win the election.[43]

The Second Cavalry Division in Rio Grande do Sul was in charge of monitoring the situation. Before the elections General Arthur Moura, the U.S. Army attaché, accompanied Colonel Newton Alvarez Rodriquez of the Estado Maior do Exército and Colonel Dickson Melges Grael of the Second Cavalry Division to the Uruguay River to view and photograph a camp of leftist militants associated with the Frente Amplio. According to Grael, Moura's visit indicated the influence exercised by the U.S. government and its support of Brazil's preparations for possible action.[44]

Moura's visit was probably one of his regular trips to military bases to gather intelligence. Whether the United States officially sanctioned Brazilian plans is unknown. Regardless, Brazilian cooperation showed that military-to-military relations were still close. It also indicated a convergence of interests resulting from the shared perception of danger from the leftist militants. That confluence of interests, however, failed to prevent the Brazilians from abrogating official military ties later.

ABROGATION OF THE MILITARY ACCORD

Gerald Ford's succession to the presidency following the Nixon resignation did not alter efforts to revitalize relations. During Ford's tenure in office Congress passed the Harkin Amendment, which conditioned a country's receipt of U.S. military assistance to the state of human rights as determined by the Department of State in an annual report. The Ford administration showed no inclination to enforce the amendment with regard to the Brazilian situation, but its successor did.

The Carter administration pursued the Harkin Amendment's intent with zeal. In the first annual report, issued in early 1977, the Department of State singled out Brazil for criticism. The government of Ernesto Geisel (1974–1979), military leaders, and even opposition leaders responded swiftly to the report. Foreign Minister Antônio Francisco Azeredo da Silveira accused the United States of interfering in Brazil's internal affairs, and opposition leader Tancredo Neves blasted the U.S. position on nuclear technology and human rights. The influential pro-U.S. chief of the Civil Cabinet, General Golbery do Couto e Silva, also found the report offensive.[45]

Nationalist feelings swelled, and on March 11, 1977, Ramiro Guerreiro, secretary general of the Itamaraty, informed Ambassador John Crimmins of Brazil's intention to cancel the 1952 military accord. In three days the accord would have celebrated its twenty-fifth birthday. Brazilian society greeted the announcement as something akin to a declaration of independence. Former ambassador to the United States Maúricio Nabuco, who helped forge the accord, joined former heads of the JBUSMC Generals Nelson de Melo, Idálio Sardenberg, and Ary Presser in praising the break. Cardinal Paulo Evaristo Arns spoke for many by saying, "A great hour in the improvement of organized civil society has arrived."[46]

A NEW RELATIONSHIP

The following September Brazil announced the termination of the U.S. Navy Mission, the JBUSMC, and an agreement on a joint aerial mapping project. Although these actions ended the formal structures of military relations, they did not end the close working relationship of the two countries' military establishments. Previously agreed on procedures mandated that the accord would remain in effect one year after the announcement of its demise. In reality JBUSMC activities continued for four years after its formal dismantling to process aid in the pipeline. The special military relationship also continued in areas of common strategic interest through the chiefs of staff and other agencies, such as the attaché offices and the Brazilian Military Purchasing Commission. Unchanged as well were joint projects such as the United International Anti-Submarine Warfare naval exercises that had been in operation since 1960 and in which Brazil and the United States were the main navies. Instead of joint military activities coming out of the work of the JBUSMC, cooperation in those activities came through direct understandings by the individual service branches.[47]

Perhaps even more indicative of a continued approximation is the field of military education. Despite the abrogation of the accord, U.S. military personnel attend Brazilian courses at the ECEME, the Centro de Operações da Selva e Ação de Commando jungle school, and the Estado Maior do Exército. Brazilians attend the U.S. Field Artillery School, the Command and General Staff school at Fort Leavenworth, the Cavalry School, and the Infantry School, as well as take *estagios* dealing with engineering, parachute, war matériel, and automotive matters. Brazilian officers also teach Portuguese at the United States Military Academy at West Point and act as liaison at the Fort Leavenworth Command and General Staff School. Brazilians have made up the largest contingent of Latin American officers attending the Inter-American Defense College in Washington for a number of years. In addition, in 1989–1991 the deputy commander of the School of the Americas at Fort Benning, Georgia, was Brazilian, and the U.S. Army continues to publish an edition of the journal *Military Review* in Portuguese.[48]

Although military-to-military ties remained close, government-to-government relations suffered during the Carter administration. Carter attempted to draw the military back into an alliance in 1980 when he sent Vernon Walters to Brazil to obtain participation in a South Atlantic treaty organization based on the NATO model. Apparently the Brazilians distrusted Carter and declined to join the initiative.[49]

REAGAN AND THE BRAZILIAN MILITARY

Ronald Reagan tried to reverse the situation when he assumed the presidency, for the perception was that the United States had to restore its credibility in the region as part of the global struggle with the Soviet Union. U.S. policy emphasized a harder anti-Cuban and anti-Soviet stance, with Brazil as an important partner. In an effort to woo the Brazilian military, Reagan dropped the human rights condition for receipt of U.S. military assistance.[50]

Brazil received no substantial aid, but the action removed an irritant in relations. Reagan also named former air force officer Langhorne Motely ambassador to Brazil and provided a $1 billion emergency bridge loan to the government. Motely, who had grown up in Rio de Janeiro and knew many Brazilian officers from a stint as a general staff officer at the Southern Command in Panama during the 1960s, bypassed regular foreign office channels and dealt directly with the military. The resulting improvement in the atmosphere led to the formation of a joint military study group in 1982.[51]

Although few concrete programs have ensued from the efforts to reform close military ties, they have generated much debate in Brazil. Brazilians worry that the Memorandum of Understanding on Military Industry, signed in 1984, could enable the United States to pressure Brazil as it has in the past. Under the conditions of the memorandum, Brazil can use U.S. technology in the production of war matériel but the United States reserves the right to restrict Brazilian export of weaponry developed from U.S. technology. Brazil's large export of military hardware to countries such as Iraq, Iran, and Libya could put the United States and Brazil on a collision course. The issue is of so much concern to the Brazilians that debate among military and arms industry leaders focuses on whether Brazil should rely on imported technology. Brazil's nuclear and missile delivery programs and U.S. desires for Brazilian military involvement in the war on drugs dominated relations through the mid-1990s and promise to be the main issues in the second half of the decade.[52]

Improved relations with the Reagan government flowed from a cooperative effort between the U.S. intelligence services and the *Serviço Nacional de Informações* (SNI, or National Intelligence Service). In 1983 Brazil acted on information Ambassador Motely gave the SNI regarding the cargoes of Libyan transport planes en route to Central America. When the aircraft stopped in Brazil for refueling, Brazilian authorities examined them and found that cargo listed as medical supplies contained arms, ammunition, and small aircraft. The following year Secretary of State George Shultz signed the Memorandum of Understanding on Military Industry with the Brazilian government for the exchange of intelligence information, views on military doctrine, and possible arms technology transfers. Shultz sought a new military agreement, but Army Minister Walter Pires refused the offer.[53]

As might be expected, problems continue to crop up in the relationship. Accusations of a leveling of Brazil with its neighbors and provision of outdated equipment did not disappear, especially in the navy. Other issues of current concern between the two nation's military establishments affect the relationship. Although the Brazilian Congress passed legislation banning the transfer of sensitive technology without government approval, heavyhanded U.S. pressure has angered many in the officer corps. Similarly, U.S. desires to curb Brazil's development of an atomic bomb and a space and missile program have irritated military and civilian leaders. U.S. pressure for the Brazilian military to become involved in the war on drugs has led to further resentment among the armed services officer corps.[54]

Relations between the Brazilian and U.S. militaries remain cordial, even though not as close as in previous decades. In light of the continued relationship the 1977 break of the accord must be seen as another adaptation to national and international realities. By 1977 the efficacy of the accord and the joint commissions was minor. Brazil produced most of its military hardware needs, and other agencies dealt with military relations as required. The demise of the old structures was simply a formal recognition of the changed environment in which bilateral military affairs were conducted in the brotherhood of arms.

Notes

1.   Bandeira, *Brasil–Estados Unidos*, 141–157; McCann, "Brazilian Foreign Relations in the Twentieth Century," 17–19; Vladimir Reisky de Dubnic,

"Trends in Brazil's Foreign Policy," in *New Perspectives of Brazil*, ed. Eric N. Baklanoff (Nashville, Tenn.: Vanderbilt University Press, 1966), 95; and Townsend, *Bureaucratic Politics*, 131.

2. E. Bradford Burns, "Tradition and Variation in Brazilian Foreign Policy," *Journal of Inter-American Studies and World Affairs* 9:2 (April 1, 1967): 195–212; Perry, "Brazilian Armed Forces," 22; and Cervo and Bueno, *História da política exterior*, 339, 344–349.

3. For contemporary descriptions of the revolt and the U.S. involvement, see Philip Geyelin, "Dominican Flashback: Behind the Scenes," *Wall Street Journal*, June 25, 1965, 1; Dan Kuzman, *Santo Domingo: Revolt of the Damned* (New York: G. P. Putnam's Sons, 1965); and Tad Szulc, *The Dominican Diary* (New York: Delacorte Press, 1965). For a somewhat biased account that nevertheless contains valuable information, see Lawrence A. Yates, *Power Pack: U.S. Intervention in the Dominican Republic, 1965–1966* (Fort Leavenworth, Kans.: Leavenworth Combat Studies Institute, 1988). For a more balanced view, see Jerome Slater, *Intervention and Negotiation: The United States and the Dominican Revolution* (New York: Harper and Row, 1970). For a more current account that focuses only on the U.S. role in the crisis, see Herbert G. Schoonmaker, *Military Crisis Management: U.S. Intervention in the Dominican Republic, 1965* (New York: Greenwood Press, 1990).

4. Yates, *Power Pack*, 146–147; and Walters, *Silent Missions*, 400.

5. Luís Viana Filho, *O Governo Castelo Branco*, vol. 2 (Rio de Janeiro: Biblioteca do Exército Editora, 1975), 434; and Walters, *Silent Missions*, 400.

6. Yates, *Power Pack*, 149.

7. Ibid.

8. Ibid., 150, 153.

9. Department of Defense to Department of State, May 25, 1965, DDRS 157-D, LC; Cel. Inf. (QUEME) Carlos de Meira Mattos, "A Força Inter-Americana do Paz na República Dominica, Participação Brasileira (FAIBRAS)," *A Defesa Nacional* 53:614 (July–August 1967): 40–41; and Yates, *Power Pack*, 153.

10. General Bruce Palmer, Jr., Oral History, January 6, 1976, 179, 184, 187, USMHI; and Palmer to Vernon Walters, April 26, 1966, "Dominican Republic Fact Sheets," Bruce Palmer, Jr., Papers, USMHI.

11. Yates, *Power Pack*, 155–156; and Slater, *Intervention and Negotiation*, 132.

12. Slater, *Intervention and Negotiation*, 98, 138–148.

13. CIA, Biographic Register, "Commander Designate of the Inter-American Peace Force (IAPF)," December 1965, DDRS 15-A, LC; and Slater, *Intervention and Negotiation*, 148–149, 152.

14. Only one Brazilian soldier died in combat; three committed suicide, and one was killed by the accidental discharge of weapons. For a complete description of Brazilian operations that avoids mention of the conflict between Alvim and Palmer, see Coronel Carlos de Meira Mattos e Oficiais do FAIBRAS, *A experiência do FAIBRAS na República Dominica* (No pub. data), Appendix 3; Meira Mattos, "A Força Inter-Americana de Paz," 40–41; and Slater, *Intervention and Negotiation*, 185.

15. Castello Branco quoted in Viana Filho, *O Governo Castelo Branco*, 430; and John W. F. Dulles, *President Castello Branco, Brazilian Reformer* (College Station: Texas A&M University Press, 1980), 138–142.

16. Estado Maior do Exército, *História do Exército Brasileiro* (No pub. data), 876–877.

17. Meira Mattos, "A Força Inter-Americana de Paz," 32; Robert Reynolds, "Brazil's Overseas Military Operations," *Military Review* 46:11 (November 1966): 91; Walters, *Silent Missions*, 400; and CIA, "Commander Designate of the Inter-American Peace Force."

18. Viana Filho, *O Governo Castelo Branco*, 435.

19. Lincoln Gordon, "Brazil's Future World Role," *Orbis* 16:3 (Fall 1972): 629; Storrs, *Brazil's Independent Foreign Policy*, 425; and Stepan, *Military in Politics*, 236.

20. Memorandum of Conversation, Kubitschek and JFK, September 15, 1961, NSF Countries—Brazil, 10/61–11/61, Box 11-13, JFK Library.

21. Dulles, *President Castello Branco*, 138–142; and Ralph G. Santos, "Brazilian Foreign Policy and the Dominican Crisis: The Impact of History on Events," *The Americas* 29:1 (July 1972): 72.

22. Dulles, *President Castello Branco*, 146–147; Viana Filho, *O Governo Castelo Branco*, 443; Department of State, Background Paper, "Brazil and Vietnam," January 23, 1967, in *Visit of President Elect Costa e Silva of Brazil, January 25–27, 1967*, DDRS 199-B, LC; Santos, "Brazilian Foreign Policy," 68; and Townsend, *Bureaucratic Politics*, 132.

23. Department of State, "Brazil and Vietnam."

24. Department of State, Background Paper, "Military Assistance to Brazil," January 19, 1967, in *Visit of President Costa e Silva of Brazil, January 25–27, 1967*, DDRS-1978, 199-B, LC; and Department of State "Brazil and Vietnam."

25. Gordon to Secretary of State, January 13, 1963, DDRS 213-A/C; Joint Chiefs of Staff, *Counterinsurgency Bluebook Fiscal Year 1966*, November 15, 1966, DDRS 242-C, LC, 180, 257. For details on AID police training in Latin America, see Huggins, "U.S.-Supported State Terror," 219–242.

26. Schneider, *Brazilian Foreign Policy*, 45, 47; Wesson, *U.S. and Brazil*, 56; and Albert Fishlow, "The United States and Brazil: The Case of the Missing Relationship," *Foreign Affairs* 60 (Spring 1982): 906. Costa e Silva was also angry at the United States for delaying aid and loans and reducing the size of embassy personnel because of his government's abuse of human rights under AI-5. See Skidmore, *Politics of Military Rule*, 103. Costa e Silva took the advanced tank officer course at Fort Knox, Kentucky.

27. John W. Tuthill, "Operation Topsy," *Foreign Policy* 8 (Fall 1972): 63–64, 69–71, 79, 85; Leacock, "Promoting Democracy," 94; and Black, *U.S. Penetration of Brazil*, 221–224. MAAGs had been established with the 1954 Mutual Security Act to perform as non-combatant advisers. Unlike in other countries, the JBUSMC acted as the MAAG in Brazil. See JCS to Secretary of Defense, May 23, 1956, Appendix F, RG-218, JCS Geographic Decimal File, 1954–1956, CCS 370 (5-25-48) Sec. 14, NA.

28. Department of State to COMUSMILGP—Brazil, October 26, 1964, DDRS 184-F, LC; *U.S. Policies and Programs in Brazil*, 54–55; Clovis Briggão, "Brazil's Military Industry: A Discussion of Recent Developments" (Toronto: Latin American Research Unit, December 1979), 22–23; U.S. Congress, Senate, Hearings Before the Committee on Appropriations, *Foreign Assistance and Related Programs FY74*, 93rd Cong., 1st sess., 1974, pt. 2; and Goldhamer, *Foreign Powers in Latin America*, 175.

29. "EUA ate 75 forneceram 50% das armas para o Brasil," *O Jornal do Brasil*, March 9, 1977, 14; Robert J. Branco, *The United States and Brazil: Opening a New Dialogue* (Fort Lesley J. McNair, Washington, D.C.: National Defense University Press, 1984), 75; Frank Craig Pandolfe, "South American Naval Development, 1965–1985," unpublished ms, 1989, 92–94; and Lars Schoultz, *National Security and United States Policy Toward Latin America* (Princeton: Princeton University Press 1987), 183. The United States remained the major arms supplier to Brazil from 1966 to 1975.

30. General Carlos de Meira Mattos, *A geopolítica e as projeções do poder* (Rio de Janeiro: Livraria José Olympio Editora, S.A., 1977), 142; General Raulino de Oliveira, "Podemos fabricar nosso armamento," *Revista do Clube Militar* 94 (February 1949): 69; "Toma nota," *Revista do Clube Militar* 90 (July–August 1948): 43; Briggão, "Brazil's Military Industry," 22–28; and Branco, *U.S. and Brazil*, 84–86. For detail on Brazil's arms industry, see Patrice Franko Jones, *The Brazilian Defense Industry: A Case Study of Public-Private Collaboration* (Boulder, Colo.: Westview Press, 1991). For the best view of Brazil's drive for autonomy in the production of military goods, see Hilton, "Armed Forces and Industrialists in Modern Brazil," 629–673.

31. Figueiredo quoted in Michael Sieniawski, "Brazil Clashes with Open-Door Policy on Arms Sales," *Christian Science Monitor* 74:224 (November 12, 1982): 15; Perry, "Brazilian Armed Forces," 23; Branco, *U.S. and Brazil*, 87; McCann, *A nação armada*, 106–108; and Scott D. Tollefson, "From Collor to Iatmar Franco: U.S.-Brazilian Security Relations and Their Implications for Civil-Military Dynamics in Brazil" (Paper presented at the Middle Atlantic Council of Latin American Studies, Pennsylvania State University, University Park, Pennsylvania, April 3, 1993).

32. "Nabuco aplaude," 19; U.S. Senate, *U.S. Policies and Programs in Brazil*, 89–90; McCann, *A nação armada*, 109.

33. General Carlos de Meira Mattos, Brasil, 92–93; Wesson, *U.S. and Brazil*, 76; and Bandeira, *Presença*, 354–368.

34. Max G. Mainwaring, "Nuclear Power in Brazil," *Parameters* 14:4 (Winter 1984): 45.

35. Juan E. Gugliamelli, *Argentina, Brasil, y la bomba atómica* (Buenos Aires: Tierra Nueva, 1976), 8; Stephan M. Gorman, "Security, Influence, and Nuclear Weapons: The Case of Argentina and Brazil," *Parameters* 9:1 (March 1979): 57; and Wesson, *U.S. and Brazil*, 76–77.

36. Gorman, "Security, Influence, and Nuclear Weapons," 157; and Wesson, *U.S. and Brazil*, 79–81.

37. Wesson, *U.S. and Brazil*.

38. Norman Gall, "Atoms for Brazil, Dangers for All," *Foreign Policy* 23 (Summer 1976): 155–201; and Wesson, *U.S. and Brazil*, 76.

39. Gall, "Atoms for Brazil"; Gorman, "Security, Influence, and Nuclear Weapons," 57; Wesson, Limits of Influence, 76, 79–81; and Branco, U.S. and Brazil, 74–75. Influential diplomat George Ball lambasted Ford and Secretary of State Henry Kissinger for not personally intervening to prevent the Brazilian-German deal. See George Ball, Diplomacy for a Crowded World (Boston: Little, Brown 1976), 266.

40. U.S. Congress, House, Hearings Before the Subcommittee on Inter-American Affairs of the Committee on International Relations, 95th Cong., 2d sess., June 27, 28, July 19, 20, August 2, 9, 1978, 77–78; Albert Fishlow, "Flying Down to Rio: Perspectives on U.S.-Brazil Relations," Foreign Affairs 57 (Winter 1978–1979): 387; Schneider, Brazil, 51; and Wesson, U.S. and Brazil, 75.

41. Branco, U.S. and Brazil, 74–75; Skidmore, Politics of Military Rule, 154–156, 196; "Harris Addresses Democrats Here," New York Times, October 7, 1971, A29; "Brazil Will Retain Curbs on Civil Liberties," New York Times, July 5, 1972, C8; and Baily, U.S. and the Development of South America, 118.

42. Embaixada do Brasil—Washington, Visita do Presidente Emílio Garrastazú Médici aos Estados Unidos da America, 7 a 9 de Dezembro de 1971, Discursos do Presidente do Brasil e comunicado conjunto (No pub. data), 2.

43. Cel. Dickson M. Grael, Aventura, corrupção, e terrorismo: A somba da impunidade (Petrópolis: Editora Vozes, 1985), 11, 13–14; and Eduardo Varela, "Invadir a Uruguai: Os planos do III exército sob Médici," O Jornal do Pais, May 23–29, 1985, 17.

44. Grael, Aventura, 15.

45. Hugo Abreu, O outro lado do poder (Rio de Janeiro: Editora Nova Fronteira S.A., 1979), 56–57; "Tancredo ve tres pontos de atrito," 15; U.S. House, Hearings Before the Subcommittee on Inter-American Affairs, 80–81; Skidmore, Politics of Military Rule, 154–156, 196–197; and Baily, U.S. and Development of South America, 125.

46. "Nabuco aplaude"; "Brasil denuncia acordo militar" and Carlos Prado, "O fim do acordo militar," Opinão, March 18, 1977, 5.

47. "Linha credito não foi usada," O Jornal do Brasil, March 12, 1977; "Acordo militar Brasil-EUA"; "Unitas preserva segurança e solidifica pan-americanismo," Revista do Clube Militar 172:44 (February 1970): 20–23; Skidmore, Politics of Military Rule, 197; Pandolfe, "South American Naval Developments," 239; and author interview with Mason. The Military Liaison Office was the last vestige of the U.S. section of the JBUSMC. It closed operations shortly after this interview.

48. Author interview, source wishes to remain unnamed, Inter-American Defense College, Fort Lesley J. McNair, Washington, D.C., June 8, 1989; and "Militares Brasileiros ja tem sua própria doutrina e dispensam a estrangeira," O Jornal do Brasil," March 12, 1977. For information on Brazilians at the School of the Americas, see U.S. Army, Catálogo de cursos para 1990 (Fort Benning, Ga.: Escuela de las Americas, October 1989). The Inter-American Defense College was founded in 1962. Each year from forty to sixty Latin American colonels and lieutenant colonels take a ten-month period of coursework.

49. Fleischer, "Brazil," 91.

50. According to Harold Molineu, the Reagan administration's backing away from the human rights emphasis in U.S. policy and moving toward one that criticized abuse by regimes of the totalitarian Left (as defined by Reagan officials) still had as a mission the "democratizing" of Latin America. See Harold Molineu, *U.S. Policy Toward Latin America: From Regionalism to Globalism* (Boulder, Colo.: Westview Press, 1986), 144–150, 176. In a newer volume Howard Wiarda depicts the Reagan administration policy toward Latin America as one of greater pragmatism and centrism. See Howard J. Wiarda, *American Foreign Policy Toward Latin America in the 80s and 90s: Issues and Controversies from Reagan to Bush* (New York: New York University Press, 1992), 25.

51. Fleischer, "Brazil"; Michael Kryzanek, *U.S.–Latin American Relations* (New York: Praeger, 1985), 157; and Fishlow, "U.S. and Brazil," 918.

52. Monica Hirst, "The United States and the Middle Powers in Latin America: Mexico and Brazil," in *Latin American Views of U.S. Policy*, ed. Robert Wesson and Harold Munoz (New York: Praeger, 1986), 100–101; and Tollefson, "From Collor to Itamar Franco."

53. Fleischer, "Brazil," 91–92. Also see *O Jornal do Brasil*, February 5, 1984, 21; February 7, 1984, 16; and February 19, 1984, 8.

54. For an excellent analysis of current issues between the United States and Brazilian militaries, see Tollefson, "From Collor to Itamar Franco."

.. 10 ..

The Brotherhood

With the close of World War II, the special military ties created between the United States and Brazil stood at a crossroads. Vast changes had occurred on the international scene with the fall of fascism and the rise of the cold war between the world's two great powers and their allies. The new post-war configuration guaranteed that old alliances would undergo a metamorphosis, but it was unclear how that transformation would evolve. Nowhere was this more evident than in the military relationship between Brazil and the United States. The assumption by the United States of the role of leader of the non-communist world, with accompanying greater responsibilities, and Brazil's drive for great nation status affected the nature of the Brazilian-American military alliance and ensured constant adjustment to maintain the special nature of the relationship.

Anti-communist cold war strategy drove military relations with Brazil after World War II, but confused U.S. policy in the early post-war period worried the Brazilians. As the exigencies of cold war geopolitics focused U.S. foreign policy elsewhere, many Brazilians came to resent the United States for giving European and Asian countries the lion's share of aid. They felt the United States had taken advantage of Brazil rather than treating it as a partner, as was expected. When asked if that view was justified, General Matthew Ridgeway replied, "I am sure we did, without question."[1]

The relationship remained close but underwent great change as both countries adapted to foreign policies shaped by new internal and international pressures. Brazil continued to be important to U.S. hemispheric defense plans, but confused U.S. policy in the early post-war period made the Brazilians question if ties remained special. Equally distressing were the multilateral approach to U.S. foreign policy, especially where it involved rapprochement with Argentina, and the struggle among government agencies for control of policy making in the United States.

Brazil cooperated with the United States despite these problems but conditioned cooperation on the amount and quality of U.S. assistance and how it affected national and/or institutional objectives. Thus, cooperation with the United States was good in creating the Escola Superior de Guerra, in signing the 1952 military accord, and in occupying the Dominican Republic. Cooperation suffered, however, in the requests for Brazilian troops for Korea and Vietnam. The same criteria applied to negotiations for the missile-tracking, radio, and LORAN radar stations and installations, but with some difference. The latter menaced neither national nor institutional objectives, which allowed Brazil to adopt a harder stance in bargaining for assistance.

The issue of U.S. aid was an important one to the Brazilians. The Truman administration attempted to provide as much assistance as it considered possible given the worldwide commitments of the United States. In March 1948 President Truman ordered the Department of State to expedite Ambassador Pawley's request for a technical mission to Brazil and told the Treasury Department to extend a stabilization loan to the wartime ally. Regarding the loan, Truman pointed out that Brazil had requested the loan at least a half dozen times without a response from Treasury. The president's support for the Inter-American Military Cooperation Act pointed to his efforts to maintain the specialness of military ties.[2]

Although the Inter-American Military Cooperation Act failed to pass Congress, Truman's support of the military's Latin American policy was one aspect of his administration's strategy to sustain U.S. economic, military, and political influence in the region. The United States did not expect an attack anywhere in the hemisphere or believe its bilateral defense alliances, especially with Brazil, would directly strengthen the West's military capabilities should there be conflict with the Soviet Union. The goal was to prevent any European or Soviet influence while undercutting nationalist, statist doctrines and policies. The dependent military relationships also provided leverage to protect U.S. investments. The primary military considerations were to standardize arms and to preserve access to Brazil's air facilities and strategic resources. CIA estimates claimed that control of those resources, along with civil air transportation, would allow the shipment of approximately 2,365 tons of matériel and between 10,800 and 27,000 troops per month to conflict areas.[3]

Both Brazil and the United States considered staffing an important part of influencing the other. The issue, however, seemed to be more a problem for the United States than for Brazil.. While the U.S. military attempted to implement its hemisphere defense program in Brazil, personnel problems of the JBUSMC limited effective operation of the commission and threatened to disrupt efforts to exert influence. Personnel problems that were solved early in the war reappeared immediately in the post-war period and caused disarray in the Rio commission, which led to bad feelings and poor cooperation. Although Washington quickly and efficiently dealt with such situations, much of the problem was the result of the arrogance of senior U.S. officers assigned to Brazil.

Interservice rivalry exacerbated personnel problems. If fuzzy U.S. foreign policy during the early post-war period disconcerted Brazilians, the petty conflicts among the U.S. Army, Navy, and Air Force delegates on the JBUSMC caused even greater concern. Each service section was an independent, autonomous unit, and disputes over jurisdiction were frequent. Members of the commission recognized that post-war service rivalry reflected poorly on the U.S. military.[4] The infighting that occurred when, as a result of the U.S. Congress's post-war economizing drive, the U.S. commission members received orders to conserve resources proved especially disruptive. The Joint Chiefs of Staff suggested that the different service branch sections of the commission pool their resources, such as transportation. Jealousies over who was to control the assigning of resources led to arguments that hindered communication among U.S. delegates and presented an embarrassing disunity to their Brazilian colleagues.[5]

Dissension between Brazilian and U.S. commission members created obstacles to cooperation as well. The problems were not new, nor were they limited to the military. Perceptions, and misperceptions, often were at the root of misunderstandings. The lack of knowledge of each other's culture and reasons for certain views on particular issues increased tensions in the relationship that could have been avoided with minimal effort. In the early stages of World War II General Miller had many disagreements with Góes Monteiro and had little respect for the Brazilian chief of staff. Miller even accused Góes Monteiro of blocking cooperative efforts and giving aid to Nazi agents in Brazil. Dean Acheson was even more disparaging after the war. In his autobiography, *Present at the Creation*, Acheson spoke condescendingly about his impressions of Getúlio Vargas during a 1952 trip to South America.[6]

Classic symptoms of culture shock often caused initial negative attitudes among senior U.S. officers assigned to the JBUSMC. Major General Robert M. Webster's first few months in Rio de Janeiro in 1950 as the chief of the air section of the JBUSMC did little to excite him about his new post. By March 1951, however, the efforts of Brazilian officers and adjustment to the new environment had caused Webster to become more enthusiastic. Noting the change in him, former chief of the air section Major General Robert L. Walsh commented that "eventually they usually get all of us."[7]

To be sure, many military and civilian leaders understood the importance of assigning knowledgeable officers to Latin America. In 1948 General Albert C. Wedemeyer, director of the U.S. Army's Plans and Operations Division, complained to Matthew Ridgeway of his difficulties in trying to impress on his brother officers in Washington the value of the region. Wedemeyer argued that it was vital for U.S. personnel to have an understanding of the temperament of the Latin American officers with whom they had to deal. Assistant Secretary of Defense H. Struve Hensel echoed Wedemeyer's complaint several years later when speaking of the MAAG. Hensel lamented the deficiency of officers equipped with the diplomatic skills necessary for service in strategic locations such as Brazil.[8]

Like many North American counterparts, Latin American officers, especially in Brazil, often cared little for the U.S. connection. A 1947 Department of State biographical sketch of Vice Admiral Sylvio de Noronha spoke of the naval officer's efforts to combat "reactionary" officers in the Brazilian Navy who resisted "the modernizing influence" of the U.S. Navy Mission. An anti-American strain in the Brazilian officer corps became glaringly evident a few years later over the issue of proposed involvement in the Korean conflict.[9] The gradual replacement of World War II–generation officers by younger men further distanced large segments of the Brazilian officer corps.

Despite anti-American or anti-Brazilian tendencies in the military establishments of both countries, personal friendships between officers was common. Before Matthew Ridgeway departed for the Rio Conference in 1947, Paul Schoppel of the Army Department wrote Comandante Raul Reis of the military household at Catete Palace asking that the U.S. general be treated as a "brother" because "he is one of us." Schoppel sent variations of the same letter to General Armando T. Trompowski de Almeida, the minister of aeronautics, and to Colonel Edmundo Macedo Soares e Silva, the governor of the State of Rio de Janeiro. Ridgeway apparently received the favored treatment Schoppel requested, for in discussing the military relationship with Brazil, he claimed that "it was very easy to work with the Brazilians," whereas the Mexicans were "stand-offish, very stiff." The Brazilian relationship was different, claimed Ridgeway. It was "closer than any of the others." The perception of a brotherhood of arms also found reinforcement in the 1972 boast of General George R. Mather, chief of the U.S. delegation to the JBUSMC in the early 1960s, that many of his old and dear friends, such as Médici and Castello Branco, were in positions of political power.[10]

Brazilian military policymakers shared the belief that influence was greater when dealing with friends. Experiences with Generals Kroner, Shugg, and Gerhardt caused the Brazilians great concern about who among the North American military were their friends. This attitude became particularly evident during the 1952 negotiations for a mutual security agreement, when opposition to the extension of the military relationship was strong in certain Brazilian military and political circles. To blunt opposition, the most powerful segments of Brazilian politics—the president, Itamaraty, and the military—recognized the need for a friendly advocate in the U.S. military. The Brazilians felt they had such a man in General Charles L. Mullins, the chief of the U.S. delegation to the JBUSMC. The problem for the Brazilians was that Mullins was due for reassignment in

October 1952 and retirement in January 1953. President Vargas, Foreign Minister Neves da Fontoura, and General Góes Monteiro expressed their concern to Ambassador Herschel V. Johnson and requested that the United States make an exception and extend Mullins's assignment in Rio. Believing that friendship equaled influence and therefore cooperation, the Joint Chiefs of Staff and the secretary of defense agreed that Mullins should stay in Brazil at least until a new military agreement had been reached.[11]

Brazilian concern over friendly advocates reflected anxiety about the relationship adapting to new geopolitical realities. To modernize its military, Brazil required the friendship of the United States and became concerned over any proposed changes in the agencies that oversaw military relations. Proposals to consolidate the various activities or to diminish their importance always met with Brazilian opposition. Conversely, the Brazilians initiated proposals to upgrade the structures of the relationship as a means of assuring Brazil's special place in U.S.–Latin American military relations. Only after Brazil developed its own arms industry did the importance of maintaining the Rio and Washington military commissions decline.

Although leaders in both Brazil and the United States believed there was a connection between friendship and influence, it would be a mistake to assume the brotherhood of arms took precedent over institutional and national concerns. Carlos de Meira Mattos's admonition to the Brazilian delegates to the Tenth Inter-American Conference in Caracas not to forget the injustice of U.S. post-war economic policy in Latin America bears this out.[12] Brazil's decision not to participate in the Korean conflict and in the Vietnam War showed that influence was tenuous at best. Personal and institutional friendship spoke less of influence and more of common views among men engaged in the same profession. The split in the Brazilian military, especially between the nationalists and the Sorbonne group, also indicates that not all members of the same institution share the same ideas on goals or the best means to achieve them. The dominance of the pro-U.S. officers in post-war Brazilian military politics, however, ensured that a special relationship with the U.S. military would continue as a staple of Brazil's foreign policy.

Brazilian geopolitical thought led the South American giant to support the Western democracies in World War I, World War II, and the post-war world. Brazil's dominant military thinkers viewed the U.S. alliance as paramount throughout most of the course of the period studied. Writing in the 1970s, Brazil's two major geopoliticians, Generals Carlos de Meira Mattos and Golbery do Couto e Silva, emphasized the relationship but regarded it as associational rather than subordinate. The U.S. tie reflected shared perceptions of the world and offered the best means to develop the military so it could carry out its mission. Nevertheless, Meira Mattos and Golbery, and many of the pro-U.S. officers, were nationalists who did not blindly follow U.S. leadership.[13]

Some scholars conclude that contact with U.S. officers and a resulting modified emulative process may have contributed to the Latin American militaries' intervention into national politics. However, other evidence suggests that the Latin Americans were not emulating the United States as much as they were following traditional cultural paths. Leaders of the Latin American militaries perceived intervention in civilian affairs as a means through which legitimate concerns received proper consideration in national decision making. Whereas the U.S. military's structured pattern of influence makes it a pressure group, the Latin American military is an active political player. Thomas Skidmore raises the same question of influence in regard to the Brazilian officer corps. Although the officer corps had been a major actor in politics since 1889, its role in policy making did not become routine until after 1930. Hence, what effect, if any, did the U.S. officers have on the political actions of their Brazilian colleagues?[14]

Alfred Stepan also questions U.S. influence in examining the Brazilian military's adoption of counterinsurgency doctrine. He cites data that show the minuscule number of officers attending U.S. service schools. More telling to Stepan was the ESG's concern with revolutionary warfare in the 1950s at a time when U.S. preoccupation was with nuclear war. Both points are valid but may ignore the fact that many Brazilian officers received training from U.S. advisers at the schools located in Brazil. In addition, according to Stepan's study, eighty percent of the generals involved in the conspiracy to overthrow João Goulart received training at U.S. service schools, which seems to lend weight to the contention that the U.S. military influenced the Brazilian military's actions.[15]

Closer examination reveals that if U.S. officers influenced their Brazilian brothers in arms, it was a case of preaching to the converted. Any influence was indirect and occurred through the supportive means of confidence building and shared beliefs. Knowledge of techniques and methods of repression was widespread and well established with or without the special relationship. Certainly, the type and amount of U.S. assistance allowed the Brazilians to place greater emphasis on different responses to new perceived threats, such as occurred with civic action and counterinsurgency. However, when the officers in control of the Brazilian military determined that a course of action did not serve national and/or institutional needs, they did not succumb to U.S. wishes. The decisions not to send troops to Korea and Vietnam are examples of this proposition. In short, Brazilian military elites needed little tutoring.

Nevertheless, throughout the course of the formal relationship Brazilian-U.S. military ties remained special. Post-war issues and the positions taken by both groups strained the friendship, whose importance faded for other reasons. Post-war relations reflected an adaption to internal and international political, economic, and social pressures. Despite the demands on the United States as the leader of the capitalist world after 1945, the government and the military tried to provide the Brazilians with military hardware and assistance in training and in extraconstitutional activities. As Robert W. Porter, commander in chief of the U.S. Southern Command from 1965 to 1969, explained, the U.S. military felt Brazil was an important element in the defense of the United States.[16]

The Brazilians felt the U.S. connection was important to its development as a great nation, supported the anti-communist crusade in international councils and in the Dominican Republic, and provided basing and communications sites. Only when internal pressures or a conflict of institutional interests arose were there differences, such as disagreements over the quantity and quality of military assistance. As Brazil and the Brazilian military evolved into their more modern present state, the need for the U.S. tie became less crucial and made a formal break possible.

Personal and institutional friendships remain close, as evidenced in the field of military education, despite the break of the 1952 accord. The Brazilian military no longer relies on the United States for arms or guidance, but neither has it severed the symbiotic relationship completely. Nevertheless, debate over a resumption of close military relations with the United States continues to be a staple of Brazilian military politics. New issues have arisen that will continue to test the nature of Brazil–United States military relations.

In 1981 Robert W. Porter articulated the reasons the United States wanted to maintain military cordiality with Brazil when he said Brazil was a country to be reckoned with in the near future. The United States should improve its ties, he argued, because "they're [the Brazilians] going to have a great influence on what happens in the western hemisphere by the year 2000." Brazil's growing military capability and economic potential make it a country to contend with in Department of Defense eyes.[17] Porter's prediction will be tested in the coming years. New issues have arisen that will continue to test Brazil–United States military relations. If reports of a Brazil-Argentina arms race, Brazilian imperial designs toward smaller neighbors, Brazilian attainment of atomic capabililties, Brazilian arms transfers, and disagreements over drug trafficking prove true, the brotherhood of arms may again become one of the dominant factors in Brazil-U.S. relations, but in an adversarial sense.[18]

NOTES

1. Ridgeway, Oral History, May 10, 1977, USMHI, 24; and Sam Pope Brewer, "Latin American Resentment Smolders over Alleged Neglect by the United States," *New York Times*, June 16, 1952, 13.

2. Truman to Robert A. Lovett, March 10, 1948; and Truman to Secretary of the Treasury, March 10, 1948, Subject Files, Foreign Affairs—Brazil, PSF-171, HST Library.

3. CIA, Intelligence Reports, "Importance to the U.S. of Latin American Civil Air Transport," ORE 22-49, October 2, 1950, PSF-256, HST Library; Baily, *U.S. and Development of South America*, 67; Carone, *A república liberal*, 63; Francis, *Attitudes of U.S. Government*, 270; Green, *Containment of Latin America*, 262, 264; and Rabe, "Inter-American Military Cooperation," 144.

4. Freeman, Oral History, 79–80.

5. Ibid.

6. Acheson, *Present at the Creation*, 667; and Hilton, *Hitler's Secret War*, 240.

7. Major General R. L. Walsh to Major General Robert M. Webster, March 2, 1951, RG-218, JCS Military Commissions, U.S.-Brazil, BDC 4060, Foreign Military Assistance Program, Box 2, NA.

8. Wedemeyer to Ridgeway, January 16, 1948, Matthew B. Ridgeway Papers, Box 10, USMHI; and Hensel to Assistant Secretary of the Army, Assistant Secretary of the Air Force, and Assistant Secretary of the Navy, May 26, 1955, RG-218, JCS Central Decimal File, 1954–1956, CCS 092 (8-22-46) (2) Sec. 12, NA.

9. Department of State, Division of Biographical Information, "Vice-Admiral Sylvio de Noronha," PSF—Trip Files, August 31–September 20, 1947, Box 103, HST Library.

10. Paul H. Schoppel to Ridgeway, Ruben de Mello, Armando T. Trompowski de Almeida, and Cel. Edmundo Soares e Silva, August 13, 1947, Matthew B. Ridgeway Papers, Personal Files, January 1947–June 1948, Box 10; and Ridgeway, Oral History, May 10, 1977, 3, 5.

11. Neves da Fontoura to Herschel V. Johnson, July 29, 1952; David Bruce to Robert Lovett, August 25, 1952; and C. P. Cabell to Secretary of Defense, September 19, 1952, RG-218, JCS Central Decimal File, 1948–1950, CCS 300 (9-24-48), Sec. 2, NA. Mullins served longer than any other American officer as chief of the U.S. delegation of the JBUSMC.

12. Roger W. Fontaine, *The Foreign Policy-Making Process in Brazil* (Ann Arbor, Mich.: University Microfilms, 1970), 193.

13. Meira Mattos, *A geopolítica e as projeções do poder*, 142–143; Child, "Geopolitical Thinking," 90–92; and Honório Rodrigues, "Foundations of Brazil's Foreign Policy," 331.

14. Skidmore, *Politics in Brazil*, 329–330; Fontaine, *Foreign Policy-Making Process in Brazil*, 169; and William E. Kane, *Civil Strife in Latin America: A Legal History of U.S. Involvement* (Baltimore: Johns Hopkins University Press, 1972), 178. Stepan points out that the military viewed itself as representing the people's concerns, referring to themselves as *o povo farda* (the people in uniform). See Stepan, *Military in Politics*, 131.

15. Stepan, *Military in Politics*, 126–131; and Alfred Stepan, *The State and Society: Peru in Comparative Perspective* (Princeton: Princeton University Press, 1978), 130–131, 240.

16. General Robert W. Porter, Oral History, 1981, USMHI, 475.

17. Ibid.; and U.S. Congress, House, Committee on Armed Services, "United States Military Posture for FY1982," Hearings on Military Posture and H.R. 26144 and H.R. 2970, 97th Cong., 1st sess., 1981, pt. 1, 109. The Department of State does not share Defense Department feelings about the Brazilian military. See U.S. Congress, House, Committee on Foreign Affairs, Subcommittee on Inter-American Affairs, *United States–Brazilian Relations*, 97th Cong., 2d sess., 1982, 39.

18. Wiarda, *American Foreign Policy Toward Latin America*, 74. Only Argentina and Brazil possess aircraft carriers among the Latin American navies. Both are of World War II vintage. See Schoultz, *National Security*, 184. For potential flashpoints in Brazil–United States relations, see Tollefson, "From Collor to Itamar Franco."

APPENDIX A
JBUSMC Country Delegation Chiefs

BRAZIL

6 Jan. 43–10 Jan. 45	Gen. Div. Crisovão de Castro Barcellos
31 Jan. 45–26 Nov. 46	Gen. Bda. Alvaro Fiuza de Castro
26 Nov. 46–10 Jan. 52	Gen. Ex. Salvador Cesar Obino
29 Apr. 53–31 Aug. 54	Ten. Brig. Eduardo Gomes
28 Jan. 55–9 Dec. 55	Maj. Brig. Ajalmar Vieira Mascarenhas
30 Dec. 55– 5 Mar. 58	Gen. Ex. Aristotles de Souza Dantas
9 Apr. 58–10 Dec. 58	Gen. Ex. João Carlos Barreto
23 Dec. 58–9 Feb. 61	Gen. Ex. Osvaldo Cordeiro de Farias
9 Feb. 61–27 Sept. 61	Gen. Ex. Nelson de Melo
27 Sept. 61–24 Jan. 63	Gen. Ex. Nestor Souto de Oliveira
24 Jan. 63–22 May 64	Gen. Ex. Nestor Penha Brasil
3 July 64–22 Nov. 65	Ten. Brig. Francisco de Assis Correa de Melo
10 Dec. 65–29 Sept. 66	Gen. Ex. Nilo Augosto Guerreiro Lima
21 Dec. 66–20 Mar. 67	Alm. Esq. José Moreira Maia
18 Apr. 67–4 Nov. 69	Alm. Esq. Murillo Vasco do Valle Silva
2 Dec. 69–29 Oct. 71	Gen. Ex. Idálio Sardenberg
29 Oct. 71–2 Dec. 71	Ten. Brig. Ary Presser Bello
2 Dec. 71–4 Nov. 74	Ten. Brig. José Vaz da Silva
4 Nov. 74–30 Aug. 77	Alm. Esq. Arnaldo de Negreiros Januzzi
30 Aug. 77–19 Sept. 78	V. Alte. Marcio de Faria Neves Pereira de Lyra

UNITED STATES

Jan. 43–May 43	R. Adm. Augustin Toutan Beauregard, USN
May 43–Feb. 43	Capt. Walter S. Macaulay, USN
Sept. 43–Feb. 45	Brig. Gen. Hayes A. Kroner, USA
Feb. 45–Mar. 46	Brig. Gen. Byron E. Gates, USAF
Mar. 46–Feb. 47	R. Adm. Leland P. Lovett, USN
Feb. 47–June 47	Maj. Gen. William H. H. Morris, USA
June 47–Sept. 52	Maj. Gen. Charles L. Mullins, USA
Sept. 52–Apr. 55	Maj. Gen. William A. Beiderlinden, USA
Apr. 55–Apr. 57	Maj. Gen. Robert F. Sink, USA
Apr. 57–June 59	Maj. Gen. William J. Verbeck, USA
June 59–Dec. 61	Maj. Gen. Raymond C. Bell, USA
Dec. 61–Sept. 64	Maj. Gen. George C. Mather, USA
Sept. 64–Nov. 66	Maj. Gen. James W. Totten, USA
Nov. 66–Nov. 68	Maj. Gen. Robert L. Linville, USA
Nov. 68–July 70	Maj. Gen. Richard J. Seitz, USA
Aug. 70–Aug. 72	Maj. Gen. George S. Beatty, Jr., USA
Aug. 72–Aug. 73	Maj. Gen. Alexander R. Bolling, Jr., USA
Aug. 73–July 75	Maj. Gen. Maurice W. Kendall, USA
July 75–Jan. 77	Maj. Gen. Charles L. Spragins, USA
Jan. 77–May 78	R. Adm. William M. Callaghan, Jr., USN
May 78–Sept. 78	Col. Billy M. Mobley, ad. interim, USAF

APPENDIX B
Military Assistance and Sales to Brazil
(Dollars in Thousands)

Military Sales Agreements

FY 1950–FY 1967	71,485
FY 1968	2,265
FY 1969	11,348
FY 1970	2,458
FY 1971	17,901
FY 1972	32,619
FY 1973	14,857
FY 1974	71,497
FY 1975	27,222
FY 1976	11,789
FY 1977	14,277
FY 1950–FY 1977	277,718

Statistics on military sales and assistance vary according to the agency or organization conducting the survey. For example, the figures in the U.S. Agency for International Development's "U.S. Overseas Loans and Grants" and in the U.S. Senate's "U.S. Policies and Programs in Brazil" do not match those of the U.S. Defense Security Assistance Agency. This is particularly true for the 1945–1950 period.

Foreign Military Sales Deliveries

FY 1950–FY 1967	39,862
FY 1968	15,684
FY 1969	18,171
FY 1970	11,655
FY 1971	2,472
FY 1972	12,918
FY 1973	23,265
FY 1974	20,800
FY 1975	38,804
FY 1976	32,676
FY 1977	9,941
FY 1950–FY1977	226,248

Foreign Military Sales Financing Program

	DOD Direct	DOD Guaranty
FY 1955–FY1967	20,868	32,388
FY 1968	10,796	7,704
FY 1969	—	—
FY 1970	—	—
FY 1971	9,400	—
FY 1972	7,889	12,000
FY 1973	14,962	—
FY 1974	20,000	25,300
FY 1975	27,500	32,500
FY 1976	—	44,000
FY 1977	—	—
FY 1955–FY 1977	111,415	153,892

Military Assistance Program: Includes Military Assistance Funded and Excludes Training

FY 1950–FY 1967	205,239
FY 1968	1,681
FY 1969	—
FY 1970	—
FY 1971	—
FY 1972	—
FY 1973	—
FY 1974	—
FY 1975	—
FY 1976	—
FY 1977	—
FY 1950–FY 1977	206,920

International Military Education and Training Program: Includes Military Assistance Service Funded

FY 1950–FY 1967	10,068
FY 1968	875
FY 1969	754
FY 1970	776
FY 1971	689
FY 1972	668
FY 1973	662
FY 1974	816
FY 1975	771
FY 1976	654
FY 1977	59
FY 1950–FY 1977	16,792

International Military Education and Training Program Deliveries/Expenditures: Includes Military Assistance Service Funded

FY 1950–FY 1967	9,342
FY 1968	1,285
FY 1969	868
FY 1970	712
FY 1971	860
FY 1972	667
FY 1973	641
FY 1974	934
FY 1975	702
FY 1976	612
FY 1977	33
FY 1950–FY 1977	16,656

Summary of Students Trained Under International Military Education and Training Program

FY 1950–FY 1967	5,082
FY 1968	590
FY 1969	620
FY 1970	555
FY 1971	482
FY 1972	300
FY 1973	279
FY 1974	258
FY 1975	273
FY 1976	218
FY 1977	—
FY 1950–FY 1977	8,657

Source: U.S. Defense Security Assistance Agency, Data Management Division, *Foreign Military Sales and Military Assistance Facts* (Washington, D.C.: U.S. Defense Security Assistance Agency, Data Management Division, December 1977).

Bibliography

Primary Sources

Manuscript Collections

Harry S. Truman Library, Independence, Missouri

Papers of Harry S. Truman
  Official Files
  Subject Files, Foreign Affairs—Brazil
  Trip Files, 31 August–20 September 1947
  White House Central Files

Papers of Dean Acheson

Merwin L. Bohan, Oral History Transcript

Paul C. Daniels, Oral History Transcript

Major General Kenner F. Hertford, Oral History Transcript

Thomas Mann, Oral History Transcript

William D. Pawley General File

Central Intelligence Agency, Intelligence Reports

Central Intelligence Agency, National Intelligence Estimates

Department of State, Division of Biographical Information

John F. Kennedy Library, Boston, Massachusetts

Papers of President Kennedy, Countries—Brazil

Central Intelligence Agency, Office of Current Intelligence

United States Army Military History Center, Washington, D.C.

Terrett, Dulaney. "Great Power Maneuvering for the Bulge of Brazil: An Episode in Defense Strategy." N.d. Historical Manuscript File.

United States Military History Institute, Carlisle Barracks, Pennsylvania

Papers of General Willis D. Crittenberger

General Paul L. Freeman, Oral History Transcript

Papers of General Charles H. Gerhardt

General George R. Mather, Oral History Transcript

Papers of General Bruce Palmer, Jr.

General Bruce Palmer, Jr., Oral History Transcript

Papers of General Matthew B. Ridgeway

General Matthew B. Ridgeway, Oral History Transcript

Lt. General Richard J. Seitz, Oral History Transcript

Lt. General Arthur G. Trudeau, Oral History Transcript

Government Publications

Declassified Document Reference System, Library of Congress, Washington, D.C.

Central Intelligence Agency. Biographic Register. "Commander Designate of the Inter-American Peace Force (IAPF)." December 1965. Declassified Document Reference System (DDRS) 15-A.

———. Information Report. "Establishment of Soviet Military Mission Tied to Soviet Offer of Aid to Brazil." August 8, 1963. DDRS 13-F.

———. Information Report. "Plans of General Olimpio Mourão Filho to Overthrow the Brazilian Government." April 30, 1963. DDRS 12-D.

———. Information Report. "Plans of Military Coup Directed by General Amaury Kruel, Minister of War, Marshall Odylio Denys, General Nelson de Mello, and Others to Discuss Plans for an Anti-Government Coup." March 13, 1963. DDRS 11-E.

———. Information Report. "Plan Within Brazilian Second and Third Armies for Coup Against Goulart Administration." April 10, 1963. DDRS 12-B.

Department of Defense to Department of State. May 25, 1965. DDRS 157-D.

Department of State. Gordon to Secretary of State. January 14, 1963. DDRS-1977 213-A/C.

———. Gordon to Mann. March 4, 1964. DDRS 84-E.

———. Background Paper. "Brazil and Vietnam." January 23, 1967. In *Visit of President Elect Costa e Silva of Brazil, January 25–27, 1967.* DDRS-1978 199-B.

———. Background Paper. "Military Assistance to Brazil." January 19, 1967. DDRS-1978 199-B.

Department of State. Division of Research for the American Republics. "An Estimate of the Political Potential of Getúlio Vargas." OIR Report No. 4324. May 9, 1947.

Foreign Policy Research Institute. *A Study of U.S. Military Assistance Programs in the Underdeveloped Areas.* Philadelphia: University of Pennsylvania. April 8, 1959. DDRS-1978 194-B.

Joint Chiefs of Staff. National Security Action Memorandum 119—"Civic Action." *Counterinsurgency Bluebook Fiscal Year 1966.* November 15, 1966. DDRS 242-D.

U.S. Army. *Catalógo de cursos para 1990.* Fort Benning, Ga.: Escuela de las Americas, October 1989.

Other Government Documents

Department of State. *Foreign Relations of the United States, 1937.* Vol. 5, *The American Republics.* Washington, D.C.: GPO, 1954.

———. *Foreign Relations of the United States, 1938.* Vol. 5, *The American Republics.* Washington, D.C.: GPO, 1956.

———. *Foreign Relations of the United States, 1940.* Vol. 5, *The American Republics..* Washington, D.C.: GPO, 1961.

———. *Foreign Relations of the United States, 1941.* Vol. 6, *The American Republics.* Washington, D.C.: GPO, 1963.

———. *Foreign Relations of the United States, 1945.* Vol. 9, *The American Republics.* Washington, D.C.: GPO, 1969.

———. *Foreign Relations of the United States, 1946.* Vol. 11, *The American Republics.* Washington, D.C.: GPO, 1969.

———. *Foreign Relations of the United States, 1947.* Vol. 8, *The American Republics.* Washington, D.C.: GPO, 1972.

———. *Foreign Relations of the United States, 1948.* Vol. 9, *The United Nations: The Western Hemisphere.* Washington, D.C.: GPO, 1972.

———. *Foreign Relations of the United States, 1949.* Vol. 2, *The United Nations; The Western Hemisphere.* Washington, D.C.: GPO, 1975.

———. *Foreign Relations of the United States, 1950.* Vol. 2, *The United Nations; The Western Hemisphere.* Washington, D.C.: GPO, 1976.

———. *Foreign Relations of the United States, 1951.* Vol. 2, *The United Nations; The Western Hemisphere.* Washington, D.C.: GPO, 1979.

———. *Foreign Relations of the United States, 1952–1954.* Vol. 4, *The American Republics.* Washington, D.C.: GPO, 1983.

———. *Foreign Relations of the United States, 1955–1957.* Vol. 7, *American Republics: Central and South America.* Washington, D.C.: GPO, 1987.

Embaixada do Brasil, Washington. Visita do Presidente Emílio Garrastazú Médici aos Estados Unidos da America, 7 a 9 de Dezembro de 1971. *Discursos do Presidente do Brasil e comunicado conjunto.* No pub. data.

Estado Maior do Exército. *História do exército brasileiro.* No pub. data.

Historical Division, Air Transport Command. "History of the South Atlantic Wing of the Air Transport Command." Microfilm, NA.

President's Committee to Study the United States Military Assistance Program. *Interim Report*. March 17, 1959.

U.S. Congress. House. *Hearings Before the Subcommittee on Inter-American Affairs of the Committee on International Relations*. 95th Cong., 2d sess., June 27, 28, July 19, 20, August 2, 9, 1978.

————. *Hearings on Foreign Assistance and Related Agencies Appropriations—1973*. 92d Cong., 2d sess., pt. 1, April 12, 1973.

————. Committee on Armed Services. *Military Assistance Advisory Groups* (Porter Hardy Report). 84th Cong., 2d sess., 1956.

————. Committee on Armed Services. "United States Military Posture for FY 1982." Hearings on Military Posture and H.R. 2614 and H.R. 2970. 97th Cong., 1st sess., 1981.

————. Committee on Foreign Affairs. Report 354. 86th Cong., 1st sess., 1960.

————. Committee on Foreign Affairs. Subcommittee on Inter-American Affairs. *United States–Brazilian Relations*. 97th Cong., 2d sess., 1982.

U.S. Congress. Senate. Hearings Before the Committee on Appropriations. *Foreign Assistance and Related Programs FY 74*. 93rd Cong., 1st sess., pt. 2, 1974.

————. Hearings Before the Subcommittee on Western Hemisphere Affairs of the Committee on Foreign Relations. *United States Policies and Programs in Brazil*. 92d Cong., 1st sess., May 4, 5, 11, 1971.

————. Appropriations Committee. *Hearings: Mutual Security Appropriations for 1960*. 86th Cong., 2d sess., 1960.

————. Committee on Foreign Relations. *Hearings: Mutual Security Act of 1952*. 82d Cong., 2d sess., 1952.

————. Committee on Foreign Relations. *The Mutual Security Act of 1960*. Report 1286. 86th Cong., 2d sess., 1960.

————. Special Committee to Study the Foreign Aid Program. *Report on United States Foreign Assistance Program: South America (Peru, Chile, Argentina, Uruguay, and Brazil)*. By David K. E. Bruce. 85th Cong., 1st sess., 1957.

U.S. Defense Security Assistance Agency, Data Management Division. *Foreign Military Sales and Military Assistance Facts*. Washington, D.C.: U.S. Defense Security Assistance Agency, Data Management Division, December 1977.

Record Groups, National Archives, Washington, D.C.

Record Group 59: Records of the Department of State
General Records of the Department of State, 1955–1959.
Office of East Coast Affairs (Brazil), 1956–1957.
Records of the Assistant Secretary of State for Inter-American Affairs (Henry F. Holland), 1953–1956. Country File (Brazil-Chile).
Records of the Department of State, 1950–1954.
Relating to Internal Political and National Defense of Brazil, 1955–1959. Microfilm 1511, Roll 8.

Record Group 218: Records of the Joint Chiefs of Staff
  JCS Central Decimal File, 1946–1947.
  JCS Central Decimal File, 1948–1950.
  JCS Central Decimal File, 1954–1956.
  JCS Central Decimal File, 1959.
  JCS Chairman's File, 1953–1957.
  JCS Combined Chiefs of Staff Decimal File, 1942–1945.
  JCS Geographic Decimal File, 1951–1953.
  JCS Geographic Decimal File, 1954–1956.
  JCS Geographic Files, 1942–1945.
  JCS Military Commissions, U.S.-Brazil.

Record Group 319: Records of the Army Staff, Plans and Operations Division
  P&O Decimal File, 1946–1948.
  P&O Decimal File, 1949–February 1950.

Memoirs

Acheson, Dean. *Present at the Creation: My Years in the State Department.* New York: W. W. Norton, 1969.

Cordeiro de Farias, General Oswaldo, Aspasia Camargo, and Wilder de Góes. *Meio seculo de combate: Dialógo com Cordeiro de Farias.* Rio de Janeiro: Editora Nova Fronteira, 1981.

Eisenhower, Dwight D. *Waging Peace, 1951–1961.* Garden City, N.Y.: Doubleday, 1965.

Guedes, Paulo Pinto. Interview by Aspasia Camargo. "E fomos para a guerra." In *Getúlio, uma história oral.* Ed. Valentina da Rocha Lima, 212–215, Rio de Janeiro: Editora Record, 1986.

Leitão de Carvalho, General Estevão. *Memórias de um soldado leglista.* Vol. 3. Rio de Janeiro: Biblioteca do Exército Editora, 1964.

Author Interviews

Lt. Colonel Daniel Mason. Military Liaison Office, United States Embassy, Brasília, Brazil, June 14, 1985.

Staff Member (source desires anonymity). Inter-American Defense College, Ft. Lesley J. McNair, Washington, D.C., June 8, 1989.

SECONDARY SOURCES

Articles and Back Chapters

Alves Silva, Jeronymo Jorge. "Evolucão histórica do militar brasileira formou sua consciência democratica." *Revista do Clube Militar* 43:168 (October 1969): 43.

Baines, John M. "U.S. Military Assistance to Latin America: An Assessment." *Journal of Inter-American Studies and World Affairs* 14:4 (November 1972): 469–487.

Barros, Alexandre de S. C. "The Formulation and Implementation of Brazilian Foreign Policy: Itamaraty and New Actors." In *Latin American Nations in World Politics*, ed. Heraldo Muñoz and Joseph S. Tulchin, 30–44. Boulder, Colo.: Westview Press, 1984.

Bell, Peter D. "Brazilian-American Relations." In *Brazil in the Sixties*, ed. Riordan Roett, 77–102. Nashville, Tenn.: Vanderbilt University Press, 1972.

Burns, E. Bradford. "Tradition and Variation in Brazilian Foreign Policy." *Journal of Inter- American Studies and World Affairs* 9:2 (April 1967): 195–212.

Child, John. "Geopolitical Thinking in Latin America." *Latin American Research Review* 14:2 (1972): 75–103.

Conniff, Michael L. "The Tenentes in Power: A New Perspective on the Revolution of 1930." *Journal of Latin American Studies* 10:1 (May 1978): 61–82.

Correa, General Antônio Jorge. "Escola Superior de Guerra—laboratório de ideias." *A Defesa Nacional* 63:667 (May–June 1976): 9–11.

Costa e Silva, Ten. Cel. Riograndino da. "O communismo e as forças armadas." *A Defesa Nacional* 38:437 (December 1950): 115–117.

Della Cava, Ralph. "Torture in Brazil." *Commonweal* 6:112 (April 24, 1970): 135–141.

Editorial. *A Defesa Nacional* 22:376 (September 1945): 5–8.

Editorial. *A Defesa Nacional* 38:438 (January 1951): 4.

Editorial. *A Defesa Nacional* 38:441 (April 1951): 3–4.

Elsey, George M. "Some White House Recollections." *Diplomatic History* 12:3 (Summer 1988): 357–364.

"Escola Superior de Guerra." *Dicionário Histórico-Biografico Brasileiro, 1930–1983*, ed. Israel Beloch and Alzira Alves de Abreu, vol. 2. Rio de Janeiro: Fundação Getúlio Vargas, Centro de Pesquisa e Documentação de História Contemporânea do Brasil, Forense-Universitária, 1984.

"Exército—fator de integração nacional." *Revista do Clube Militar* 43:165 (June 1969): 10–11.

"Extracto do discurso proferido pelo General do Exército Diwght [*sic*] D. Eisenhower na Escola de Estado Maior do Brasil, em 6 de Agosto de 1946." *A Defesa Nacional* 33:388 (September 1946): 263.

Filho, Ten. Cel. Adelardo. "Problemas do Brasil." *A Defesa Nacional* 37:430 (May 1950): 71–80.

Fishlow, Albert. "Flying Down to Rio: Perspectives on U.S.-Brazil Relations." *Foreign Affairs* 57 (Winter 1978–1979): 387–405.

———. "The United States and Brazil: The Case of the Missing Relationship." *Foreign Affairs* 60 (Spring 1982): 904–923.

Fleischer, David V. "Brazil." In *The Latin American Military Institution*, ed. Robert Wesson, 89–93. New York: Praeger, 1986.

Francis, Michael J. "Military Aid to Latin America in the U.S. Congress." *Journal of Inter-American Studies* 87:1 (February 1982): 396–397.

———. "The United States at Rio, 1942: The Strains of Pan Americanism." *Journal of Latin American Studies* 6:11 (May 1974): 77–95.

Gall, Norman. "Atoms for Brazil, Dangers for All." *Foreign Policy* 23 (Summer 1976): 155–201.

García, Ten. Cel. J. H. "A outra guerra." *A Defesa Nacional* 37:430 (May 1950): 95–96.

Gomez, Rosenda A. "The Marxist Approach to Latin America: Marx, Lenin, Stalin, and Mao." In *The Political-Military Defense of Latin America*, ed. Bruce B. Mason, 3–7. Tempe: Bureau of Governmental Research, Arizona State University, 1963.

Gordon, Lincoln. "Brazil's Future World Role." *Orbis* 16:3 (Fall 1972): 621–631.

Gorman, Stephen M. "Security, Influence, and Nuclear Weapons: The Case of Argentina and Brazil." *Parameters* 9:1 (March 1979): 52–65.

Hilton, Stanley E. "The Armed Forces and Industrialists in Modern Brazil: The Drive for Military Autonomy (1889–1954)." *Hispanic American Historical Review* 62:4 (November 1982): 629–673.

———. "The Brazilian Military: Changing Strategic Perceptions and the Quest for Mission." *Armed Forces and Society* 13:3 (Spring 1987): 329–351.

———. "The United States, Brazil, and the Cold War, 1945–1960: End of the Special Relationship." *Journal of American History* 68:3 (December 1981): 599–624.

Hirst, Monica. "The United States and the Middle Powers in Latin America: Mexico and Brazil." In *Latin American Views of U.S. Policy*, ed. Robert Wesson and Harold Munoz, 87–105. New York: Praeger, 1986.

Huggins, Martha K. "U.S.-Supported State Terror: A History of Police Training in Latin America." In *Vigilantism and the State in Modern Latin America: Essays on Extralegal Violence*, ed. Martha K. Huggins, 219–242. New York: Praeger, 1991.

Kaplan, Stephen S. "U.S. Arms Transfers to Latin America, 1945–1974: Rational Strategy, Bureaucratic Politics, and Executive Parameters." *International Studies Quarterly* 6:11 (December 1975): 399–431.

Langley, Lester D. "Military Commitments in Latin America, 1960–1968." *Current History* 56:334 (June 1969): 346–384.

Leacock, Ruth. "Promoting Democracy: The United States and Brazil, 1964–1968." *Prologue* 13:2 (Summer 1981): 77–99.

Lopes de Oliveira, Solon. "Uma opinião." *A Defesa Nacional* 38:444 (July 1951): 128.

Mainwaring, Max G. "Nuclear Power in Brazil." *Parameters* 14:4 (Winter 1984): 40–46.

Malan, Pedro Sampio. "Relações econômicas internacionais do Brasil (1945–1964)." In *História geral da civilização brasileria*. Vol. 3, *O Brasil republicano*. Vol. 4, *Economia e cultura (1930–1964)*, ed. Boris Fausto, 51–106. São Paulo: DIFEL, 1984.

Martins de Mello, Cel. Humberto. "A restruturação do exérctio." *A Defesa Nacional* 33:384 (May 1946): 14–15.

McCann, Frank D. "The Brazilian Army and the Problem of Mission, 1939–1964." *Journal of Latin American Studies* 12:1 (May 1980): 107–126.

———. "Brazilian Foreign Relations in the Twentieth Century." In *Brazil in the International System: The Rise of a Middle Power*, ed. Wayne A. Selcher, 1–23. Boulder, Colo.: Westview Press, 1981.

———. "The Brazilian General Staff and Brazil's Military Situation, 1900–1945." *Journal of Inter-American Studies and World Affairs* 25:3 (August 1983): 299–324.

———. "The Formative Period of Twentieth-Century Brazilian Army Thought, 1900–1920." *Hispanic American Historical Review* 64:4 (November 1984): 737–765.

———. "The Military." In *Modern Brazil: Elites and Masses in Historical Perspective*, ed. Michael L. Conniff and Frank D. McCann, 47–80. Lincoln: University of Nebraska Press, 1989.

Meira Mattos, General Carlos de. "Doutrina política revolucionária Brasil—potência." *Revista do Clube Militar* 44:174 (April 1970): 16–18.

———. "A Força Inter-Americana de Paz no República Dominica, Participação Brasileira (FAIBRAS)." *A Defesa Nacional* 53:614 (July–August 1967): 31–42.

Nunn, Frederick M. "Military Professionalism and Professional Militarism in Brazil, 1870–1970: Historical Perspectives and Political Implications." *Journal of Latin American Studies* 4, pt. 1 (May 1972): 29–54.

Oliveira, General Raulino de. "Podemos fabricar nosso armamento." *Revista do Clube Militar* 94 (February 1949): 68–69.

Pang, Eul-Soo. "Brazil's Pragmatic Nationalism." *Current History* 68:401 (January 1975): 5–10.

Paterson, Thomas G. "Bearing the Burden: A Critical Look at JFK's Foreign Policy." *Virginia Quarterly Review* 54:2 (Spring 1978): 193–212.

Perry, William. "The Brazilian Armed Forces: Military Policy and Conventional Capabilities of an Emerging Power." *Military Review* 58:9 (September 1978): 10–24.

Poppino, Rollie. "The Early Cold War Years." *Current History* 56:334 (June 1969): 340–345.

Powell, John Duncan. "Military Assistance and Militarism in Latin America." *Western Political Quarterly* 18:2, pt. 1 (June 1965): 382–393.

Quadros, Jânio. "Brazil's New Foreign Policy." *Foreign Affairs* 40:1 (October 1961): 19–27.

Rabe, Stephan. "Inter-American Military Cooperation, 1944–1951." *World Affairs* 137:2 (Fall 1974): 132–149.

Ransone, Jr., James F. "The Grand Alliance." In *The Second World War: Europe and the Mediterranean*, ed. Thomas E. Griess, 182–211. Wayne, N.J.: Avery, 1984.

Reisky de Dubnic, Vladimir. "Trends in Brazil's Foreign Policy." In *New Perspectives of Brazil*, ed. Eric N. Baklanoff, 78–100. Nashville, Tenn.: Vanderbilt University Press, 1976.

Reynolds, Robert. "Brazil's Overseas Military Operations." *Military Review* 46:11 (November 1966): 85–91.

Rodrigues, José Honório. "The Foundations of Brazil's Foreign Policy." *International Affairs* 38:3 (July 1962): 324–338.

————. "The Foundations of Brazil's Foreign Policy." In *Latin American International Politics: Ambitions, Capabilities, and the National Interests of Mexico, Brazil, and Argentina*, ed. Carlos Alberto Astiz, 196–215. Notre Dame, Ind.: University of Notre Dame Press, 1969.

Rosenbaum, H. Jon. "Brazil's Foreign Policy and Cuba." *Inter-American Economic Affairs* 23:3 (Winter 1969): 25–46.

Santos, Ralph G. "Brazilian Foreign Policy and the Dominican Crisis: The Impact of History on Events." *The Americas* 29:1 (July 1972): 62–77.

"Segurança e desenvolvimento." *Revista do Clube Militar* 43:166 (July 1969): 8–10.

Sieniawski, Michael. "Brazil Clashes with Open-Door Policy on Arms Sales." *Christian Science Monitor* 74:244 (November 12, 1982): 15.

Smith, Joseph. "American Diplomacy and the Naval Mission to Brazil, 1917–1930." *Inter-American Economic Affairs* 25:1 (Summer 1981): 73–91.

————. "United States Diplomacy Toward Political Revolt in Brazil, 1889–1930." *Inter-American Economic Affairs* 37:2 (Autumn 1983): 3–21.

Távora, Juarez. "Escola Superior de Guerra." *A Defesa Nacional* 61:475 (February 1954): 111–120.

"Toma nota." *Revista do Clube Militar* 90 (July–August 1948): 43–44.

Tuthill, John W. "Operation Topsy." *Foreign Policy* 8 (Fall 1972): 62–85.

"Unitas preserva segurança e solidifica pan-americanismo." *Revista do Clube Militar* 172:44 (February 1970): 20–23.

Villar de Queiroz, J. M. "Bloco ocidental: Problemas, políticos, econômicos, e militares." *Revista Brasileira de Política Internacional* 6:2 (September 1963): 431–454.

Winkelman, Major Colin K., and Captain A. Brent Merrill. "United States and Brazilian Military Relations." *Military Review* 63 (June 1983): 60–73.

Books

Abreu, Hugo. *O outro lado do poder*. Rio de Janeiro: Editora Nova Fronteria S.A., 1979.

Agee, Philip. *Inside the Company: CIA Diary*. Harmondsworth, England: Penguin, 1975.

Andrews, Craig Neal. *Foreign Policy and the New American Military*. Beverly Hills, Calif.: Sage Publications, 1974.

Archdiocese of São Paulo. *Brasil: Nunca mais*. With a preface by Dom Paulo Evaristo Arns. Petrópolis: Editora Vozes, 1985.

Arruda, Antônio de. *ESG: História de sua doutrina*. São Paulo: Editores GRD, 1980.

Bacchus, Wilfred A. *Mission in Mufti: Brazil's Military Regimes, 1964–1985*. New York: Greenwood Press, 1990.

Baily, Samuel. *The United States and the Development of South America, 1945–1975*. New York: New Viewpoints, 1976.

Ball, George. *Diplomacy for a Crowded World*. Boston: Little, Brown, 1976.

Bandeira, Luiz Alberto Moniz. *Brasil–Estados Unidos: A rivalidade emergente (1950–1988)*. Rio de Janeiro: Editora Civilização Brasileira, 1989.

———. *O Governo João Goulart: As lutas sociaisno Brasil, 1961–1964*. Rio de Janeiro: Editora Civilização Brasileira, 1978.

———. *Presença dos Estados Unidos no Brasil*. Rio de Janeiro: Editora Civilização Brasileira, 1973.

Barber, Willard, and C. Neale Ronning. *Internal Security and Military Power: Counterinsurgency and Civic Action*. Columbus: Ohio State University Press, 1966.

Benevides, Maria Victoria de Mesquita. *O Governo Kubitschek: Desenvolvimento econômico e estabilidade política*. Rio de Janeiro: Paz e Terra, 1979.

Berle, Adolf A. *Latin America—Diplomacy and Reality*. New York: Harper and Row, 1962.

Black, Jan Knippers. *Sentinels of Empire: The United States and Latin American Militarism*. New York: Greenwood Press, 1986.

———. *United States Penetration of Brazil*. Philadelphia: University of Pennsylvania Press, 1977.

Branco, Robert J. *The United States and Brazil: Opening a New Dialogue*. Fort Lesley J. McNair, Washington, D.C.: National Defense University Press, 1984.

Brayner, Floriano de Lima. *Recordando os bravos: Eu convivi com eles—Campanha da Itália*. Rio de Janeiro: Editora Civilização Brasileira, 1977.

Burns, E. Bradford. *The Unwritten Alliance: Rio Branco and Brazilian-American Relations*. New York: Columbia University Press, 1966.

Carone, Edgard. *A república liberal*. São Paulo: DIFEL, 1985.

Cervo, Amado Luiz, and Clodoaldo Bueno. *História da política exterior do Brasil*. São Paulo: Editora Atica S.A., 1992.

Child, John. *Unequal Alliance: The Inter-American Military System, 1938–1978*. Boulder, Colo.: Westview Press, 1980.

Coelho, Edmundo Campos. *Em busca de identidade: O exército e a política na sociedade brasileira*. Rio de Janeiro: Forense-Universitária, 1976.

Comissão de Relações Públicas do Exército. *O seu exército*. N.p.: N.p., 1967.

Conn, Stetson, and Byron Fairchild. *The Framework of Hemisphere Defense*. Washington, D.C.: Office of the Chief of Military History, Department of the Army, 1960.

Cooke, Morris L. *Brazil on the March: A Study in International Cooperation*. New York: McGraw and Hill, 1944.

Coutinho, Lourival. *O General Góes depoe*. Rio de Janeiro: Livraria Editora Coelho Branco, 1956.

Couto e Silva, General Golbery do. *Aspectos geopolíticos do Brasil*. Rio de Janeiro: Biblioteca do Exército Editora, 1957.

DeConde, Alexander. *A History of American Foreign Policy*. New York: Charles Scribner's Sons, 1963.

Degler, Carl N. *Affluence and Anxiety, 1945–Present*. Glenview, Ill.: Scott Forseman, 1968.

Dreifuss, Rene A. *1964: A conquista do estado; ação política, poder, e golpe de classe*. Petrópolis: Editora Vozes, 1981.

Dix, Robert H. *Colombia: The Political Dimensions of Change*. New Haven: Yale University Press, 1967.

Dulles, John W. F. *Carlos Lacerda, Brazilian Crusader*. Vol. 1, *The Years 1914–1960*. Austin: University of Texas Press, 1991.

———. *Castello Branco: The Making of a Brazilian President*. College Station: Texas A&M University Press, 1978.

———. *President Castello Branco, Brazilian Reformer*. College Station: Texas A&M University Press, 1980.

———. *Unrest in Brazil: Political-Military Crisis, 1955–1964*. Austin: University of Texas Press, 1970.

———. *Vargas of Brazil: A Political Biography*. Austin: University of Texas Press, 1967.

Dutra, Eloy. *IBAD, sigla da corrupção*. Rio de Janeiro: Editora Civilização Brasileira, 1963.

Estado Maior do Exército. *História do Exército Brasileiro*. No pub. data.

Fishlow, Albert, and Abraham F. Lowenthal. *Latin America's Emergence: Toward a U.S. Response*. New York: Foreign Policy Association, 1979.

Flynn, Peter. *Brazil: A Political Analysis*. Boulder, Colo.: Westview Press, 1978.

Fontaine, Roger. *Brazil and the United States: Toward a Maturing Relationship*. Washington, D.C.: American Enterprise Institute for Policy Research, 1974.

Francis, Michael J. *Attitudes of the United States Government Toward Collective Military Arrangements with Latin America, 1945–1960*. Ann Arbor: University Microfilms, 1974.

Fulbright, J. William. *The Arrogance of Power*. New York: Random House, 1966.

Goldhamer, Herbert. *The Foreign Powers in Latin America*. Princeton: Princeton University Press, 1972.

Goldman, Eric. *The Crucial Decade—and After, America 1945–1960*. New York: Vintage Books, 1960.

Goldwert, Marvin. *Democracy, Militarism, and Nationalism in Argentina, 1930–1966: An Interpretation*. Austin: University of Texas Press, 1972.

Gomes da Costa, Joffre. *Marechal Henrique Lott*. Rio de Janeiro: N.p., 1960.

Grael, Cel. Dickson M. *Aventura, corrupção, e terrorismo: A somba da impunidade*. Petrópolis: Editora Vozes, 1985.

Green, David. *The Containment of Latin America: A History of the Myths and Realities of the Good Neighbor Policy*. Chicago: Quadrangle Books, 1971.

Grow, Michael. *The Good Neighbor Policy and Authoritarianism in Paraguay: United States Economic Expansion and Great Power Rivalry in Latin America During World War II*. Lawrence: Regents Press of Kansas, 1981.

Gugliamelli, Juan E. *Argentina, Brasil, y la bomba atómica*. Buenos Aires: Tierra Nueva, 1976.

Haines, Gerald K. *The Americanization of Brazil: A Study of U.S. Cold War Diplomacy in the Third World, 1945–1954.* Wilmington, Dela.: SR Books, 1989.

Heath, Jim F. *Decade of Disillusionment: The Kennedy-Johnson Years.* Bloomington: Indiana University Press, 1975.

Hernandez, Erenesto. *Colombia en Corea.* Bogotá: Imprenta de las Fuerzas Armadas, 1953.

Hilsman, Roger. *The Politics of Policy Making in Defense and Foreign Affairs.* New York: Harper and Row, 1971.

Hilton, Stanley E. *Brazil and the Great Powers, 1930–1939: The Politics of Trade Rivalry.* Austin: University of Texas Press, 1975.

————. *Hitler's Secret War in South America: German Military Espionage and Allied Counterespionage in Brazil.* Baton Rouge: Louisiana University Press, 1981.

Hodges, Donald. *Argentina, 1943–1976: The National Revolution and Resistance.* Albuquerque: University of New Mexico Press, 1976.

Hovey, Harold. *United States Military Assistance: A Study of Policies and Practices.* New York: Praeger, 1965.

Johnson, John J. *The Military and Society in Latin America.* Stanford: Stanford University Press, 1964.

————. *Political Change in Latin America: The Emergence of the Middle Sectors.* Stanford: Stanford University Press, 1958.

Jones, Patrice Franko. *The Brazilian Defense Industry: A Case Study of Public-Private Collaboration.* Boulder, Colo.: Westview Press, 1991.

Kane, William E. *Civil Strife in Latin America: A Legal History of U.S. Involvement.* Baltimore: Johns Hopkins University Press, 1972.

Kryzanek, Michael. *U.S.–Latin American Relations.* New York: Praeger, 1985.

Kuzman, Dan. *Santo Domingo: Revolt of the Damned.* New York: G. P. Putnam's Sons, 1965.

LaBak, Amir. *1961: A crises renuncia e a solução parlamentárista.* São Paulo: Editora Brasiliense, 1986.

LaFeber, Walter. *Inevitable Revolutions: The United States and Central America.* Expanded ed. New York: W. W. Norton, 1984.

Leacock, Ruth. *Requiem for Revolution: The United States and Brazil, 1961–1969.* Kent, Ohio: Kent State University Press, 1990.

Leitão de Carvalho, Estevão. *A serviço do Brasil na Segunda Guerra Mundial.* Rio de Janeiro: Biblioteca do Exército Editora, 1952.

Levinson, Jerome, and Juan de Onis. *The Alliance That Lost Its Way: A Critical Report on the Alliance for Progress.* Chicago: Quadrangle Books, 1970.

Lieuwen, Edwin. *Arms and Politics in Latin America.* Rev. ed. New York: Praeger, 1961.

————. *U.S. Policy in Latin America: A Short History.* New York: Praeger, 1965.

Lyra Tavares, General Aurélio de. *O Exército Brasileiro visto pelo seu ministro.* Recife: Universidade de Pernambuco—Imprensa Universitária, 1968.

Mascarenhas de Morães, Marshall João B. *The Brazilian Expeditionary Force by Its Commander.* Translated from the 2d ed. No pub. data.

McCann, Frank D. *The Brazilian-American Alliance, 1937–1945.* Princeton: Princeton University Press, 1973.

————. *A Nação Armada: Ensaios sobre a história do Exército Brasileiro.* Trans. Silvio Robim. Recife: Editora Guararapes, 1982.

Mecham, John Lloyd. *The United States and Inter-American Security, 1889–1960.* Austin: University of Texas Press, 1961.

Meira Mattos, Cel. Carlos de. *A experiencia do FAIBRAS na República Dominica.* No pub. data.

————. *A geopolítica e as projeções do poder.* Rio de Janeiro: Livraria José Olympio Editora, S.A., 1977.

————. *Brasil: Geopolítica e destino.* Rio de Janeiro: Biblioteca do Exército Editora with Livraria José Olympio Editora, 1975.

Molineu, Harold. *U.S. Policy Toward Latin America: From Regionalism to Globalism.* Boulder, Colo.: Westview Press, 1986.

Moreira, Marcilio Marques. *De Maquiavel a San Tiago: Ensaios sobre política, educação, e economia.* Brasília: Editora Universidade de Brasília, 1981.

Moreira Alves, Maria Helena. *State and Opposition in Military Brazil.* Austin: University of Texas Press, 1988.

Morel, Edmar. *O golpe começou em Washington.* Rio de Janeiro: Editora Brasiliense, 1965.

Moura, Gerson. *Autonomia na dependência: A política externa brasileira de 1931 a 1942.* Rio de Janeiro: Editora Nova Fronteira S.A., 1980.

Nunn, Frederick M. *Yesterday's Soldiers: European Military Professionalism in South America, 1890–1940.* Lincoln: University of Nebraska Press, 1983.

Pach, Jr., Chester J. *Arming the Free World: The Origins of the United States Military Assistance Program, 1945–1950.* Chapel Hill: University of North Carolina Press, 1991.

Parker, Phyllis R. *Brazil and the Quiet Intervention, 1964.* Austin: University of Texas Press, 1979.

Parkinson, F. *Latin America, the Cold War, and the World Powers, 1953–1973.* Beverly Hills, Calif.: Sage, 1974.

Penna, J. O. de Meira. *Política externa, segurança, e desenvolvimento.* Rio de Janeiro: Livraria AGIR Editora, 1967.

Rabe, Stephen G. *Eisenhower and Latin America: The Foreign Policy of Anti-Communism.* Chapel Hill: University of North Carolina Press, 1988.

Reisky de Dubnic, Vladimir. *Political Trends in Brazil.* Washington, D.C.: Public Affairs Press, 1968.

Rostow, Walt W. *The Stages of Economic Growth: A Non-Communist Manifesto.* 2d ed. Cambridge: Cambridge University Press, 1960.

San Tiago Dantas, Francisco Clementino de. *Política externa independente.* Rio de Janeiro: Editora Civilização Brasileira, 1962.

Santos, Cel. Francisco Ruas, ed. *Marechal Castello Branco: Seu pensamento militar, 1946–1964*. Rio de Janeiro: Imprensa do Exército, 1968.

Schneider, Ronald M. *Brazil: Foreign Policy of a Future World Power*. Boulder, Colo.: Westview Press, 1976.

———. *"Order and Progress": A Political History of Brazil*. Boulder, Colo.: Westview Press, 1991.

———. *The Political System of Brazil: Emergence of a "Modernizing" Authoritarian Regime, 1964–1970*. New York: Columbia University Press, 1971.

Schoonmaker, Herbert G. *Military Crisis Management: U.S. Intervention in the Dominican Republic, 1965*. New York: Greenwood Press, 1990.

Shoultz, Lars. *Human Rights and United States Policy Toward Latin America*. Princeton: Princeton University Press, 1981.

———. *National Security and United States Policy Toward Latin America*. Princeton: Princeton University Press, 1987.

Silva, Helío. *Golpe ou contragolpe?* Rio de Janeiro: Editora Civilização Brasileira, 1975.

Skidmore, Thomas E. *Politics in Brazil, 1930–1964: An Experiment in Democracy*. New York: Oxford University Press, 1967.

———. *The Politics of Military Rule in Brazil, 1964–1985*. New York: Oxford University Press, 1988.

Slater, Jerome. *Intervention and Negotiation: The United States and the Dominican Revolution*. New York: Harper and Row, 1970.

Smith, Joseph. *Unequal Giants: Diplomatic Relations Between the U.S. and Brazil, 1889–1930*. Pittsburgh: Pittsburgh University Press, 1991.

Smith, Robert Freeman, ed. *The United States and the Latin American Sphere of Influence*. Vol. 2, *Era of Good Neighbors, Cold Warriors, and Hairshirts, 1930–1982*. Malabar, Fla.: Robert E. Krieger, 1983.

Sodré, Nelson Werneck. *História militar do Brasil*. 2d ed. Rio de Janeiro: Editora Civilização Brasileira, 1968.

Souza, Jr., General Antônio de. *O Brasil e a Terceira Guerra Mundial*. Rio de Janeiro: Biblioteca do Exército Editora, 1959.

Stacchini, José. *Março 64: Mobilização de audacia*. São Paulo: Companhia Editora Nacional, 1965.

Starling, Heloisa Maria Murgel. *Os senhores das Gerais: Os novos inconfidentes e o golpe militar de 1964*. Petrópolis: Editora Vozes, 1986.

Stepan, Alfred. *The Military in Politics: Changing Patterns in Brazil*. Princeton: Princeton University Press, 1971.

———. *The State and Society: Peru in Comparative Perspective*. Princeton: Princeton University Press, 1978.

———, ed. *Authoritarian Brazil: Origins, Policies, and Future*. New Haven: Yale University Press, 1973.

Storrs, Keith Larry. *Brazil's Independent Foreign Policy, 1961–1964: Background, Tenets, Linkage to Domestic Politics, and Aftermath*. Ithaca: Cornell University Press, 1973.

Szulc, Tad. *The Dominican Diary.* New York: Delacorte Press, 1965.

————. *Segurança nacional, problemas atuais.* N.p.: José Alvaro Editora, S.A., n.d.

Townsend, Joyce Carol. *Bureaucratic Politics in American Decision Making: Impact on Brazil.* Washington, D.C.: University Press of America, 1982.

Vasconcelos, Cel. Qema Osny. *2 Guerra Mundial.* Curso de Preparação. N.p.: Escola de Comando e Estado Maior do Exército, 1969.

Viana Filho, Luís. *O Governo Castelo Branco.* Vol. 2. Rio de Janeiro: Biblioteca do Exérctio Editora, 1975.

Victor, Mario. *Cinco anos que abalaram o Brasil (de Jânio Quadros ao Marechal Castelo Branco).* Rio de Janeiro: Civilização Brasileira, 1965.

Walters, Vernon. *Silent Missions.* Garden City, N.Y.: Doubleday, 1978.

Weis, Warren Michael. *Cold Warriors and Coups d'Etat: Brazilian-American Relations, 1945–1964.* Albuquerque: University of New Mexico Press, 1993.

Wesson, Robert G. *The United States and Brazil: Limits of Influence.* New York: Praeger, 1981.

Whitaker, Arthur P. *The United States and the Southern Cone: Argentina, Chile, and Uruguay.* Cambridge, Mass.: Harvard University Press, 1976.

Wirth, John D. *The Politics of Brazilian Development, 1930–1954.* Stanford: Stanford University Press, 1970.

Wiarda, Howard J. *American Foreign Policy Toward Latin America in the 80s and 90s: Issues and Controversies from Reagan to Bush.* New York: New York University Press, 1992.

Yates, Lawrence A. *Power Pack: U.S. Intervention in the Dominican Republic, 1965–1966.* Fort Leavenworth, Kans.: Leavenworth Combat Studies Institute, 1988.

Dissertations

Barros, Alexandre de. "The Brazilian Military: Professional Socialization, Political Performance, and State Building." Ph.D. diss., University of Chicago, 1978.

Fontaine, Roger W. *The Foreign Policy-Making Process in Brazil.* Ann Arbor, Mich.: University Microfilm, 1970.

Krause, Theresa Louise. "The Establishment of United States Army Air Corps Bases in Brazil, 1938–1945." Ph.D. diss., University of Maryland, 1986.

Lanoue, Kenneth Callis. "An Alliance Shaken: Brazil and the United States, 1945–1950." Ph.D. diss., Louisiana State University and Agricultural and Mechanical College, 1978.

Weis, Warren Michael. "Roots of Estrangement: The United States and Brazil, 1950–1961." Ph.D. diss., Ohio State University, 1987.

Wolfe, Joel W. "The Rise of Brazil's Industrial Working Class: Community, Work, and Politics in São Paulo, 1900–1955." Ph.D. diss., University of Wisconsin, 1990.

Newspapers and Magazines

"Acordo militar Brasil-EUA ainda dura um ano." *O Jornal do Brasil* (Rio de Janeiro), March 12, 1977, 20.

"Ainda as nossas bases são ocupada." *Imprensa Popular* (Rio de Janeiro), March 28, 1948, 1.

"Auto suficiência." *O Radical* (Rio de Janeiro), November 7, 1950, 2.

"Brasil denuncia acordo militar com EUA." *O Jornal do Brasil* (Rio de Janeiro), March 12, 1977, 1, 19–22.

"Brazil will retain Curbs on Civil Liberties." *New York Times*, July 5, 1972, C8.

Brewer, Sam Pope. "Latin American Resentment Smolders Over Alleged Neglect by the United States." *New York Times*, June 16, 1952, 13.

Collação, Tomas. "Muito." *Correio da Manha* (Rio de Janeiro), March 29, 1951, 1.

———. "Tropas." *Correio da Manha* (Rio de Janeiro), October 18, 1952, 1.

"Em Berlim ou mais para leste." *A Noite* (Rio de Janeiro), June 20, 1951, 1, 9.

"EUA ate 75 forneceram 50% das armas para o Brasil." *O Jornal do Brasil* (Rio de Janeiro), March 9, 1977, 14.

"Exame de consciência." *Correio da Manha* (Rio de Janeiro), December 1, 1950, sec. 2, 1.

Geyelin, Philip. "Dominican Flashback: Behind the Scenes." *Wall Street Journal*, June 25, 1965, 1.

"Harris Addresses Democrats Here." *New York Times*, October 7, 1971, A29.

Kluckhohn, Frank L. "Brazilians Cooler to U.S. Occupation." *New York Times*, January 5, 1946, 4.

Leite Filho, Barreto. "Nova fase nas negociações Brasil-EE.UU: Para defesa do continente americano." *O Jornal* (Rio de Janeiro), February 20, 1957, 1.

Lincoln Gordon Interview. *Veja* (São Paulo), March 9, 1977, 1.

"Linha credito não foi usada." *O Jornal do Brasil* (Rio de Janeiro), March 12, 1977, 1.

"Militares brasileiros ja tem sua própria doutrina e dispensam a estrangeira." *O Jornal do Brasil* (Rio de Janeiro), March 12, 1977, 1.

"Nabuco aplaude o ato de Geisel." *O Jornal do Brasil* (Rio de Janeiro), March 12, 1977, 19.

"O Brasil e a situação internacional." *Correio da Manha* (Rio de Janeiro), December 9, 1950, caderno 2, 1.

O Estado de São Paulo (São Paulo), December 23, 1950, 1.

"O General Dutra com a palavra." *Correio da Noite* (Rio de Janeiro), April 3, 1945, 1.

O Jornal do Brasil (Rio de Janeiro), February 5, 1984, 21; February 7, 1984, 16; and February 19, 1984, 8.

"A política externa e as forças armadas." *Correio da Manha* (Rio de Janeiro), December 7, 1950, sec. 2, 1.

"A posição do Brasil." *Diário de Noticias* (Rio de Janeiro), December 7, 1950, 4.

"A posição do Brasil." *Diário Carioca* (Rio de Janeiro), December 29, 1950, 4.

Prado, Carlos. "O fim do acordo militar." *Opinião* (São Paulo), March 18, 1977, 5.

"Tancredo ve tres pontos de atrito entre Brasil e EUA." *O Jornal do Brasil* (Rio de Janeiro), March 9, 1977, 15.

"Truman quer a nossa escravização." *Hoje* (São Paulo), April 26, 1947, 1.

Última Hora (São Paulo), June 19, 1951, 1.

Varela, Eduardo. "Invadir o Uruguai: Os plano do III exército sob Médici." *O Jornal do Pais* (Rio de Janeiro), March 23–29, 1985, 17.

"Vargas fixa os rumos do futuro governo." *O Jornal* (Rio de Janeiro), November 5, 1950, 1–2.

Unpublished Material

Briggão, Clovis. "Brazil's Military Industry: A Discussion of Recent Developments. Working Paper 37. Toronto, Canada: Latin American Research Unit, December 1979.

Burgess, Mike, and Daniel Wolf. "The Concept of Power in the Brazilian Higher War College (ESG)." Working Paper 27. Toronto, Canada: Latin American Research Unit, December 1979.

Pandolfe, Frank Craig. "South American Naval Development, 1965–1985: A Four Nation Survey." Photocopy, 1989.

Tollefson, Scott D. "From Collor to Itamar Franco: U.S.-Brazilian Security Relations and Their Implications for Civil-Military Dynamics in Brazil." Photocopy of paper presented at the Middle Atlantic Council of Latin American Studies, Pennsylvania State University, University Park, Pennsylvania, April 3, 1993.

Index